STATE
OF A
UNION

ALSO BY JERRY OPPENHEIMER

Idol: Rock Hudson, The True Story of an American Film Hero

Barbara Walters: An Unauthorized Biography

*The Other Mrs. Kennedy, Ethel Skakel Kennedy: An
American Drama of Power, Privilege, and Politics*

Just Desserts: The Unauthorized Biography of Martha Stewart

STATE
OF A
UNION

Inside the Complex Marriage
of Bill and Hillary Clinton

JERRY OPPENHEIMER

HarperCollins*Publishers*

HarperCollins books may be purchased for educational, business, or sales promotional use. For information please write: Special Markets Department, HarperCollins Publishers Inc., 10 East 53rd Street, New York, NY 10022.

FIRST EDITION

Designed by Elliott Beard

Library of Congress Cataloging-in-Publication Data is available upon request.

ISBN 0-06-019392-1

00 01 02 03 04 ❖/RRD 10 9 8 7 6 5 4 3 2 1

In Memory of Dorothy Oppenheimer (1918–1999)
and Jeanne Altman (1917–1999)
Women of Valor

CONTENTS

THE LETTER

SHE SAW THE LETTER the minute she walked into his room. It was impossible to miss it, lying there neatly, open, on his desk. The room itself was the usual mess, jumbled piles of books and papers and cast-off clothes casually strewn everywhere. The letter alone seemed to have been carefully placed, an orchestrated touch. She froze, staring at it. Was she meant to read it? Was she not?

He had told her to drop by his house, using her key to get in, to pick up a few things for his overnight trip, yet another stop on the campaign trail. A young candidate, especially one running for Congress for the first time, was on the road constantly. He had asked her specifically to go to his desk, to find some papers he needed. Had he left the letter where he knew she would be sure to find it? He wasn't the sort of person who forgot things like that—everyone already knew Bill Clinton never forgot anything. He must have known.

Marla Crider approached the desk warily, feeling a bit queasy. But she couldn't ignore it. He had to know she would see it, he must want her to read it.

"Dear Bill," she read, the handwriting sharp, emphatic, instantly recognizable. Even years later, she was still able to recall most of the words.

"I still do not understand why you do the things you do to hurt me," the letter began. "You left me in tears and not knowing what our relationship was all about," she read.

"I know all your little girls are around there," it continued, "if that's what it is, you will outgrow this. They will not be with you when you need them. They are not the ones who can help you achieve your goals. If this is about your feelings for—" (and here she saw her own name, staring up from the paper) "this too shall pass. Let me remind you, it always does."

What you're feeling now, the letter implied, isn't real. Don't trust it. Listen to your head, not your heart.

"Remember what we talked about," it went on. "Remember the goals we've set for ourselves. You keep trying to stray away from the plan we've put together.

"Take some time, think about it, and call me when you're ready," the letter ended. It was signed, of course, as she had known it would be, "Hillary."

Marla stood over it a long time, frozen, confused. She was a bright girl, a college senior, perceptive about people, but she was only twenty-one, with all the normal romantic ideals of that age. She had started seeing Bill months ago, when she had begun working for the campaign; at first, it had been a casual connection, but with time, the feelings had deepened. He was fresh from the East, only twenty-seven, with a brilliant pedigree, Georgetown/Oxford/Yale, a man on the move, charismatic, energetic; she was just a kid from Fayetteville, drawn to the excitement of a campaign.

Yet they had, in fact, a great deal in common—both had grown up in small Arkansas towns and had Arkansas roots going back several generations; both even had a touch of Cherokee ancestry in their backgrounds. The state was in their blood, its people and history, even its smells— pine trees, barbecue smoke—deeply embedded in their souls. Both had a strong background in politics; her uncle was a respected judge in the area. Each came from down-to-earth folks—her father and grandfather, just like his grandfather, owned a grocery store. Even their birthdays were the same day, August 19. It was no surprise they had gravitated to each other. Both were young, attractive, politically idealistic, Democrats to the core. It had all, up to now, seemed completely natural.

This letter, though, seemed to be talking about something utterly outside her experience. A plan that needed to be adhered to? Some sort of strange pact? Goals. Achievement. What did any of this have to do with love? Just what kind of relationship was this?

Marla had known, of course, that Bill had a girlfriend, Hillary, who had lived with him at Yale, and was now up in Washington, working for the Watergate committee, and who had made several trips down to see him. She knew he was very serious about Hillary, that he was in love with her—but that there was no actual engagement, no firm assurance that anything permanent would ensue.

She had been impressed by Hillary's obvious intelligence, the fact that she was a Yale Law School graduate, working at a high-profile job. Not by her looks, of course. After the first time she'd met her, she'd even said to him, "You all have a lot in common *intellectually*, don't you?" When he agreed, she added, almost to herself, "Then that's got to be it." Annoyed, he had snapped at her not to be a snob.

It hadn't just been Hillary's looks, though—the heavy glasses, unruly brown hair, lack of makeup, long granny-style dresses so out of place in 1974 northwest Arkansas. It had been her attitude, too. She peered through her thick lenses at the workers in the campaign head-quarters as if they were an alien species, with their slow drawls, their easy laughs, their genial Southern manners. Her own manner was abrupt, cool, businesslike. She seemed to trust none of them, to feel they were all far below her intellectual level. Only with some of the faculty members at the University of Arkansas, in Fayetteville, did she seem to feel comfortable.

Hillary and Bill had had a huge fight after her last visit, Marla knew; for several days, there had been none of Hillary's usual calls from Washington. Nothing surprising in the fact she had written him—it was something any woman might have done under the circumstances. But this letter! She wasn't using feminine wiles, she was literally trying to argue him back into the relationship, point by point—as if she were the lawyer, and he was the jury. And what a relationship! A studied plan; a course of action you could "stray from." Just what was this, anyway?

Subdued, Marla gathered up the papers and clothes she had come to get and left the house, driving slowly back to headquarters. Her mind swirled, trying to grapple with the letter's implications. Clearly, a vital, intense connection existed between Bill and Hillary. But it was not the sort of bond she had ever seen before; there was, in fact, something a bit chilling about it. There was genuine emotion, true: you left me in tears, she had said, but how much was organized plan? Could two people forge a true commitment from an intellectual blueprint? Was such a thing even possible? Desirable? What you're feeling now isn't important, the letter had said. It will pass—it always does. Remember our plan.

What would happen if such an alliance became permanent? What would get pushed aside—as mere feelings that don't matter? What happened to feelings deferred? The poet Langston Hughes had asked the same question once, about dreams—did they just dry up, he wondered, like a raisin in the sun? Or sink like a heavy load?

Or do they explode?

In the end, Marla never asked Bill about the letter. She couldn't. She brought it up to a friend, one of the campaign managers, who just laughed—of course Bill had left it out on purpose for her to see, he assured her. That was just the sort of thing he would do. She decided finally he wanted her to realize the relationship with Hillary was *not* set in stone, that *nothing* was sure, yet, and he wanted her to know this. Or maybe he wanted her to understand he had no choice? That the plan was already in place and needed to be followed? She could never bring herself to ask him directly.

But the sudden stark glimpse she'd had into the workings of their relationship, and the question she'd had, standing over the letter—just what kind of relationship was this?—continued to prey on her mind for years, through his governorship, through his presidency, through all of the scandals, and his impeachment.

Marla Crider had no way of knowing, of course, that twenty-five years later, the same question would virtually paralyze the entire country. And that no one—neither friend nor enemy nor pundit nor shrink—would have the answer.

THE MEETING

THEY MET CUTE. Or at least, that was the story that would be told again and again in the following years—at private interviews and public press conferences, in speeches and books, to small groups and large, so many times that eventually many Americans—who had never thought to wonder for a minute how the previous forty-three presidents had met their wives, or why they should care—could reel it off faster than they could their own family tales. Even *Current Biography of 1993* referred to it as an "oft-repeated tale."

Almost always, too, it was told exactly the same way, in almost the same words (a manner that invariably makes policemen suspicious when interrogating suspects), and given rich cinematic flourish: Hillary Rodham, then in her second year at Yale Law School, was bent over her books in the law school library; Bill Clinton, newly arrived from Oxford, was standing across the room, talking to a student who was trying to convince him to try out for the Yale Law Journal. She looked up; their eyes locked. Hillary then got up, "walked the entire length of the law library," as Bill liked to put it, stood foursquare in front of him, and confronted him directly.

"If you're going to keep looking at me and I'm going to keep looking back, we at least ought to know each other. I'm Hillary Rodham."

And Bill the smooth, Bill the charmer, Bill who'd never been at a loss for words in his life, was struck so dumb he couldn't come up with his own name.

For the *Man from Hope* video shown at the 1992 Democratic convention, the two told the story in tandem, à la vaudeville, the camera cutting first to one, then the other, with Bill coming in for the punch line—"I couldn't remember my name!"

Seven eventful years later, speaking at a fundraiser for Hillary's not-quite-yet-announced New York senate campaign, he pulled the tale out again, adding a few premeeting touches.

Actually, he said now, he had first noticed her in class (though since he was a first-year student and she was second year, the chance of their ever having a class together was slim to none). "She was an interesting, compelling-looking woman, so I followed her out of class. And I got right behind her and I said, 'No, this is nothing but trouble.' And then I kind of stalked her around the law school for two or three weeks."

The library scene, however, remained basically the same. "Hillary slams down the book and she walks across the library and she looks at me and says, 'Look, you have been staring at me for weeks, and I've been staring back. So at least we ought to know each other's name. I'm Hillary Rodham. What's your name?'

"I couldn't remember my name!"

The fundraiser audience dutifully laughed, though scarcely anyone could have been hearing the story for the first time. Later, talking to reporters on Air Force One, the president explained why he'd considered Hillary Rodham trouble—"I thought I would fall in love with her, and I didn't want to fall in love."

Maybe not, though up until then, Bill Clinton had been steadily falling in love with one woman after another, with no noticeable reservation.

The cute-meet story, of course, could be true, word for word. But like so many other things with the Clintons, it is unlikely it was the whole truth.

Paul Fray, an early friend and political operative who served as campaign manager for Clinton's 1974 congressional campaign, remembers quite a different version—one he heard directly from Hillary herself.

"I asked her one day, 'Where were you when you met Bill?'" he said.

"She said, 'I was standing there in the registration line.'

"I said, 'Well, how did the conversation start?'

"She said, 'Oh, you know—he just sort of asked me where I was from and I told him I was from Illinois—and the next thing I knew, his leg was rubbing up against mine!'"

Not the best tale for a fundraiser, perhaps—or for a convention, or for *Current Biography*. Still, it does have a definite ring of reality to it. Fray loved it, and foolishly tried to push for more—"Gee, what was he trying to do, Hillary?"—which brought her up quick, earning him an icy stare and a stern, "Don't let your imagination go crazy."

"I said, 'Hey, it's clear you bit for the bug.' She got a little pissed off, like she thought I was putting her down, but I was really trying to congratulate her in a way," he explained. "She *knew* what that boy was about from the beginning."

There are other reasons to take the established story with a grain of salt. Despite the repeated punch line—"I couldn't remember my name!"—there was little about Hillary Rodham's physical appearance at the time that would render a young man speechless. By all reports, she cut a distinctly unprepossessing figure at Yale, with her Coke-bottle glasses, drab brown hair, somewhat solid shape. She was rarely seen in anything but shapeless clothing, and eschewed makeup of any kind. "I don't think she cared that much, and anyway, it was kind of hip then not to look great," fellow classmate Art Kaminsky offered, diplomatically.

By those standards, Hillary was as hip as they came.

"Everyone wanted to date the same two girls in that class, Myra Goldenberg and Sharon Coleman," said classmate Michael Medved, then a strong anti-Vietnam activist who has since become a well-known conservative media critic. "Then there was a whole range of women who were sort of worth considering. Hillary wasn't in either of those groups. She was heavier, there was no aura of availability. She wore those sweatshirts, socks and sandals, big baggy black pants. She was everybody's den mother, everybody's friend—that was what she was putting out."

Medved for one is sure the cute-meet tale is bogus. "I think the thing about him seeing her in the library is garbage," he said. "Not a chance. I'm sure if God has videotapes somewhere, and you could replay it, you'd see." The leg-rubbing story sounded a lot realer, he thought. On the other hand, Bill's stuttering reaction could have been simple embarrassment at being confronted so directly by someone he'd made an offhanded pass at earlier.

But if her looks were not the drawing card, that doesn't mean there was nothing about her that might attract keen interest, particularly from a newly arrived Bill Clinton. A second-year student, Hillary was already well established at Yale, a formidable presence, when Bill arrived in fall 1970. She had arrived on campus the year before, already a celebrity of sorts. Everyone knew about the speech she had given at her Wellesley commencement, in which she had confronted Senator Edward Brooke, the graduation speaker, and that Hillary's remarks had received wide media attention. Hillary's star status was assured, at least in certain rarified circles. People at Yale knew who she was. In a class full of celebrities—and everyone at Yale Law School considered him or herself a celebrity to some degree—she stood out.

Hillary took to Yale immediately; even more than at Wellesley, perhaps for the first time in her life, she found herself in a community where she felt instantly at home, filled with social activists, students as brilliant and ambitious as she was herself. One of a handful of women (thirty-five in a class of 265), Hillary shone—she impressed her professors, made friends with ease. At the moment that Bill Clinton first met her, she was the one at the center of the "in" scene; he was the newcomer, the interloper, looking to ingratiate himself. It was not a moment that would be repeated until decades later when they had come full circle, when Hillary moved out of the White House to begin her own political career, and he would remain alone, a lame-duck commander in chief.

Hillary, in her second year at Yale Law School, was in her element, a confident and happy young woman, and it showed. Classmates describe her as warm, generous and openhearted, always ready to help; the sort of person who asked how you were doing and seemed to really listen to the answer. There was not a trace of the acid wit so many would note later on.

"Universally popular," Medved said. "Someone you could talk to, could laugh with. It's hard to think of anyone at law school who disliked her, and most people did have people who disliked them. She was so exceptionally sunny, mature, confident, kind, generous."

"She had a great laugh and could light up a room. I was very nerdy and she was very nice to me," remembered Steve Hadley, who would later serve as assistant secretary of defense under George Bush. She had, also, "a real sense of presence, a sense she was a player, even then. Which is amazing when you think about it." At one point during their first year, a famous law professor came to speak, and students were invited to the reception. Most of them stood back, cowed, unable to say anything to the great man. Not Hillary. "She walked right up to him, 'Hi, I'm Hillary Rodham.' Not only could she pull it off, she could then engage him in a terrific conversation, the guy obviously enjoyed it."

But she was also "a very outgoing, fun person," said Hadley. "I think somehow that's gotten lost."

Kwan Kwan Wang, her suitemate that second year, also remembers her kindness. "I never heard her say anything negative or snide about anybody," she said. A native of Burma, Wang had never seen snow before, and was somewhat nervous at the prospect. The first snowfall found Hillary at her door, demanding she come out with her; she drove her around New Haven for hours so she could take in the scene, get used to it. Wang was entranced. "You've got to enjoy it now; tomorrow it's going to be all slush," Hillary instructed.

Hillary provided a comforting, sympathetic ear to many Yale males, worried and anxious about the draft. The war was on everyone's mind then, and Yale, especially during Hillary's first year, was a hotbed of antiwar activity. "Everybody believed Yale in the spring of 1970 was going to be the seat of some major revolutionary action," said Jerry Hafter, a classmate. "They had all the store windows boarded up, police were on the lookout for snipers on the roof. Then in the middle of that—Kent State happened." Many never recovered from the shock. "It was like, we're the center of the universe, the smartest people in the world, and lo and behold, the great revolutionary event takes place out there? Not here? It took everyone's breath away."

Many of the students, by then, had been forced to come to some kind of terms with the problem—Hafter, who had been at Oxford, had signed up with ROTC the summer before entering Yale, along with many others. The Yale ROTC unit was almost completely made up of law students who were there for one reason only, protection against the draft; the commander, a liberal type, had announced that if anyone wanted to get out after they received their draft number, he would allow it. Some did leave; Hafter stayed—his lottery number, when it came down, was a precariously low 55. "But there were lots of people at the law school doing what [Bill] might have done," he said.

Years later, during the 1992 campaign, Hillary herself expressed some regret that he hadn't. "Oh, Jerry, our life would be so much easier if Bill had just gone out and marched around with you guys," she complained to Hafter. Considering all the attention being paid in the press to Clinton's draft problems at that time, Hafter thought that was a pretty fair statement.

Everyone knew Hillary; Bill was the new kid in town, much as he had been years before, as a six-year-old, when he'd first moved to Hot Springs from Hope, a situation that had been very difficult for him, friends believed. But he'd learned long ago how to remedy that—you strode into the thick of the crowd, grabbed a hand (or rubbed a leg), introduced yourself, and let loose a wave of Southern charm. It had always worked before.

Not everyone at Yale was impressed by these tactics, though. "Eddie Haskell," said Medved judiciously. "It didn't occur to me at the time, but thinking back, it fits perfectly." (Haskell was the smarmy adult-pleasing kid on *Leave It to Beaver*.) "The sense was that this was a guy who was there for the main chance, who knew exactly who to suck up to. It was like a Sammy Glick kind of thing. He was so eager to please, so much on the make." Bill had an almost courtly demeanor, rather like the young Elvis; his conversation was dotted with "ma'ams" and "sirs." This did not necessarily endear him to his fellow students.

"What did he see in Hillary? The establishment, and an available female. Keep in mind there were very few women, and they were taken," Medved said bluntly. "You took what you could get."

But whatever motives prompted the meeting, and however it actually occurred, there is no question that once it took place, the connection forged between Bill and Hillary was immediate, total, and powerful. On both sides. A number of friends have wondered if Bill was Hillary's first real romance. "If so, it could be the Rosetta stone, the key to everything," one said hopefully. Bill wasn't—she'd seriously dated at least two men in college, and was still somewhat involved with one she'd met in Washington during a summer internship. Kwan Kwan Wang remembers her talking about how difficult it was to break off a longtime relationship. She managed it, however, with some dispatch. Once Bill came on the scene, there was room for no one else.

He was Southern, exotic, fresh from his Rhodes scholarship to Oxford, with an ambition as oversized as the watermelons grown in his native Hope, Arkansas, which he bragged about to anyone who would listen—they were the largest in the world, he said, often. An inordinate number of people from his past have sworn over the years that they always knew where he was headed. There's no particular mystery to that—Bill had told nearly all of them himself, long ago.

"You're going to sleep in the Lincoln bedroom some day," he announced to his mother's close friend Marge Mitchell one day, out of the blue.

"Really," she drawled, unimpressed. "How'm I going to get there?"

"Because I'm going to be president," Bill told her, grandly. "He was a little annoyed at me, that I questioned him," she recalled. It showed doubt; he wasn't used to doubt. Even if it was understandable, given the situation: he was only twelve years old at the time.

Many at Yale Law School had political ambitions; it just wasn't considered good form to mention them. You were supposed to keep those things close to your chest, in the traditional tight-lipped Ivy League manner. "Everybody at Yale Law School back then was thinking about running for political office, being involved in politics somehow," said Medved. "But it was not cool to talk about it." Bill, though, talked about it all the time. "Everybody knew he saw himself as a man of destiny," said Medved. "He intended to go back and help his state, he said often. But there was a sense in which it was more than that, that he was going back to save his state."

People tended to see him as an operator; on the other hand, most thought his prospects were probably pretty good, coming as he did from a small Southern state. "At that time, in the media and culture, there was this huge stereotype of the big-bellied Southern sheriff," noted Medved. "Anyone with a Southern accent was thought to be a racist, a KKK'er. And here was Bill Clinton—he was like this exotic specimen of the enlightened Southerner, someone who had transcended his poor benighted background, was strong on civil rights—there was this immediate assumption he would have this glittering political future, coming from Arkansas."

The other thing everybody at Yale knew about Bill, even from the beginning, had to do with his appetite—for food. "That was the overwhelming impression," said Medved. "The one thing, if someone said, what do you remember about Bill Clinton."

Though he had dated a great many women, and had had a few slightly kinky experiences at Oxford, he was *not* known as a skirt-chaser. Food, though, was another matter; everyone knew how Bill felt about food. Many a classmate was treated to the sight of Bill swallowing a baked potato whole, or ingesting an entire pizza in record time. "Anyone who thinks this guy never inhaled never saw him around a pizza," said one.

"I specifically remember him showing off swallowing those potatoes. 'Look, Ah'm gonna make this potato disappear.' In it went and down, like a snake," said Medved. "It was almost a macho thing with him—like look how much I can eat, look how manly I am. People talked about it behind his back—did you see what Bill Clinton ate?"

Hillary, though, with her plain Midwest accent, her bland suburban roots, was oblivious to any criticism. She was smitten. Proudly, she introduced Bill to her friends. She collared Steve Hadley in the library excitedly. "I've just met this fabulous guy, he's really special," she said, pulling him across the room, to where Bill was standing.

"He was sort of larger than life, big Afro haircut," said Hadley. "I was short-haired, in Navy ROTC uniform, and had these big glasses. And he decided in about thirty seconds I was pretty nerdy—he was absolutely right, of course—and we never said anything much to each other again. But she clearly, from the very start, saw this guy as something special."

"Over the top," was how Medved viewed her reaction. "She was dazzled, right from the beginning. It was, 'You know who I'm seeing right now—Bill Clinton! Can you believe it, lucky me. Look what I've landed.'"

However the relationship would change over time, however many complicated intellectual and emotional components it would come to include, in at least one way, Bill and Hillary were no different from millions of other young couples—part of the initial fusion consisted of a powerful physical attraction. They were the sort of couple who were all over each other in public, often to the embarrassment of others. "A suprisingly hot couple," Medved put it. "Could not keep their hands off each other. You didn't think of Hillary that way. But lots of pawing—him pawing her, but her pawing him, too. It was embarrassing, like, okay, great, you have this relationship—please. They were so thrilled to be together." According to a female classmate, once they moved in together, "they shut that door and didn't come out for a year. They fucked each other's brains out."

Not an atypical college romance, in that way. But there were other, less typical sides. Even at the start, Bill's absolute conviction that he was headed directly for high political office operated as a strong aphrodisiac, fueling the romance. It was a conviction Hillary bought into immediately, a future she desired.

Both Medved and Bill had worked on Joe Duffey's senate campaign that fall. It had ended badly, with Duffey going down resoundingly in defeat. A short time later, Medved ran into Bill and Hillary, at the law school. Medved was still mourning the loss, but Hillary was full of optimism.

"Poor baby, I know you put your heart and soul into that campaign," she said. "But don't worry, pretty soon Bill will be there, in the Senate, working for the [antiwar] cause, and everything will be okay."

It seemed a ludicrous idea to Medved, looking at her oversized, grinning boyfriend, who was wearing a particularly outlandish bright yellow shirt with brown stitching that day, and who looked, like he always looked to Medved, for all the world like he'd just swallowed a canary—totally pleased with himself. Cringing inwardly, he managed a weak smile. You could joke with Hillary about nearly everything, but not about Bill, not then, not ever.

It seemed, to many, an incongruous pairing. Partly it was simply their looks: Bill was noticeably attractive, Hillary not. "You would not have normally said, oh, there's a couple that goes together," said Art Kaminsky.

But others, even at the start, wondered about the regional disparity, too. Hafter, who came from Mississippi and had gotten seriously involved with a Pittsburgh girl while at Yale, knew people wondered the same thing about his relationship, whether it would work out, since he like Bill was committed to going home.

"I was dating a girl, Martha Munsch, who'd been kind of a feminist leader, she'd been the sports editor of a Pittsburgh newspaper before coming to Yale, and the first woman journalist to insist on going into men's locker rooms. So she was kind of a little star, like Hillary was a big star. She was very Northern-oriented, and I was sure I was going back to the South. Things just never worked out.

"A number of people back then thought our relationship was like Bill and Hillary, that they were so far apart, from different poles, it couldn't be bridged over," said Hafter, who had known Bill at Oxford, and considered him basically a good old boy, a can-do type, no intellectual—"but then, I was a good old boy myself; maybe he exaggerated those traits around me.

"It was clear Bill was going back to Arkansas—everyone knew that. People felt it wouldn't work out." Why would a powerhouse like Hillary, whom everyone expected great things from, want to bury herself in Arkansas?

There were also enormous differences in personality, temperament, and approach to the world between the two—though for the most part, those differences only worked to lock in the relationship, each so clearly had what the other lacked. Even then, Hillary was the cool logician, the strategist, the pragmatist, impatient with high-flung rhetoric, able to cut through the guff—even in the early days of her infatuation, friends remember her bringing him up short, telling him to get to the point, give it a break, or even, occasionally, just plain shut up. Bill, meanwhile, was always the emotional reactor, the wild man, all intuition and gut and razzle-dazzle. In class Hillary was the eternally well-prepared student; Bill the guy who would postpone studying to the last minute, then grab someone else's notes on the way out the door. At Oxford, he had avoided getting a degree completely.

"I've seen it said that a lot of Americans at that time did not get degrees at Oxford," said Hafter. "That's really not true. Actually it was very unusual for an American not to earn a degree when there." Bill, though, had been there "more for the experience," he felt. "You didn't see him hanging around the library."

Both Hillary and Bill did well at Yale. But then, doing well at Yale was not as hard as most people thought.

"The basic trick to Yale Law School was getting in, not getting out," said Richard Atkinson, who graduated in 1974 and eventually ended up teaching law at the University of Arkansas. "There was relatively little class ranking back then. You could get away with a lot and people were pretty relaxed about it."

"It's a secret about Yale Law School very rarely revealed," said Art Kaminsky. "It's a wonderful place, but a joke when it comes to any sort of academic pressure. Doesn't exist. The year I got there, 1968, we got rid of grades—it went to pass-fail. It was a pretty laid-back place even before that, and this made it extraordinarily more laid-back." It certainly left plenty of time and energy for getting involved in campaigns, protests, off-campus activities.

Forever after, people would debate about which one of the two was smarter—it almost came down to which sort of mind you preferred. Certainly, though, it was Hillary's brain that got top rating at Yale—she was the one with the true lawyer's mind, people felt. Later, others would give the nod to Bill. "Hillary is smart the way you're smart. Bill Clinton is a whole n'other dimension," Arkansas journalist Gene Lyons remembers hearing from a friend, Dave Criner, back in the 70s.

It would be Hillary, though, who would always impress lawyers the most. Kaminsky remembered Hadley telling him he thought Hillary had been "not just the smartest woman, the smartest *person* at law school," though Hadley himself has no memory of the comment ("She was smart but everyone was smart," he shrugged).

Bill himself went along with the Yale appraisal of Hillary's capability—he decided almost immediately that Hillary was smarter than anyone else, and never wavered from that belief. It was, in fact, practically the first thing Paul Fray remembered him saying about her, long before he brought her down to Arkansas for a visit. "He told me she was the smartest woman he'd ever met, brilliant beyond compare," he said.

Bill and Hillary would never strike people as an obvious match; over the years, many would puzzle over the relationship, in a growing crescendo that reached a peak during the Monica Lewinsky scandal—a time when nearly everyone in the country was pondering the mystery.

One writer, Charles McCarry, produced a fast-paced riff with *Manchurian Candidate* overtones about the rise of a Clinton clone (*Lucky Bastard*, 1998), offering his own sly theory: his Hillary figure is a Marxist operative, assigned to the candidate back in college, who has been trained carefully in the use of (or withholding of) sex, among other techniques. Wacky as it was, it reflected the thoughts of many—Hillary was the dragon lady, the controller, the political dominatrix, the one with a master plan; Bill the (somewhat) innocent dupe, the raw talent; he the bleeding heart, she the tough pragmatist committed to keeping him in check. Not unreminiscent of that other famous couple to come out of the South—Colonel Tom Parker and his Elvis.

There was some credence to this view, of course—just as there was some credence to the later one, which saw Hillary as a decent, loyal help-mate bearing up stoically in the face of a flagrantly misbehaving husband. But it was never that simple.

The truth was that both Bill and Hillary saw in each other the possibility of a dream fulfilled—and the dream was never less than the presidency, the most powerful office in the land. He saw her, from the start, as the one woman who could help him get there; she saw him as the one man who could make it. It is ridiculous to argue that they were like any other two kids in love; they weren't. Their love for each other was infused by the dream, it was part and parcel of it, inseparable from the beginning.

The dream was never of sheer power alone—power, yes, but power to do good works, to help people. Still, achieving the power was the primary task. Believing this, believing in the inevitability of their ultimate achievement, united them in a virtually unbreakable bond, an irrevocable pact.

They were not, of course, the first couple to have come together through dedication to a mutual goal. But the sheer purity and unwavering intensity of the Clintons' aim—not to mention its target—would forever set them apart. Surely no other couple in history ever set out to occupy the White House with such unswerving dedication, such sheer confidence, such unity of purpose.

They believed they were going there, and that they should be there. Bill had been telling people he was going to be president since childhood; soon after they met, Hillary started telling people the same thing. Even those who believed in Bill early on had their doubts; those who heard the announcement from Hillary were even more dubious. It seemed ludicrous, impossible, a kind of joke.

When actually it was nothing of the kind. It was, in fact, exactly what they meant to do.

But at the time, their friends only knew that Bill and Hillary had fallen hard for each other—and that however odd it might seem, however strange a combination, it looked like the real thing.

Mary Lee Fray, Paul's wife, who had known Bill for years, knew at once this relationship was something special.

"Bill had never ever talked about being in love before. But when he called to tell me about Hillary, his voice tone changed. He talked about her heart, her feelings. I'd never heard this before with anybody." In the past, Mary Lee had fixed him up with a number of girls—Sharon Evans, who'd been Miss Arkansas and was a college friend of hers from Ouachita Baptist; even a young brunette sometime singer named Gennifer Flowers, who belonged, as Mary Lee had at the time, to the Young Republicans club.

"But he'd never talked about anyone like he was talking about Hillary. He said, 'This person has the biggest heart. You two have so much in common. You'll love her. You'll absolutely adore her.'"

The minute the conversation ended, Mary Lee called her mother in Alexandria, Virginia—her parents, the Saunders, had gotten to know Bill well, when he was at Georgetown. "Bill's in love," she told her. "The love bug has bitten!"

HILLARY'S POLITICAL ROOTS

I<small>F</small> H<small>ILLARY</small> <small>INHERITED</small> her political savvy, keen sense of strategy, and backroom deal-making from anyone, it was from her late great-uncle, George Beale Rodham. Of his generation, George Rodham was one of the rare shining lights—an aberration in a family of under-achievers. Like George, Hillary has been the shooting star of her generation of Rodhams, seemingly a genetic fluke, completely at odds with the rest of her family.

George in his day, and Hillary in hers—and there are a few others—were the intellectually gifted Rodhams, the doers, the activists, whose accomplishments stand out starkly against the lackluster backdrop of the family as a whole. For the most part the Rodhams were remarkable only for their incredible blandness, simplicity, lack of education and drive. "Ordinary, that's the only way I can describe them—except for a few," a Rodham family observer noted.

They were, for the most part, a collection of exhausted laborers, blistered farmers, clock-punching millworkers, by-the-book civil servants, baby-making machines, drab loners, prudish spinsters, lonely bachelors, and sad drinkers. And even some of those few who had bright futures went into some sort of mysterious intellectual free-fall zone, their lives ending miserably and tragically.

Amazingly, for all that has been written about the Clintons, little is really known about the Rodhams whose genealogical tree has been left virtually unexamined. In fact, knowing those family roots helps to decipher Hillary's enigmatic persona and offers some clues into her complex partnership with her husband.

Compared to the Clintons of Hot Springs—a family with a history devoid of elected politicians before "Billy Jeff" came along—a few of the Rodhams of Scranton, including even Hillary's father, sought distinction in the political arena, seeing themselves as an amalgam of New York's legendary "Boss Tweed" and Chicago's "Bathhouse John" Coughlin crowd. The political Rodhams were backroom politicians, fixers, purveyors of patronage, operators.

The seed of the Rodham politico strain first blossomed with George Rodham, who was born on November 19, 1889, in the family's first homestead on U.S. soil, a drab, wood-frame house at 1103 Blair Avenue in the coal dust–polluted, dreary city of Scranton, in northeastern Pennsylvania, a melting pot of Italian, Irish, Polish, German, and British immigrants who came mostly to work in the mines and in the lace factory. The Rodhams were so poor that whenever the Susquehanna River overflowed its banks one or more of their low-lying houses would be flooded and filled with silt.

George Rodham was the lucky thirteenth child of Hillary's paternal great-grandparents, Isabella Simpson Bell Rodham and Jonathan Rodham, who was six years his wife's junior. To keep food on the table for his enormous brood, Jonathan Rodham worked in the mines. Later he became one of Scranton's finest, walking a beat, twirling a nightstick, often patrolling his own neighborhood in the poor, crime-riddled North Scranton Precinct.

The Rodhams' neighborhood had been a peaceful, predominately white Anglo-Saxon Protestant enclave until right after the turn of the century, when there came a huge influx of Italians into the precinct. With the immigrants came the enforcers from the old country, members of the "Black Hand," the Mafia crime organization.

"There were shootings, knifings, and dynamitings," remarked Nick Petula, a Scranton historian, who documented some thirty-five murders in the Rodham neighborhood between 1905 and 1919—and more slayings, and other forms of mayhem after that.

"The crimes were mostly Italian against Italian," Petula said. "Mostly it had to do with extortion. The store owners, even the miners, paid them so much a month in protection money so they wouldn't bother you—it might even be a penny a week. The mob just made sure they had to pay something to show who was in control. If people didn't pay there were slashings—marking of people, Wild West–type shootouts on street corners. People would tumble out of a bar, guns blazing away."

After eleven years as a beat cop, Jonathan Rodham was forced to leave the department—family lore says it had to do with Scranton's patronage politics; he was appointed by one mayoral administration and booted out by another. He eventually went into the florist business with one of his sons.

By the time Jonathan and Isabella had arrived in Scranton from Durham, England, in the early 1880s, they had already brought nine children into the world, virtually one a year. (The eighth was Hillary's grandfather, Hugh Simpson Rodham.) The remaining four children were born in Scranton.

Since churning out babies was her sole occupation, Isabella kept detailed records on the births. A neatly written log in her handwriting found in a Rodham attic showed the precise day of the week when each child was born. She had "2 on a Monday, 4 on a Tuesday, 2 on a Thursday, 1 on a Friday, 2 on a Saturday, 2 on a Sunday."

The Rodhams' first, Thomas Bell Rodham, born April 23, 1868—he was one of the two Thursday children—was precocious, sensitive, the only Rodham to finish secondary school at that point, let alone go on to college. Jonathan could never have afforded his son's tuition on his meager wages, but the extraordinarily bright boy won a scholarship while in Scranton public school to attend Keystone Academy, a community college, where he excelled.

He then set his sights on becoming a doctor—a doctor in a family of miners and laborers—gaining admission to prestigious Medico-Chirurgical College, in Philadelphia, which later became a part of the University of Pennsylvania.

After graduating in 1897, he married a local girl, Georgia Lackey, with whom he had a son and two daughters. The young physician settled in Scranton and established a modest family practice, making home visits to patients in a horse and buggy until he could afford his first car. During his career he delivered at least fifteen hundred babies, he often boasted.

Highly respected and well liked—a man with a keen mind—he received a mayoral appointment to the Scranton Board of Health, and also served on the city's school board. And he dabbled behind the scenes in local Republican politics. Until Hillary came along, all of the Rodhams were staunch members of the G.O.P.

In 1936, at sixty-eight, Dr. Rodham suffered a stroke and was forced into retirement, which was spent collecting books and listening to baseball games on the radio. "After he had a series of strokes I had a hard time understanding what he was saying, except for when it came to the cuss words," recalled Donald Rodham, the first cousin of Hillary's father, Hugh, and Jonathan Rodham's nephew. "Hillary has his brains, and sometimes his mouth." The good doctor—the first of the few extraordinary Rodhams—died on June 15, 1948, at eighty, some eight months after Hillary was born.

Jonathan and Isabella Rodham's last child was George, the one from whom Hillary, family members believe, inherited her political genes. "He was the only *elected* politician in the family. And he was the only big-time politician the family had until Hillary came along," said a Rodham. "And it's still to be seen whether she'll ever get elected like George was."

Oddly, in her entire life in politics, Hillary has never publicly discussed her family's political roots, among a number of other family secrets.

George was big as a bear and strong as a bull, an intimidating figure. He stood over six feet and weighed at least 225 pounds. He had big heavy-set shoulders, a barrel chest that narrowed to a skinny waist, and spindly legs. In his tailored pinstripe suits and pinstripe shirts, with his neatly parted and combed hair, rimless eyeglasses, and earnest look, he resembled the actor George Reeves who played TV's Superman. As a young man he became a heavy drinker, found that he and liquor didn't mix, went on the wagon, and forever banned booze from his home.

Like many of the Rodham men he looked like a bruiser. As his son Donald diplomatically stated years after his father's death, "Because of my dad's physical stature he earned your respect. But I wouldn't say he was a tough guy. He was a very, very quiet type individual. He did not come out and display his emotions. He did not discuss his problems or his political dealings freely. I would say that's the sign of a good politician."

For almost half his life, Rodham earned a modest living for his family as a surveyor and mining engineer for the Hudson Coal Company. But his real world—and real clout—emanated from his involvement in Scranton Republican politics.

Early on Rodham caught the eye of Lackawanna County Republican ward leader and political boss Bernie Harding, and soon became his protégé.

Harding didn't look the role of the backroom politician, the cigar-chomping deal-maker in the movies. He was courtly, schoolteacherish in his manner and appearance, a pol who never touched a cigar, or a woman. He attended Catholic mass every day, and was good to his mother. But underneath that facade he was formidable—equally feared and respected by his many political enemies.

As one Scranton political insider offered, "Bernie was a black widow spider disguised as a ladybug."

While there's supposed to be a separation between church and state, Rodham came to Harding's attention because of work he did for St. Paul's Lutheran. Rodham had a knack for generating income for the church coffers by promoting highly successful fundraising dinners sponsored by the Ladies Auxiliary. Harding attended a couple of the affairs, saw the people lined up and the money rolling in, and instantly had visions of voters and campaign contributions dancing in his head.

"Bernie saw my father as an organizer," Donald Rodham observed. "He saw him as someone who could bring people together. He thought he would be invaluable to get people into the club."

The Lackawanna County Independent Republican Club was, in fact, a club in name only—an invention of Harding's that he conceived in the early 1930s. As veteran *Scranton Times* political reporter, associate editor, and columnist Joseph X. Flannery, recalled: "The club was a facade that Bernie Harding used to get him standing in the Republican party and it gave him a tremendous amount of leverage within the party. It wasn't a club per se. They didn't have a clubhouse. They didn't have membership. But Bernie had many, many, many friends in power. He built an umbrella over them and called it the Lackawanna County Independent Republican Club. He was able through that process over the years to get a number of good jobs for himself where he was able to direct patronage. He became extremely powerful."

And his protégé was none other than Hillary's great-uncle, George Rodham. "If Bernie was George's mentor, you can believe George was a major power figure in Scranton," Flannery said.

With Harding's support Rodham served two consecutive four-year terms—from 1942, a few weeks after war was declared, through 1949—as a powerful Scranton councilman-at-large. He also became president of Harding's Lackawanna County Independent Republican Club.

Like Bernie Harding, George Rodham had become a political boss.

During his second year in office, Rodham figured in a scandal from which even "Boss" Harding couldn't protect him. In the same election in which Rodham won his city council seat, Scranton voters welcomed a new mayor, successful local undertaker and former city treasurer Howard J. Snowdon, a reformer. Snowdon hoped to rid the city of street crime—several years earlier, for instance, George Rodham's own wife was hit over the head with a blackjack during a mugging. A higher priority for Snowdon, though, was to wipe out corruption and vice in the city: since the turn of the century wide-open prostitution and illegal gambling had been a way of life in Scranton.

Gambling took the form of slot machines that were operated in private clubs and taverns throughout the city, including Rodham's district, where cops on the take, it was assumed, looked the other way. "Gambling, sometimes clandestine, but at other times wide open and politically 'protected' flourished," according to Nick Petula, in his 1989 book, *Scranton Once Upon a Time.*

"The slot machines were illegal," said Flannery, "but the risk of being arrested was very low. The machines raised quite a bit of revenue for the clubs. One administration after another knew they were there, but the politicians weren't going to pick a fight with the American Legion post, the VFW, the Elk's club or the Daquino Society."

In June 1943, however, Mayor Snowdon changed the rules when he ordered a police raid on Daquino Hall, in Rodham's district.

"Daquino was an Italian society and because it was in his district, Rodham represented the club," Flannery said. "The Italian membership was beholden to Rodham for fighting their battles. But Snowdon cracked down on the slots. He was a very self-righteous person."

According to press reports at the time, Rodham was furious. He charged that Daquino Hall had been singled out by the mayor and the police department in retaliation for his opposition to the Snowdon administration. One account in the *Scranton Times* stated: "Rodham alleged that the police had served orders on the club, which is in the councilman's own district and where he has a large personal following, while other clubs and similar organizations having the same 'concessions' for the use of their memberships were allowed to continue unmolested.

"Rodham's friends volunteered the information that in making his charges at yesterday's council meeting, he was not so much defending the operation of slot machines in the Daquino Hall clubrooms, but was protesting the singling out of that organization while other clubs— several within a stone's throw of City Hall—were permitted to enjoy the privileges without interference by the city authorities." The mayor ignored Rodham's allegations.

While Rodham attended council meetings once or twice a week— he was paid $3,600 a year for the post—he conducted most of his political business in secrecy, in the backyard of his modest North Scranton house, a location where no one could overhear what favors were being dealt and what deals were being made.

His son Donald recalled: "People would come down the alley and show up in the yard. My father would have all kinds of conversations out there that no one, including my mother or I, was privy to. They would come in the back gate and my dad would look up and see them and then say to me, 'Just go in the house.' My mother would look up and say 'What are you doing here.' I'd say, 'Mom, Dad's got a visitor.' She'd say, 'Who is it?' and I'd say, 'I don't know.' And that occurred frequently."

Sometimes those seeking help from the councilman were troubled members of the Rodham family.

"Many times my dad would be called upon to help one of the [Rodham] families out of some kind of scrape," he said. "They would pop up every once in a while."

Among them were George's own brother, Robert Bell Rodham, and his wife, Anna May Wittick Rodham. Robert, a great-uncle of Hillary's, was one of the ne'er-do-well Rodhams—a drinker, a laborer, the tenth of Jonathan and Isabelle Rodham's brood.

Probably with some help from the councilman, Anna May Rodham, whose husband was in and out of the picture, scraped together enough money to buy a fleabag hotel and a beer-and-gin joint—Robert was the bartender—on Franklin Avenue in the heart of Scranton's infamous red-light district. She named the place Rodham's Hotel.

While there's no evidence on record that Hillary's great-aunt by marriage was a madam, it's probable that Rodham's Hotel offered a haven for ladies of the evening and their clientele who needed inexpensive short-term lodging. Related drinking, fights, and disturbances caused police problems.

Donald Rodham remembered that the hotel-owning Rodhams visited with his father on any number of occasions, seeking his help.

"When you've got that kind of business, you do run into certain types of problems," he said. "Sometimes my dad would have to go down and put in a word and get the magistrate to look the other way for a little while. Obviously, once you get a little bit of politics involved, you could straighten anything out."

The houses were a rite of passage for local boys. Petula, who did research on the city's red-light district, said he had been regaled with joyous accounts about the houses, the madams, and the girls from a wide circle of local men, ranging from his own father to his more senior teaching colleagues. "They'd tell me when they were young men they'd go to the different houses, knew the names of the madams, how much each house charged, and how they were run."

In his book, Petula wrote, ". . . the red-light district in downtown Scranton became notorious up and down the East Coast. . . .These operations ran so openly it was rumored that huge bribes were paid to city officials. . . . Many people joked that after coal, the houses were Scranton's leading industry."

A longtime Rodham family friend revealed that Hillary's father,

Hugh, savored reminiscing with a few close pals from the old days about losing his virginity in one of the houses. "Hugh used to talk on and on about how sexy the girls were and how they taught him everything he knew about women," the friend asserted. "Hugh said it was the happiest time of his life. But Hugh was a big bragger so it's hard to tell whether he was telling the truth or not. He certainly wasn't known as a ladies' man like his son-in-law, Bill."

If, in fact, Hugh Rodham was a Scranton "John," he was in excellent company.

When writer Norman Mailer came to the city in the 1980s to be honored at the University of Scranton, Joe Flannery chatted with him at a reception afterwards, and learned that the famous author had visited the city many years earlier. "You know," Mailer told Flannery, "I lost my virginity here." Mailer went on to describe how, when he was a teenager, he and a friend from New York had heard about the Scranton whorehouses, saved up their money, and came by bus to the city to enjoy their first sexual experience. "Mailer said that after they got home they had smiles on their faces for a couple of weeks," Flannery recalled.

The New York Yankees often played exhibition games in Scranton, and the city became one of Babe Ruth's favorite stops, too. After a day of visiting schools and orphans and hospitals promising he'd hit a home run for some bedridden young fan, the "Sultan of Swat" would waddle off to his favorite "house" for his own form of batting practice. "The Babe loved it here," said Petula, who also wrote a book on baseball. "The old-timers say the main reason for Ruth's coming here was the girls."

However, all of that changed with World War II and the administration of George Rodham's nemesis, Mayor Snowdon.

Near Scranton, in the town of Tobyhanna, was a bustling military depot where troops were trained and Italian prisoners of war confined. For the soldiers, the Scranton whorehouses became their prime source of recreation. Prostitutes from around the country descended to service the servicemen. When the base commander at Tobyhanna learned that the venereal disease rate among his troops had reached epidemic proportions he ordered an investigation that led directly to Scranton's red-light district. He made the city off-limits to his troops, which cut sharply into Scranton's economy. A high-level meeting between the military and the mayor resulted in a crackdown and virtually overnight most of the houses were padlocked, and the madams and the girls arrested or driven out of town. The troops were then permitted to return for their weekend and evening passes.

With the end of the war, and the demise of the red-light district, Anna Rodham's musty hotel fell on even harder times and she was now advertising "furnished rooms." After getting her and her husband out of constant jams, George Rodham had all but disowned them as relatives. "My dad did what he could to help, and gave advice, but after a while he stayed pretty much clear," Donald Rodham said. "There were some people in the Rodham family whom my father did not socialize with or do business with."

Anna Rodham's son, Robert Jr., who had enlisted in the army just before Pearl Harbor, returned from the Pacific theater "shell-shocked, an emotional wreck, and an alcoholic," a family member said. His father had died in June 1944, at the age of sixty, the victim of a hard life of drinking, smoking, and general carousing. Robert Jr., a cousin of Hillary's, took his father's place as the bartender at the run-down and soon-to-be defunct Rodham saloon.

As a boy, Robert had been close to his uncle Dr. Thomas Rodham, who had found him to be bright and had taken a personal interest in him. The doctor encouraged his nephew and gave him a number of his books, including medical texts. When Robert graduated from high school with honors, the doctor promised to finance his college education. Rodham thought his nephew might be the second physician in the family, one of that small breed of exceptional Rodhams. But Robert was a disappointment. "George Rodham tried to help him and so did my grandfather," recalled Hillary's brother, Anthony Dean (Tony) Rodham. "But Bob Rodham had some mental problems. My grandfather took care of him. My uncles took care of him."

Despite his bleak life, Bob was a bit of a braggart, a big talker. "He boasted that his family was prominent," Petula said. "He bragged about his uncles, Dr. Rodham and Councilman Rodham. One day he said, 'Gee, my cousin Hillary married a guy who's governor of Arkansas.' At the time I kind of blew it off."

When Robert Rodham died of lung cancer in 1981, virtually penni-

less and toothless—the drinking and smoking had taken their toll—
Petula bought the Rodham's house from his widow. "I helped her move
out," he said. "She gave me all the old medical books from college from
the 1890s that had belonged to his uncle Thomas. She also gave me
Bob's dog tags and his military records. I threw it all in my cellar. But after
Bill Clinton's election as president I knew it would be of interest."

SCRANTON LIFE

LIFE WAS RAW AND SPARSE for the Rodhams of Scranton. Hillary's paternal grandfather, Hugh Simpson Rodham, spent as many as sixteen hours a day, often working double shifts, in the huge, two-story brick factory on the banks of the Lackawanna River that housed Scranton Lace Works. In winter, he worked bundled up against the biting cold winds that wailed off the water and into the plant, carrying choking coal dust from the mines a half mile away, and in summer the heat was as intense as the blast furnaces of the nearby steel mills.

For fifty-two of his eighty-six years Rodham operated and later supervised work on one of Scranton Lace's enormous Nottingham looms, throbbing, clunking monsters that stood as tall as a small office building, and weighed as much as a commercial airliner. Today, workers wear industrial-strength headphones to keep out the thunderous noise in the factory, but back then Rodham could only plug cotton into his ears to deaden the incessant hammering.

"I started on the lowest job, folding tablecloths. But once I got in, I didn't leave. It was very hard to get a job at Scranton Lace," recalled Rosie Nemeth, who was an employee for more than fifty-six years.

"You had to have somebody like a relative already working there, some kind of an in. I think whatever religion you belonged to had a bearing on getting in, too. There were mostly all Protestants, some Catholics. I can't remember any Jews."

Rodham never missed a day of work, even if he was sick. With a wife, Hannah, whom he met when she was working as a winder in a silk mill, and three growing boys to house, clothe, and feed, he couldn't afford to lose a penny of his meager wages.

The upside, however, was that his job was guaranteed for life. The local families who had founded Scranton Lace were aware of the difficulties of training new weavers, and therefore were paternalistic toward their highly prized employees. Besides giving Rodham job security, the company also loaned him the down payment on a small two-family house—each having six rooms—at 1040–42 Diamond Avenue; he rented out the second unit for decades to supplement the family income.

Many years after his death, Rodham's middle son, his namesake, Hugh Ellsworth Rodham—Hillary's father—and later, Hillary's brother, Tony, wore a medal around their necks, a simple family heirloom left by the patriarch as a reminder of his hard work, his dedication to his trade, his toughness, his spirit and grit. "To Hugh Rodham," the undated inscription reads, "for recognition of his 25 years of service to the Scranton Lace Company."

Neighbors thought the world of Hugh and Hannah Rodham, according to longtime family friend Marjorie Rodney. "I can't say enough about them," she emphasized years later. "Hugh and Hannah were people to use as role models, churchgoing people, generous people, people who were always there for you when you needed help. They helped my late husband Guy get work and always gave him a good reference."

Bob Clarke, a close friend of Hillary's father agreed. "They were a typical American family, the Rodhams were, the kind of family that has made this country so strong—grand people, God-fearing, law-abiding, and well-liked in the community."

But they also were very private, and some say secretive. No one ever really got to know them.

"You had to know them to be accepted by them," explained Marjorie Rodney. "They were close-knit, friendly only to a point, not allow-

ing people to get too near them. They held you at arm's length. Mr.
Rodham was friendly, but just to a degree. He made you very welcome
at church organizational meetings. But there was always that distance.
If the Rodhams knew you well you were always welcome, but they kept
their guard up."

Every night, Hugh Rodham returned to his small house exhausted
from his labors. The job gave him little time to spend with his family,
except on Sundays when they all went to the nearby Court Street
Methodist Church, and on Friday nights when Hugh and Hannah
played high-stakes pinochle with neighbors.

Because of Hugh's rigorous work schedule, the upbringing of his
sons—Willard, born in 1907; Hugh Jr., born in 1911; and Russell, in
1918—rested with their mother, a big-boned, thick-legged, heavyset,
plain-looking, sharp-tongued woman. Hannah was a strict disciplinarian whose explosive temper and quick hand sparked fear in her sons.

"Life was tough for my father and his brothers," said Tony Rodham,
who had heard the stories about Scranton life from his father, Hugh.
"Dad said my grandmother Hannah, who died before I was born, was
stern and tough and had to be. She ran the house and had to control
the boys because my grandfather worked sixteen hours a day at the lace
factory." Of the Rodham brothers, Hillary's father turned out to be
most like his mother—a sometimes frightening tyrant.

Hannah Rodham also was known as a rabid bigot who railed against
anyone who didn't hold her beliefs. "There weren't that many Jews
around Scranton," a family observer said. "But she was known to get
wound up talking about them. There were more Catholics in the city
and she hated them with a passion, too. She used all the stereotypes.
So the boys heard that sort of thing growing up. The Jews this, the
Catholics that. Mrs. Rodham was decent and hardworking, but she
also was ignorant and uneducated. She just didn't know any better."

The Rodham boys, according to their first cousin, Donald Rodham,
were different as night and day. "Willard was sort of a follower. He was
content to sit at home and smoke a cigar and have his beer, and who
cared when tomorrow came and what it brought. Willard didn't care,
really. After he finished high school, he spent the rest of life at home

with his mom and dad. He had a girlfriend, but he never got married.

"Russell was by far the most intelligent. He was the best educated. He had a lot of book knowledge. He was the brilliant one with the most potential.

"Hugh, on the other hand, was much more of a mover and shaker. He wanted to make a name for himself in the world. He wanted to make money. He did things on his own. He was more or less of a self-starter."

Like many of the Rodham men, Willard was a hefty fellow. Bob Clarke said that when he looked at Willard he saw Babe Ruth. Along with his beer drinking and cigar smoking, Willard loved to eat, and he ballooned larger and larger, finally topping off at some 260 pounds. Friends nicknamed him "Graf" for the zeppelin. His taste in food was simple—meat and potatoes, liver and onions, burgers and fries.

After taking a two-year course at Scranton-Lackawanna Business College, where most of his classmates were young women learning shorthand and typing, Willard got a job with the Scranton Department of Public Works through the good graces of his politician uncle, George Rodham. Through patronage, Willard warmed a chair on the city payroll for twenty-eight years until his death. His official job title was "engineer and surveyor."

Hillary's brother, Tony, observed that their uncle Willard "was something else—happy, gregarious, fun-loving. He never did anything but work for the city of Scranton. He just had very few cares about anything."

The matriarch, Hannah, died of cancer on October 28, 1952, at the age of seventy, two days after her granddaughter Hillary's fifth birthday. Her estate was valued at $628, consisting of thirty shares of Scranton Lace Company stock, and eight shares of stock in the Scranton Bank & Trust Company.

With the death of his mother, Willard pledged to dedicate his life to taking care of his aging father. For the next thirteen years he cooked and served him, and sat with him at night listening to the radio or watching television. But when Hugh Rodham died at eighty-six on March 5, 1965, Willard was devastated. His father's will permitted him to remain in the house, valued at $10,000, and profit from the duplex rental unit as long as he continued to pay the real estate taxes and keep the property in good condition. The patriarch also left his three sons a cabin, valued at $4,500, that he had purchased years earlier at Lake Winola, about twenty miles northwest of Scranton. The place was handed down to Hillary's father who held on to it for "sentimental reasons" but felt "it was a big pain in the neck coming back to see it every summer," Hillary's mother told family friend Guy Rodney.

After Rodham's funeral and burial in the family plot at the Washburn Street Cemetery, fifty-seven-year-old Willard sank into a deep depression, seeking seclusion in the house where he lived all of his life. "I didn't see him around for a while and thought, my goodness, what's happened to Willard," remembered Rodham family friend and neighbor Hazel Price. "Nobody could get an answer when they called him, so the man across the street put up a ladder and opened a window. He opened the front door for the police and they found Willard dead, sitting on the toilet. That's the way he died." Willard had passed away on April 10, 1965, five weeks after his father. While the coroner's report stated that Rodham had died of coronary artery thrombosis due to arteriosclerosis, his nephew Tony Rodham had a different interpretation of his uncle's sudden demise. "He died of loneliness. When my grandfather died, Uncle Willard was lost."

Willard left his estate—the family homestead, the cabin, and a $50,000 stock portfolio that included shares in General Electric and Marathon Oil—to Hillary's father, who later sold the homestead to Hazel Price. "Hugh decided to sell it, quite frankly, when Bill Clinton was running for Congress down in Arkansas. I'll be very blunt—they needed the money for the campaign.

"Hugh did not take everything out of the attic. There were personal family letters, and a lot of family photographs. Later, I sent a lot of it on to Hillary at the White House. It's funny but Hugh Rodham just said 'Do whatever you want with that junk up there.'"

THE MYSTERIOUS DR. RODHAM

IN SEPTEMBER 1962, the youngest of the Rodham brothers, Hillary's uncle Dr. Russell David Rodham, died suddenly and tragically at the age of forty-four. As Tony Rodham recalled, "Uncle Russell was the genius of the family, and he died a terrible death. My father was afraid to tell his father that his youngest son had died. The youngest isn't supposed to die before his father."

Unlike his brothers Hugh and Willard, Russ Rodham was movie-star handsome: square-jawed, lean, with dark curly hair, and a hint of James Garner in his looks. Though he stood only five feet nine, he had a strong body from swimming competitively in high school. But most of all, he was a driven, intellectual dynamo—and an operator.

After graduating from Scranton's Central High where he was president of the class of 1932, he went to Pennsylvania State University, at the time a tuition-free state school with mediocre academic standards. If the Rodhams had had the money, Russ could easily have gained admission to one of the great premed Ivy League schools such as the University of Pennsylvania.

For Rodham, Penn State offered few challenges, and even his rigorous premed curriculum was a snap, leaving him with time for other pursuits. "Russ was always looking for a deal—a way to make money," recalled Dr. William Potter (Pete) Rumsey, a close friend and fraternity brother in the Penn State class of '39. "He started and ran a booming flower business, selling corsages to all the fraternities when they had big dances. He hired other students to help him. He was a real hustler, an entrepreneur, and he did well at it. He was very, very bright, intent on getting good grades, and also intent on making good money."

Despite his academic and entrepreneurial confidence, though, Rodham often appeared wound up, anxious, under some kind of unseen pressure. "Russ was a very, very tense guy," Rumsey noted. "He talked fast—rapid-fire. He'd start to stutter. You could see the stress. Today, you'd say the guy was totally wired." To cope with his anxiety, and whatever demons he was trying to keep in check, Russell began drinking.

Rodham had no great cause in wanting to become a doctor, no burning wish to help mankind by finding a cure for cancer. As Rumsey observed, "It was quite simple—Russell wanted to be successful and make money. That's what always impressed everybody about him—that he was striving for success. And he worked harder. He was a go-getter. Everybody just accepted the fact that Russell would make it big in the field of medicine."

During the four years they were fraternity brothers and classmates headed for medical school, Rumsey noticed that Rodham rarely talked about his family, and never once invited him to visit in Scranton. However, in one of their few discussions about life at the Rodham homestead, Russell made reference to his mother's parochialism, and the probable reason why he'd never proffered an invitation to his close college pal.

"It happens that I'm Catholic and Russ was not," Rumsey said. "He was a Methodist and he once told me, 'If my mother knew I roomed with a Catholic, she'd have a fit.' He told me they were very bigoted about religion. I was a little bit offended, but I don't think Russ was that way."

Rodham was accepted at Jefferson Medical School, in Philadelphia, which had strict religious quotas—at the time, no more than ten Jewish students were permitted in each class. "I felt anti-Semitism from students and faculty," recalled Dr. Leonard Davitch, one of Rodham's few Jewish classmates. "One professor of medicine would never have a Jewish resident; there was a urology professor who hated Jews. You'd hear things said. It wasn't always pleasant."

The day after Labor Day 1939, Rodham met the other members of the class of '43. It was an extraordinary group of bright young men — one would invent the heart-lung machine, and one of the class's mentors would devise Maalox — but all of them faced a dark future. The flames of war in Europe, they knew, would eventually engulf them; the Nazis had invaded Poland; Britain and France had declared war on Germany.

Rodham, who decided to specialize in obstetrics and gynecology, was invited to join a number of prestigious student medical organization: the Alpers Neurological Society, the Hare Medical Society, the Moon Pathological Society, and the Gross Surgical Society. He became business manager of the yearbook, *The Clinic*; president of The Academy, a social organization; and a member of Kappa Beta Phi, a party-oriented fraternity, where Rodham was in charge of food service.

"He had a brilliant future in medicine," Davitch stated. "He was very capable, a good student, interested in everything. Whenever there was a discussion, when we'd stand outside and talk about medicine, Russ was always in the center of it. He was amiable and always smiling, *always*. But sometimes with these people who smile all the time you have to wonder what's going on underneath."

Like his pals at Penn State, there were things about Rodham that bothered a number of his medical school colleagues. "I soon discovered he was a wheeler-dealer, and always seemed to have an ulterior motive," recalled Dr. Rudy Hecksher, who was Rodham's roommate for a time, and a fellow intern. "Russell could manipulate things. He was a good operator, a good politician. I pictured him as a U.S. senator, or the next president of the United States."

Members of his circle were shocked when they learned that Rodham, described as "an intern with dollar signs in his eyes," had begun quietly soliciting patients who came into the accident ward for treatment. As they sat waiting for help, Rodham appeared in his white coat and stethoscope, and spirited them into a deserted examining room, where he treated them and charged them for his services, which was both illegal and unethical. Rodham gleefully boasted to a colleague that he was generating far more money than he had ever made with his flower business at Penn State. One medical school chum compared him to "an ambulance chaser, except the patients came to him on a silver platter, unwittingly."

Eventually, Rodham's clandestine operation came to the attention of outraged Jefferson administrators. "I heard the hospital caught up with his little private practice and he had to discontinue it," Hecksher said. A smooth talker, Rodham got out of the jam without any known disciplinary action being taken against him. He was lucky—a fellow intern had recently been dismissed because, as a prank, he had prescribed "Elixir Dixie Bellis"—a brand of gin—on a chart for a patient.

Rodham also was earning quite a reputation as a playboy—attending parties, seducing nurses. "He was screwing around with a lot of them," Davitch recalled, "beautiful girls from upstate." Rodham also had become a regular at two neighborhood bars, Curley's, and Chassey's, and for a time roomed with a heavy drinker who later died of alcoholism. Their room, in the fleabag Clinton Hotel around the corner from the hospital, became the setting for boozy weekend parties. "There was lots of beer and hard liquor," recalled Rumsey, who'd come over for the weekend from Temple University, where he was a medical student. "And there were girls of course, nurses we knew."

Rodham's fraternity sponsored an annual near-orgy called the "Black and Blue Ball" at a fancy downtown hotel. Members of the police riot squad were assigned to keep the peace because of the wild carousing by the inebriated couples. A gossip column in an issue of *The Clinic*, which described some of the shenanigans, clinically noted: "Russ Rodham having trouble with his external ocular movements"—meaning he was so drunk his eyes were rolling around in his head.

At one point Rodham shocked his friends with the proclamation that he had become engaged to an attractive nurse from the Pennsylvania Dutch country who worked in the obstetrics ward at Jefferson. "Russ called me 'Doody-boy,' sort of a play on my name," said Rudy Hecksher, "and he told me about the engagement to this very nice nurse. I knew her myself because I had worked on the ward. She was a good-looking brunette—sweet, small, quiet, and pleasant. They seemed like a good match. But Russ said to me, 'Doody-boy, it's fun being engaged, but I have no intention of marrying that gal.' And I thought, 'Isn't this strange?'

But I didn't say anything because I didn't think it was my business. They had actually sent out the invitations. Then several of my friends said he didn't marry her, that on the day of the wedding he just didn't show up."

Because of the war and the military's dire need for doctors to treat the wounded, Rodham's class was put on an accelerated schedule, attending classes through the summer of 1942, and graduating in March instead of May 1943. The usual year-long internship also was cut to nine months, ending on December 31, 1943. On January 4, 1944—with the Yanks landing at Anzio, with reports that thousands of GIs were being tortured by the Japanese, and with the RAF bombing Berlin—twenty-seven of the twenty-eight interns in the Jefferson class of '43 were shipped off to serve their country.

Only one, Dr. Russell Rodham, stayed behind.

While Rodham had joined the ROTC at Jefferson and had received an officer's commission in the Army Reserves, he managed to avoid active duty until the war was over by maneuvering to become the class's chief resident. As a result, a number of his classmates came to think of him as a slacker. "I always thought he got that job at Jefferson to avoid going into combat. I believe everyone thought that who knew Russ," Rumsey said. Hecksher, who served overseas in the Army Transportation Corps, observed, "Russ didn't want to go into the service. He did everything he could to keep out. Anyone who had the privilege of living with him could see what was going on."

Rodham, it's believed, had ingratiated himself with several highly respected doctors at Jefferson who felt he was both brilliant and troubled, and might have helped him avoid the war. Recalled fellow intern Dr. Bernard Miller: "Jefferson was kind of a closed little family. They always looked after their own in a very kindly, helpful way. I think that is what happened. There were some unsavory tales about Russ at that time, something about alcohol or drugs, something untoward. I think it was just a matter of someone being helpful to him."

According to military records, Rodham eventually did go on active duty, but not until July 7, 1945—two months after Germany surrendered, and a month before Japan capitulated. The farthest he served from the family homestead in Scranton was at a peaceful army convalescent hospital in sunny Daytona Beach, Florida. Discharged as a Medical Corps captain on April 17, 1947, he was photographed in uniform proudly wearing the World War II Victory Medal, and the American Campaign Medal.

After the war Rodham's classmates—even his best pals—lost track of him, and they said he never made any effort to contact them. Some believed he had begun an obstetrics practice, but could not locate him. Others speculated his apparent disappearance had to do with his embarrassment or guilt about his military service. There was even a rumor that he had taken his own life.

In fact, about the time his niece Hillary was born in Chicago, Rodham had quietly returned to Scranton with a wife, Elizabeth, and a baby. They moved for a time into the family homestead with Hugh, Hannah, and Willard. "Elizabeth was a nurse, a Southern girl, and at some point they had a daughter, Kimberly," said Hazel Price, who lived in the other half of the Rodham's duplex on Diamond Avenue. "One day I just came out on the porch and Russell said, 'Hazel, I want you to meet my wife.' She was a very nice, very attractive girl with dark blond hair, kind of petite. Kimberly had the lighter hair too, and the lighter eyes."

Not long after, Rodham established a general medical practice in town, and he, his wife, and their baby moved into "a traditional doctor's house" where his rented office was located. However, within a year or two his life fell apart: his marriage ended, he closed his practice, and he disappeared from Scranton. There are contradictory accounts of what happened because, as Hazel Price pointed out, "The Rodhams were a very closed family when it came to family troubles. They just didn't talk about them. You couldn't even say to his mother or dad, 'How's Russell?' because they'd just clam right up. There was just such a cloud of mystery. It was all very hush-hush, and nobody would talk about it."

One story offered up by the family came from Hillary's mother, Dorothy Rodham, who told Scranton friend Marjorie Rodney's husband that Russell had stopped practicing medicine after being beaten severely while examining a prisoner of war patient at a local Veterans Administration hospital. While there was such a POW camp in the Scranton area, at the Tobyhanna army complex, there is no record that a Dr. Russell Rodham had ever worked in, or consulted there, or for that matter, at any VA hospital in the country.

In fact, for years Rodham had been battling with bouts of depression that became more severe after he returned to Scranton. After closing his practice, he quietly moved to the Chicago area and stayed with his brother Hugh's family in Park Ridge, when Hillary was about four years old.

"When Uncle Russell went through his depression he came to our house and was taken care of by my father," Tony Rodham acknowledged. "He stayed at our house for a *long* time. He was not happy. He had a sad life. In Chicago he drifted about doing different jobs. My father helped him out financially. It was really kind of sad because Uncle Russell was a great guy. He'd always bring Hillary and me and my brother Hughie gifts. He'd come over on Christmas morning and set up the train. He was what every kid should have as an uncle."

With financial help from his brother Hugh, Russell Rodham bought and moved into a small apartment building on Broadway in a run-down section of Chicago. For a time he worked as a salesman, according to Tony Rodham, possibly selling medical supplies.

By the early '60s, Rodham's life was in ruins. Depressed and drinking, he lived alone in his small walk-up apartment, and the one-time golden boy of the family—the former star of his medical school class—eked out a meager living working as a bartender in a nearby restaurant called the Ivanhoe, a former Prohibition-era speakeasy and hangout for gangster Al Capone.

"That's so shocking and very strange if you knew the Rodham family," observed Marjorie Rodney. "Being Methodist, they didn't believe in alcohol. They were brought up without being familiar with that type of behavior. They were very straitlaced. Their church meant a great deal to them."

Shortly after two on the afternoon of September 4, 1962, Rodham fell asleep while smoking a cigarette in a frayed easy chair in the grimy and dimly lighted basement of his building. Firemen rushed him to Illinois Masonic Hospital where he was pronounced dead on arrival from extensive burns. A brief story the next day in the *Chicago Tribune*, headlined "Bartender Dies in Fire in Broadway Flat," quoted unnamed friends as saying Rodham "had been ill since receiving antirabies shots after being bitten by a dog two months ago." Years later his nephew Tony Rodham observed, "It was very sad what happened to Uncle Russell. He had a brilliant future, a hard life, and a tragic end."

A number of curious things happened following Rodham's death, all attributable to Hillary's father. For instance, as the informant on the death certificate, he stated that Russell had never been married, but military records and the accounts of friends showed otherwise. In his poorly typed will naming his brother as executor, Russell Rodham had left a fourth of "what little I have . . . to Clarine for her kindness and 1/2 of what Clarine gets is to go to Kim Bales. The money is to be kept in the form of War Bonds, until she finishes high school. In case she wants to go to college. Hugh be sure and see that my will is followed." Tony Rodham identified Clarine as his late uncle's girlfriend "who I'm sure was helping him through his problems." He said he did not know the identity of Kim Bales, whose first name is the same as that of the toddler Russell Rodham said was his daughter when he had returned to Scranton years earlier. Tony Rodham said he had never heard from his parents that his uncle had ever been married or was a father.

The timing and wording of Rodham's obituary in the *Scranton Times* also was odd. It appeared on October 14, more than a month after his death. Moreover, the obituary, which was placed by Hillary's father, was filled with falsehoods and misleading statements. It said that Rodham had died on October 9, and that he had been "a practicing physician" in Chicago. It did not state how he had died. The accompanying photograph showed Captain Russell Rodham in his army uniform "as he appeared in 1945," and noted that he had returned to Scranton following the war—suggesting that he had participated in the conflict. The obituary also misstated that "military rites" were conducted at the funeral in Chicago.

"I picked up the evening paper and there was Russell's picture," recalled Hazel Price. "That was how I knew he had died. Quite frankly, none of the Rodhams ever talked about it."

THE WORLD'S GREATEST SALESMAN

IF HILLARY INHERITED HER DRIVE, her ambition, her guts, and her arrogance from anyone, it was from her father, Hugh, who spent his entire working life as a salesman. Bob Clarke, who bonded as a life-long friend of Hugh's when they played in the outfield together at Scranton's Central High, observed, "When my wife and I see her on TV, we look at each other and say, 'Well, she's just like Hugh, oh yes.' Hillary has her father's courage, indomitable will to succeed, and ability to cast off obstacles."

Another close Rodham family observer was less diplomatic in comparing father and daughter: "Hugh was the consummate pitchman, a great bullshit artist," he asserted. "Hillary is a more sophisticated, better educated, and a far brighter version of him. Hugh made it selling curtains to hotels and motels, and Hillary made it selling Bill Clinton and herself to the American people."

Rodham began earning his reputation at Central High where he was a poor student, but was big and tough enough for sports. For a baseball game against Blair Academy, for instance, he had a friend chauffeur him to the playing field in a borrowed open touring car while he sat in the back, one leg over the windowsill, puffing a big cigar, trying to look like the playboy scion of one of the Vanderbilts.

Donald Rodham, Hugh's first cousin, never forgot the rush Hugh seemed to derive from watching him practically choke to death. "At Lehigh University, where I got a degree in chemical engineering, I was smoking cigarettes. And it was nice of my cousin Hugh to teach me how to chew tobacco. The only thing he didn't teach me to do was spit. I swallowed it. I thought my bottom was coming up. It was horrible. And Hugh just laughed and joked about it. I said, 'It might be funny to you, but I'm about to die here!' It was horrible. Hugh didn't care. That's the kind of guy he was."

Rodham, whose high school grades were a disaster, was accepted at Penn State because of a sports scholarship arranged through family political connections. He had no interest in academics; his main course of study was physical education. On campus, he divided his time between a jock group called the Friars, and drinking with his fraternity brothers at Delta Upsilon socials.

In the years after Hillary became famous, articles and books suggested that her father had been a college football star. But the only information Penn State had about his pigskin career was that he had "lettered in football." But for years after he graduated in 1935 with a B.S. degree in education, Rodham often bragged about his gridiron prowess and complained about his playing field injuries.

In fact, Rodham was more bench-warmer than all-American, according to a number of Penn State alumni, such as Pete Rumsey, who was in premed at Penn State with Russell Rodham and was a member of Delta Upsilon.

"I've heard people say he was a football star, but he wasn't," contended Rumsey. "Hugh was on the football squad, but to my knowledge he didn't play much. He may have gotten in a game or two. One of my fraternity brothers, older than I, said he never knew of Rodham *ever* playing. The impression I had when I met Hugh was that he was a loudmouth who boasted a lot." Another fraternity brother, Robert Seigler, described Rodham as "a bag of wind. He was all for getting out of anything he didn't have to do, academically and in the frat house. He didn't leave a good impression. And he was no Knute Rockne."

In terms of personality and physical appearance Rodham resembled his favorite 1950s television character, the portly loudmouth Ralph Kramden. And like Kramden, Rodham was constantly searching for the big score, the gold ring, the one spectacular get-rich-quick scheme that would put him on Easy Street. When, among other lost endeavors, a plan to make it big in parking lots bombed, or when a gambit to become a real estate mogul failed, Rodham always was able to make a buck selling draperies, the product he knew best, the business he learned as a young man in Scranton where he grew up during World War I and the Depression.

"Dad was the world's *greatest* salesman," boasted Tony Rodham, a salesman himself. "I witnessed him pitching clients and he was relentless. He knew the ins and outs, and he knew the customer better than the customer knew himself. There are certain techniques you use for selling and one of them is that the first time you get a 'no' you know that's not really a 'no,' it's only an objection. He would cover the objection and continue to close. If he went out for a sale, he always made the sale. You never saw him lose a sale. Our father was *the* best closer I've ever met in my life."

Rodham acknowledged that his father's salesmanship abilities were analogous to those of the amusing aluminum siding hucksters portrayed in *Tin Men*, and the slick Florida land peddlers represented in *Glengarry Glen Ross*. "It's very true," he said. "Dad could sell anybody anything. Pardon the old expression, but he could sell refrigerators to Eskimos."

One of those Hugh Rodham had sold a bill of goods to early on was a young woman from Scranton. It was the summer of 1937 and love was in the air. So was the famed aviatrix, Amelia Earhart, whose plane had gone down in the Pacific at virtually the same moment Hugh went down on his knees to propose to his first true love. While Hugh and his girl had been neighbors since childhood, and had dated a bit in high school, it wasn't until they started working together at Scranton Lace that they had become serious about each other.

A hulking fellow who wasn't much of a ladies' man, Rodham had good reason to court the girl. Despite her long hours in the factory to help support her poor family—she was an only child whose father worked in the mines and did some farming—the twenty-two-year-old cut a cute figure, with long, shiny, dark brown hair. Moreover, she had had her blue-green eyes on Hugh ever since his football-playing days in high school.

"Hugh was pretty forward," she recalled almost sixty-three years later, at the age of eighty-four, speaking for the first time about their relationship. "He was very conceited because of the football. His friends had a lot to do with his being forward. He was hero-worshiped, being a football player in high school. I went to some of the games. I think that was my attraction in a nutshell. Playing football was attractive. It's ridiculous, but people look up to them. But he wasn't a good student, very ordinary. He was smart in a street way, not in a book way. Then he got into college with a grant because he was a football player. I didn't see much of him during college, not until he came back and we worked together at Scranton Lace."

They took romantic walks along the river, and went to an occasional movie, and dinner. He professed his love to her, and soon proposed marriage. She joyfully said yes to being Mrs. Hugh Rodham, and on July 28, 1937, the couple strolled arm in arm to city hall and took out a marriage license, good for sixty days. Hugh explained that because of the tough times—the Depression was at its peak—he couldn't afford to buy her an engagement ring, and she understood. "No one did that in those days," she said. "No money."

"Being it was the Depression, we had no plans for the future," she continued. "We had no idea where we would live. But we thought we were in love. We were very, very young, and you misconcept [sic] love, if you know what I mean. You think you're in love, but you're not."

Around the time of his engagement Rodham had grown tired of working as a laborer lifting boxes at Scranton Lace, and couldn't bear the thought of spending a lifetime at the factory like his father. Despite what his fiancée believed, the ambitious Rodham's future was constantly, obsessively, on his mind.

Rodham's pal, Bob Clarke, remembered a night in a coffee shop when Hugh exploded with frustration over his plight in life. "It was after college and he was working for the lace works. Hugh was talking about what he wanted to do, and he displayed his dissatisfaction about remaining in Scranton the rest of his life. He said, 'Damn it, Bob, I'm not going to hang around here and be just another'—and I don't know whether he said 'flunky' or not—but that's what he meant. He wanted to get into his own business eventually. He said, 'I'm going to go to Chicago and strike it rich.' Hugh was a forceful fellow. He was fearless. He had big plans for himself."

Rodham got a chance to show his drive and ambition when Scranton Lace offered him a sales job—there weren't too many young men with college degrees around. Part of his territory included Chicago, where many of the firm's clients, mail-order houses like Sears & Roebuck and Spiegel, were located.

It was there in the Windy City, during one of his early business trips—with his fiancée back home counting the days—that Rodham fell hard for a thin, brown-eyed, brunette, and buxom 18-year-old office girl named Dorothy Howell, who worked for another company two floors below Rodham's regional office in the Merchandise Mart.

In no time flat, Dorothy had stolen Hugh's heart, and the Scranton girl's groom-to-be. "He didn't tell me he'd met someone else," she snapped years later. "He just dropped our engagement completely. He went away and that was it, and I went on with my own life."

About a year and a half later, she married a weaver like Hugh's father at Scranton Lace. "He was very different, very intellectual, the opposite of Rodham," said the woman, who was widowed in 1984. "I never knew where Hugh was until I started hearing that Hillary Clinton was his daughter."

Did she have any regrets about losing Hugh Rodham to Dorothy Howell? "I'm glad I didn't marry him," she declared. "I wouldn't want to be the mother of Hillary. I don't think much of her. I think she's very forward, too."

With a new woman in his life, Rodham also found a new job—selling draperies and quilts for a company called Barrett Textiles, located in New York City's garment district. After some training in Manhattan, Rodham was assigned as a salesman to work the territory west of Ohio. To be closer to Dorothy, and his customers, he made a permanent move to Chicago. On the side, he also continued representing Scranton Lace, seemingly a conflict of interest since the two firms were competitors. Like a winning candidate campaigning, Rodham was constantly on the road selling, glad-handing, downing a few shots and beers with potential clients, and soon he became one of the company's big-commission boys. "That's when he got his background in how to run his own company," observed Donald Rodham.

"Hugh was a hotshot," a colleague recalled. "He'd sit back, light a cigar, and act like he was some kind of mogul. He was a very ambitious, driven guy, with big dreams. Practically from the day he got to Chicago he told me over and over, 'I'm going to be president of my own company—mark my words.'"

Like Hugh, Hillary's mother had come from poor and parochial roots. But unlike Hugh, who had fled Scranton because it wasn't big-time enough for him, Dorothy Emma Howell didn't have any grand plan for herself. Emotionally battered, she had taken flight to escape a grim upbringing filled with hardship, disappointment, and distrust.

Dorothy's story began in Chicago where she was born in June 1919 on South Michigan Avenue, in a poor neighborhood of servants, clerks, and janitors. Her mother, Della Murray, was only fifteen and her father, Edwin Howell, a city fireman, was just seventeen, when they were married by a Baptist minister in June 1918, with Della's parents' permission. Because of her poor circumstances, the early marriage, and the pregnancy, Della had never received a formal education. Five years after Dorothy's birth, the Howells had another daughter, whom they named Isabelle.

In her best-selling, ghostwritten book, *It Takes a Village*, Hillary noted that her maternal grandparents "were too young for the responsibilities of raising children, and they decided they no longer wished to be married. . . . When my mother was only eight years old and her sister barely three, her father sent them alone by train to Los Angeles to live with his parents, who were immigrants from England."

Hillary described Dorothy's paternal grandmother as a "severe and arbitrary disciplinarian who berated her constantly, and her grandfather all but ignored her." The girls' father "was an infrequent visitor" and their mother [Della] "vanished . . . for ten years."

When Dorothy was fourteen, she fled her grandparents' home in the conservative, parochial town of Alhambra, and took a job as a live-in babysitter for a family that allowed her to continue her high school education. The woman of the household was a "college graduate" who gave Dorothy "books to read, challenged her mind, and emphasized how important it was to get a good education. She also provided a role model of what a wife, mother, and homemaker should be," Hillary wrote.

Living in that family "healed" Dorothy of what could have become "lifelong wounds," her daughter maintained, and her "character took shape in response to the hardships she experienced in her early years."

As a result of her childhood, Dorothy Rodham had developed "a strong sense of social justice and her respect for all people, regardless of status or background. . . ."

Though brief, it was a story of mythic proportions. And no one would have any reason to question the facts. It seemed so candid, and honest. As it turned out, though, Hillary's account of her mother's roots was far from complete.

In the summer of 1999, four years after Hillary's book was published and while she was revving up for her New York senatorial campaign, new details surfaced about Dorothy Rodham's life in the most unlikely of places, a national Jewish newspaper, the *Forward*.

Acting on a tip, the weekly retained the services of a genealogist who determined from yellowed public records that Hillary's grandmother's second husband, whom she married in 1933, was a Jewish businessman from Chicago by the name of Max Rosenberg. Moreover, the Rosenbergs had had a daughter of their own, Adeline—nicknamed "Addie"—who was Hillary's half aunt, and Dorothy Rodham's half sister.

For years Hillary had kept the Rosenbergs' existence a closely guarded secret, despite the fact that Max and Addie Rosenberg had been an integral part of Rodham family life, for better or for worse. But after the story broke, Hillary—who never mentioned a Jewish connection to the Rodham family though she made her ties to the Methodist Church well known—confirmed having fond childhood memories of Max Rosenberg, of spending fun afternoons with him.

Among those who had welcomed the Rosenberg revelation, who had been stewing for years over Hillary's secrecy about it, and who firmly believed Hillary, or her people, were behind the leak for political reasons, was Oscar Dowdy, Hillary's first cousin, the firstborn of Dorothy Rodham's sister, Isabelle. Three years older than Hillary, Dowdy has been an intimate part of the Rodham family melodrama, an eyewitness to many of the family's struggles, scandals, triumphs, and tragedies.

To underscore the tight bond between the Rodham and Dowdy families and Max Rosenberg, Dowdy pointed out that his younger brother, Max, who was born an epileptic and slightly retarded, was

Rosenberg's namesake. And he noted, too, that his aunt Dorothy's kids—Hillary, Hughie, and Tony—had as youngsters considered Rosenberg their grandfather because Edwin Howell, their biological maternal grandfather, had vanished.

"We would do the typical family things with Max whom I fondly call my grandfather," said Dowdy. "We'd get together for dinner at restaurants, or for holidays and birthdays. We did family things together. Everyone went to Grandma Della's house. Max helped Hillary's father and my father in many ways. I never once heard Hillary talk about how she lived in an apartment next to mine in a building that Max owned. Max would take Hillary and me to a child amusement park called Hollywood Kiddieland in Chicago. I would have been six, seven, eight years old and Hillary was three years younger than me. We were all very close."

In 1926, according to public records, Edwin Howell filed for divorce from Della. In his petition, he painted Hillary's maternal grandmother as a harridan. He said that one day in January 1926 he had come home from work and Della "insisted on wanting to go out, which she had been doing right up to date for a period of five or six months . . . I couldn't go. I worked most all the time. She became abusive and angry, and scratched and bit me, flared up at me."

His allegation was supported by one of Della's three sisters, the married Frances Czeslawski, who testified that she witnessed her sibling's "violent temper" and the fight with her husband. "She wanted to go some place, and I guess Mr. Howell didn't have the circumstances to take her," she testified. "She flew at him and scratched his face." Another witness, an employer of Edwin Howell's, also came forward to corroborate the violent confrontation.

In 1927, nine years after Edwin and Della were married, their divorce was finalized. Della was considered an unfit mother and custody of the couple's two daughters was awarded to Edwin Howell. He immediately shipped off Dorothy and Isabelle to California to live with his parents, which is the period Hillary discussed in *It Takes a Village.*

While there's no reason to doubt Dorothy's Rodham's tale of woe while living with her paternal grandparents, there's no eyewitness support for the story, either. Asked about his cousin Hillary's published account, Oscar Dowdy stated, "That's a lot of gray area. My mother

[Isabelle, Dorothy's sister] didn't tell me a lot. She just said that somehow they ended up in California. It's pretty ancient history. I couldn't elaborate."

After the divorce from Edwin Howell, Della immediately began dating, which was no big surprise. As Dowdy remembered his grandmother, "She was a fun-loving party girl."

In fact, Della Howell was quite a dish—a flirtatious brunette with hazel eyes, a round face speckled with freckles, ivory skin, full lips, a voluptuous figure on a tiny frame, and a mischievous twinkle in her eye.

Apparently that's what first attracted Max Rosenberg, who had an eye for the ladies. "My grandmother was a pretty hot number," observed Dowdy, "and Max used to flirt a lot, too. I remember when he'd take me out to a restaurant when I was a little boy, he'd flirt with all the women. So I'm sure Della had no trouble getting his attention, and that Max got turned on by her."

Otherwise, Della and Max appeared to have very little in common. They had come from entirely different worlds: Della, the gentile hotsytotsy, and Max, the Jewish operator. Della was enthralled by Max's power, business acumen, and bank account—a far cry from the *schlepper* she had been married to, though maybe not as good-looking.

But Max wasn't chopped liver, either.

"His smile was as wide as his face," a Rodham family member vividly recalled. "He was happy, smiley. Max was a slight man. He always wore dark-rimmed glasses. He had that Jewish nose, and he had that Jewish accent going, too. If you just bumped into him and had a casual conversation there would be absolutely no doubt that the man was Jewish."

By his early thirties, when he met Della during the Depression, Rosenberg already was a savvy, successful young entrepreneur.

"Max had come from desperate poverty," Dowdy recounted. "He was a self-made man. When he was very young he worked as a printer's apprentice. Part of his duty was to go down to the neighborhood tavern with a couple of bucks and buy beer by the bucket and sell it to the printers."

Later, Rosenberg made money in the stock market, bought a big apartment building in Chicago, and had lucrative real estate investments in Florida. "He would buy every bad mortgage he could get his hands on and he sometimes foreclosed and resold the same house several times," said Dowdy. "Max was a wheeler-dealer, a hustler. He was very outgoing, he had a very strong business sense, he knew politics, he was a hell of a motivator of friends and relatives, and he was very demanding. Business was pretty much it for him, making the almighty dollar.

"I can remember words from him that he got himself in a big jam with the Internal Revenue Service, and that he basically paid his way out of it. He was pretty good at concealing things. He said, 'All right fellas, this is what I'll give you,' and they accepted it. Another time, and I don't know when it was, or what the circumstances were, but he was in jail. Mob connections? There was just a lot of hearsay about how he sometimes got things done. You'd almost think he had to know those people.

"After the war I remember hearing stories about how he had stockpiled rationed goods such as tires. Things that were rationed he had his hands on. For the most part he was making sure the family had stuff. But he could have been selling it, too. He was a pretty shrewd character."

Rosenberg was also encouraging, and lovable, a man who despised failure and worshiped success.

Tall, slim, blond, and blue-eyed Helen Rutherford Dowdy, for one, said she was absolutely charmed by Rosenberg, whom she had first met in 1962, at sixteen, after she got married to Oscar Dowdy, then just eighteen, in what was a veritable reenactment of his grandmother Della's teenage marriage.

Unlike other members of their families, Helen Dowdy noted, Rosenberg was "supportive and encouraging," especially when she and Oscar faced a bumpy period a couple of years into wedded life. "Max was like, 'Damn it, if you want this to work, you get home and put on something sexy and you seduce him, and that's all there is to it.' That was Max—he said what he thought," she said.

While Max had money, personality, and streetsmarts, Della Murray, on the other hand, was an uneducated, unemployed, and unsophisticated wildcat—a "*shiksa kurvah*," as Max's mother, Mollie Rosenberg, contemptuously referred to her when she learned that her son was serious. To Mrs. Rosenberg, a member of the Hebrew Immigrant Aid Society, the Sisterhood of Agudas Achim North Shore congregation, and a Yiddish newspaper reader, Della was "*goyische* trash." Despite his mother's strong feelings, Max, thirty-two, popped the question and Della, thirty-one, accepted. It was not a fancy affair: the two of them hopped into a cab and drove to Chicago city hall where they were married in a civil ceremony. Mollie Rosenberg was furious when her son called her to tell her the news. "There was a bit of a rift between Max and his mom," Dowdy learned years later. "She was upset because, of course, he married a gentile."

Over the years, Della and Max would battle furiously, and their religious differences often came into play. During fits of temper, hotheaded Della, who refused to convert to Judaism, hurled anti-Semitic epithets at her husband.

"I can remember a lot of arguments," said Dowdy. "Many times they revolved around money. Max gave Della probably just about anything anyone could want, but it wasn't hers. Max had control. I can remember my grandma and me having a conversation one time and Grandma saying, 'I wish I had ten thousand dollars.' And Max said, 'Well, what would you do with it?' And she couldn't really give him an answer. He said, 'I'll go get you ten thousand tomorrow, just tell me what you want to do with it.' Della had a pretty good life, but it was a control thing. It was always Max's money."

In fact, to this day, it is a mystery to family members why Della and Max had hooked up in the first place. Oscar Dowdy, who had lived with them for a time during his childhood, theorized that besides the physical attraction, Max wanted to save Della "from her wild side" and help her to settle down.

"I think he saw in her some good qualities that needed some nurturing," he observed. "She was pretty wild and probably a lot of times not very ladylike and he was determined to help teach her how to be a classy lady. And I think he tamed her down to some extent, but she was still a party person."

A year after Max and Della tied the knot, fifteen-year-old Dorothy, and her ten-year-old sister, Isabelle—Oscar's mother—returned to Chicago from California for their first meeting with their new stepfather, Max. Isabelle stayed, but Dorothy despised Max from the moment they met, and stubbornly decided to return to the West Coast against her mother's wishes. She apparently felt that life with the family for whom she was worked as a domestic was a better choice for her than remaining with her mother—and her new husband.

What had sparked Dorothy's animosity toward Rosenberg?

Della had promised Dorothy—who desperately wanted to go to college—that Rosenberg would pay for her tuition, according to Dowdy. But Della apparently had made the pledge without Rosenberg's knowledge, and had used it as an inducement to convince Dorothy to return home. Moreover, it's believed, Della had overstated the type of education that Rosenberg was in fact willing to finance—he was thinking about sending her to a secretarial or vocational school, not a four-year college. When Dorothy found out, she was livid.

Her hostility was fierce, and she held a lifelong grudge against Max Rosenberg, causing tension and tumult within the family for years. Dorothy's resentment of Rosenberg, some family members have asserted, influenced Hillary's feelings about him, too, and is probably the reason for her failure to ever reveal their connection. Dorothy also came to detest her half sister, Addie, Max and Della's daughter.

In 1936, Della Rosenberg petitioned the Cook County Superior Court to grant her custody of Dorothy and Isabelle, stating that Max Rosenberg wanted to adopt them. She charged that her ex-husband, Edwin Howell, had "failed, neglected and refused to make suitable provision for herself and their two children." She told the court that in her new circumstances as the wife of a businessman she was "abundantly able to support, maintain and educate" the girls.

Court papers noted that Max Rosenberg "is as much interested in the welfare of said children as if they were his own; and he is desirous if such a result could be legally consummated, to adopt them as his own."

The Rosenbergs were confident about winning the custody battle, having established themselves in the community as a financially sound and stable family. In 1934, a year after their marriage, Della gave birth to Addie, the only child Della would have with Rosenberg, and the couple bought a comfortable two-bedroom, red brick bungalow at 6341 Campbell Avenue, in a Jewish section of Chicago's middle-class Rogers Park neighborhood.

While Dorothy chose to remain in California working as an au pair, her mother Della had reinvented herself as something of a young Chicago matron. She now had the means to send out the laundry rather than to do it herself, to hire her own girl to clean, cook, and watch Addie and Isabelle. From Max, who wore tailored suits and bought a new car every year, she had received a couple of minks, and a glittering diamond engagement ring to show off.

"They always lived well," Oscar Dowdy noted. "It was certainly upper middle class. Over the years they would travel to Europe. When Cuba was open it was a hot party area, and they went to Havana a few times. They spent a lot of time in Florida."

But for some unspecified reason, according to the court records, the judge didn't buy the Rosenberg's case, and ruled that custody of Dorothy and Isabelle remain with their father.

"For years, the family has been stymied as to why the court ruled that way. My only feeling is that they looked back on Della as having basically abandoned my mother and Aunt Dorothy years earlier," Oscar Dowdy stated. "Reading between the lines it had to do with Della not being a fit mother originally."

Despite the court's decision, however, there is no evidence that Edwin Howell ever had custody of his daughters, or that they had ever lived with him. "Their father Edwin just disappeared completely," said Dowdy. "Over the years, there was very little conversation about him from my mother, or Aunt Dorothy. I do remember a comment from my mother and Dorothy about what a son of a bitch he was. I would strongly doubt they ever tried to find him." Edwin, however, hadn't acted alone in abandoning Dorothy and Isabelle. Their mother, Della, had been a coconspirator as well. Yet, her daughters didn't feel the same animosity toward her as they did toward their father. "I think from all indications what Della did to them was long forgiven and they loved their mom," Dowdy observed. "Whether they did or didn't understand the circumstances of what happened years and years ago they certainly got past it."

In 1937, eighteen-year-old Dorothy Howell returned to Chicago. Seemingly, the only good that had come out of her hellish years in California was that she was able to complete her high school education. "Our mother had a tough life, it wasn't pleasant," maintained Tony Rodham. "She eventually came back to Chicago to see her mother."

Back in the Windy City, Dorothy and Della reconciled their differences. But Dorothy—furious over the college tuition issue—contemptuously rejected Max's overtures to make her part of his family. Instead, she moved in with an aunt, Florence Zapel, another sister of Della's, who was married to a civil engineer, Elmer Zapel. "Our mother decided to stay in Chicago, and struck out on her own, got her own job, and that's when she met our father," Tony Rodham said.

HUGH RODHAM RUNS FOR OFFICE

To downtrodden Dorothy Howell, Hugh Rodham seemed like a prince out of a fairy tale who had come to rescue her from the evils of the world. Eight years Dorothy's senior, he appeared to her as a father figure of sorts. She was overwhelmed by his confidence and tough-mindedness, impressed that he'd been to college—something she wanted desperately for herself—awed by his big talk of big things for himself in the future, and unbothered by his domineering and gruff manner, behavior to which she had become inured during her difficult childhood. All that was important to her was that Hugh Rodham made her feel wanted, and gave her a sense of security for the first time in her life.

But whether Dorothy Rodham truly ever loved her husband is a question some family members would be asking themselves decades later after observing what they viewed as a cold and unaffectionate union.

Rodham had wanted to get married right away—after all, he'd virtually left his fiancée at the altar for Dorothy. But she was in no rush. "I think she was afraid of marriage," a Rodham family member said. "She saw what her father had done to her mother. She'd been kicked around a lot as a kid. She wanted to wait and see."

Dorothy soul-searched about getting married and dated Hugh for some five years before she decided to say yes, a decision clearly speeded up by the war and by a fear of losing him.

In the immediate aftermath of the attack on Pearl Harbor on December 7, 1941, hundreds of thousands of able-bodied men lined up at enlistment centers to fight for their country, and hundreds of thousands of others were drafted. But Rodham remained a civilian until October 20, 1942, when he went on active duty in the Naval Reserve.

Previous books and articles dealing with the Rodhams and the Clintons cite 1942 as the year of Hugh and Dorothy's marriage, but without a specific date, place, details, or substantiation. "I don't know whether they were married in 1942, but it was before he went in the navy, that I know," Tony Rodham said. "My mother told me they got in the car and they drove down to a place called Coal City, Kentucky, or Coal City, Tennessee, and they got married. I have no idea why they chose that place. I don't know why they didn't get married in Chicago—it was never explained to me."

Oscar Dowdy said he was told in December 1999 by his mother, Isabelle, then seventy-five and in poor health, that she remembered being present at her sister and Hugh's nuptials. "In fact, my mother said she remembered that Grandma Della and Grandpa Max were there, too, and she thinks my mother's namesake, Aunt Isabelle, was present. My mother said, 'We all just piled in the car and went down to Kentucky. They were married in, or very near, Louisville.' She had no memory why they had gotten married down there, but she said she tagged along. From what she remembered, it was just a civil ceremony."

However, a search failed to turn up a certificate of marriage for Hugh Rodham and Dorothy Howell in county and state records in Kentucky, Tennessee, Illinois, and Indiana, between the years 1940 and 1950.

To add to the mystery, a newspaper item about Hugh Rodham written in 1947 stated that he was single.

On the other hand, Rodham's will, which was written on September 4, 1987, showed that he had bequeathed Dorothy's "diamond engagement ring to his granddaughter Chelsea Clinton," which suggests, at the least, that Hugh had given Dorothy a ring to cement their bond.

On December 14, 1999, a formal request was made to Hillary's White House spokeswoman, Marsha Berry, for the date and place of Dorothy and Hugh Rodham's wedding, but she has never responded with the information. The question, therefore, remains: where and when were Hillary's parents legally married?

Hugh Rodham spent his entire three years of service to his country at the Great Lakes Naval Training Center, in Waukegan, Illinois, located just north of his adopted hometown of Chicago. There, he got recruits into shape for the war raging in the Pacific and in Europe. At thirty-one, the robust and fit fabrics salesman had parlayed his physical education studies at Penn State into a cushy assignment as an instructor in a navy conditioning and self-defense program named after the boxer Gene Tunney.

While Dorothy continued to hold down an office job in Chicago, with Hugh in the service nearby, her sister Isabelle remained at home with Della and Max. She was working as a waitress when she met Oscar Dowdy Sr. "in some little nightclub in Chicago," said their son, Oscar Dowdy Jr. "My mom was basically a stay-at-home, sheltered person. She was probably nineteen, and he was already in the navy. It was one of those wartime marriages—not a long courtship."

A drifter who had made his way to Chicago from Hopewell, Virginia, where his poor, uneducated Scottish-English family worked on a farm, Dowdy Sr. had enlisted in the navy and was undergoing training at Great Lakes. Because of his marriage to Isabelle, and because he and Rodham were stationed together, the brothers-in-law became close friends. But Dowdy Sr. was always viewed by the Rodham family—and even his own—as inferior, a loser.

"Uncle Oscar was not one of the brightest men in the world," observed Tony Rodham. "He would argue with you about everything you could possibly imagine. He knew more about everything there was in the world than anybody else, when in fact he didn't know anything. So my mother asked my dad to keep a watch over him while they were in the navy together because he was married to her sister."

But while shrewd Hugh Rodham managed to secure his safe stateside assignment in the training brigade for the duration, naive Oscar Dowdy Sr. was shipped off to combat assignments in the bloody South Pacific, first to the Philippines, and then to New Guinea, where he was serving when his namesake, "little Oscar," as Oscar Dowdy Jr. was known, was born on March 12, 1944.

"What I heard was that Uncle Hugh could have kept him from having to go overseas," Dowdy recounted. "But my dad probably said the wrong things to the wrong people. I remember Uncle Hugh used to say, 'If your damn old man would have listened to me and kept his mouth shut he would never have been over on that stinkin' island.'"

Isabelle and little Oscar stayed with Della and Max until Dowdy returned from the war. "I don't think my dad saw me face to face until I was about eighteen months old," Dowdy said.

Dorothy, meanwhile, refused to accept Rosenberg's hospitality, and is said to have stayed with the Zapels, seeing Hugh virtually every weekend when he got a pass. The closest her husband ever got to combat during his hitch was going to war movies, and catching the newsreels while on weekend pass with his bride. "But you'd think he'd survived the Bataan death march and was John-fucking-Wayne the way he strutted around in his uniform," recalled a wartime friend of Hugh's. "He was the perfect drill instructor. He loved to criticize, to lord it over people, to play the tough guy, to be in control."

It was while Hugh was at Great Lakes that one of Dorothy's worst fears from childhood had been rekindled: that of being abandoned.

"I heard the story from my aunt Addie that Dorothy suspected Uncle Hugh was seeing another woman, and Hugh and Dorothy got into a big fight and Hugh pushed Dorothy," Dowdy revealed. "Somehow Grandpa Max heard about it and he just got furious and went after Hugh with a baseball bat, and was chasing Hugh around some parked cars, and was going to beat the shit out of Hugh with the bat.

"No matter how much Dorothy rejected Max, she was part of the family so he was still defensive of her. He was very pro-family. That was his nature. Hugh and Dorothy reconciled and tempers cooled off and Max more or less made it clear to Uncle Hugh that, 'If anything goes on again like this and I hear about it, I'll kick your ass.' Hugh was afraid of Max. Almost everybody was."

With the enlisted rank of chief petty officer, and a couple of routine service ribbons, Rodham returned to civilian life on September 28, 1945, a few weeks after the Japanese surrender, and got his old job back at Barrett Textiles, where he was soon promoted to sales manager.

With postwar housing tight, Max Rosenberg made an offer to Hugh Rodham that he couldn't refuse—a rent-free apartment in the Charlotte, Rosenberg's yellow brick, six-story, seventy-flat building at 5722 North Winthrop Avenue, in Chicago's Rogers Park section, the same area where Max and Della lived.

Hugh, who throughout his marriage would be notoriously tight with his money, eagerly accepted Rosenberg's offer. At first Dorothy balked, her bitterness toward Rosenberg still blinding her, but in the end she reluctantly went along with her husband's decision to take advantage of Rosenberg's generosity.

The Charlotte was a typical middle-class, mid-rise Chicago apartment house with a passenger elevator, a lobby switchboard manned by a telephone operator who also buzzed in visitors, and a neatly furnished small vestibule where the tenants' mailboxes were located. Rosenberg gave the Rodhams a second-floor, one-bedroom, one-bath with kitchenette unit adjacent to a similar flat he had given to the Dowdys—Oscar, Isabelle, and little Oscar.

After his discharge from the navy, Dowdy had taken a job as an auto mechanic at a Buick dealership, but when he lost that job Rosenberg made him the Charlotte's superintendant after getting him into the janitor's union. Dowdy would remain a janitor for the rest of his working life.

Despite Dorothy's animosity toward Rosenberg, Hugh Rodham and Max had forged a bond, in spite of their imbroglio over his alleged cheating on Dorothy. "They were both hustlers. They understood each other," Dowdy observed. "And I think Max admired Hugh. Max realized that Hugh was trying to do something with his life, and Hugh would listen to Max and take Max's advice. But my father used to frustrate Max and Hugh because he wouldn't do anything to improve himself.

"Over the years Max helped Hugh with financial matters and gave him business advice and probably loaned him money. Unlike my aunt Dorothy, Uncle Hugh didn't have a problem with Max. Hugh probably told Dorothy, 'Hey, get over it.' But she never did. Dorothy cursed Max, but I never heard anything from Hugh in a bad way about him. They became pretty good buds."

The Rogers Park neighborhood where the Rodhams lived was bordered by Lake Michigan and the city's northern limits. The community was a melting pot of first- and second-generation Jews, Germans, English, and Irish. There was a mix of respectable housing and churches; two big schools, Mundelein College and Loyola University; and a blighted, thickly populated ghetto dubbed "the Jungle." A published lurid description of the area stated, "On 'Maid's Night Off,' domestics from all the swank North Side and suburban homes come there to get drunk and picked up, and the boys are waiting to help them."

But with the postwar boom came plans to rejuvenate the deteriorating neighborhood: new apartment buildings, offices, and stores were on the drawing boards.

With the building explosion, and with Detroit's assembly lines working overtime to supply a postwar, car-hungry America, Hugh Rodham envisioned Rogers Park and the rest of Chicago strangling in traffic. With dollar signs spinning in his head, he speculated that he could make a killing in parking lots. He went to Max Rosenberg, who liked the idea and was even willing to financially back Rodham for a piece of the action. Their only obstacle was zoning laws, which the two men agreed had to be changed.

With Rosenberg's counsel, Hugh Rodham decided to become the first Rodham to run for public office since George Rodham, the Scranton city councilman. As Rosenberg told Hugh over and over, "Money is important but politics is power."

Rodham got the required signatures from several hundred Rogers Park residents, which qualified him to put his name on the ballot to run for alderman for the Forty-ninth Ward, which encompassed Rogers Park. A victory would make him one of the fifty members of the Chicago City Council, which he hoped would give him the power to get the needed zoning changes.

"Dad was in the process of buying parking lots, and he was being shut out by some big parking lot company at the time," Tony Rodham acknowledged. "He had some land he wanted to buy and they wouldn't let him turn it into a parking lot, so he wanted to get elected as an alderman and change the zoning laws so he could have a parking lot."

Rodham would claim to friends years later that he had already forged a friendship with a powerful politician, a shrewd Irishman by the name of Richard J. Daley, who would become known as "the last of the big-city bosses" because of his iron-fisted control of Chicago politics through widespread job patronage. Though Daley wouldn't be elected to his first term as mayor until 1955, he had garnered considerable power as an Illinois state representative and senator from the mid-1930s through the mid-1940s, and was about to be appointed Illinois director of revenue around the time Rodham decided to run for office.

"Dad was working at Barrett Textiles and had bid on a job in city hall when he first met Daley," explained Tony Rodham, based on stories his father had told him. "Dad was a big Daley person. He had great connections with Daley. While my father was a staunch Republican and Daley was a Democrat, politics makes strange bedfellows. If you needed something from Cook County, or you needed something from the city of Chicago, Daley was the guy who could get you what you needed."

Tony Rodham noted that his father had learned about the "I scratch your back, you scratch my back" school of politics "from his Uncle George in Scranton."

Oddly, in all of her years in the political arena, Hillary has never publicly discussed her father's venture into politics, and none of the writers of the many books and articles about the Rodhams and the Clintons had uncovered that facet of her father's life. Clearly, Hillary had found distasteful her father's foray into politics. She had entered the political world with Bill with a seemingly high-minded mission that unrealistically precluded the kind of backroom wheeling and dealing that was the hallmark of politicians such as her great-uncle George Rodham, or Chicago's "Boss" Daley, or even her own father, who hoped political office could help line his pockets with parking lot profits.

"The reason why Hugh decided to get into politics in the first place, and the political alliances he forged in Chicago, embarrassed Hillary," a close family friend observed. "She didn't want to be connected to any of it. She wasn't proud of why her father had thrown his hat in the ring. Probably more importantly, she felt it wouldn't help Bill or herself politically if the people of Arkansas and the country knew about it. It's part of Hillary's weirdness."

Weirdness or not, it's true that there were no lofty ideals, and no high-minded goals attached to Hugh Rodham's decision to throw his hat in the ring. Parking lot zoning, and getting it approved in his favor, was the sole reason he had decided in mid-1946 to run in the February 25, 1947, Chicago aldermanic election. It was all about making money for himself and his silent partner and mentor, Max Rosenberg, whom his wife resented.

But Rodham had hidden his true agenda from the voters. In his filing, and in subsequent newspaper profiles about his candidacy, he sounded like a social reformer.

The powerful *Chicago Tribune* of February 21, 1947, said he supported "rebuilding of slum areas and development of housing as [the] first problems to be tackled. He favors cheaper transportation and more emphasis on training policemen, particularly in criminology."

In the influential community newspaper, the *Rogers Park News* of February 20, 1947, a thumbnail sketch said Rodham, "Cites [the] need for solving housing problem. Favors directorship plan for schools with an open forum each month to discuss problems. Against city hall payrollers. Favors extensive competitive exams to qualify for municipal employment."

He also fudged his true party affiliation. A lifelong conservative Republican (until Hillary married Bill), Rodham described himself as an independent. There also were a number of other discrepancies. In one account he claimed he had lived in Chicago for twenty years, more then twice the time of his actual residency. In another, he listed his marital status as single. One concerned Rogers Park resident, Elmer Crane, filed an objection with the election commission citing "irregularities" in Rodham's aldermanic petition. But apparently no action was taken against Rodham who remained in the race.

Rodham must have known when he began campaigning—introducing himself to rush-hour commuters at the elevated subway stations in the Forty-ninth Ward, ringing doorbells, shaking hands with housewives on the street, kissing babies—that he had little chance of actually winning. He was up against a fierce opponent, a political "boss" named Frank Keenan, an independent Democrat, who had controlled the Forty-ninth for a dozen years as alderman and committeeman, and would continue to dominate for some years to come.

Keenan had been endorsed in the 1947 race by an organization called Independent Voters of Illinois as the most outstanding Democrat incumbent in the city council for trying to get taxicab licenses for returning veterans who faced a Checker–Yellow Cab monopoly in the city.

Years later, Selig Drezner, one of the other candidates, observed that, "Keenan was very formidable. He had the press backing him. Keenan ingratiated himself with the veterans who wanted to be cab drivers and he became their spokesman. He threw parties for the neighborhood kids in the theaters. He did what he wanted to do. He was the boss. He was the consummate politician. I was trying to tell the voters at the time that the son of a bitch was a crook, that power stuff went on, that there were kickbacks. But you couldn't convince the newspapers to print anything against him. He had them all lined up and that was it. After a while you knew you couldn't win."

At the time, Drezner was a twenty-five-year-old lawyer who had commanded a gunboat in the Pacific during the war. As supporters and campaign workers, he had a small army of returned veterans and young people, among them a jokester friend from high school named Shecky Green.

"Frankly," acknowledged Drezner, " I got into that race primarily to get my foot into politics. Later, I got a job as a state's attorney in Cook County. I became friends with people like Adlai Stevenson and Richard Daley. And Rodham probably did it for business reasons, to get his name known. I would assume very seriously that it was a business ploy." Drezner said he had no knowledge of Rodham's parking lot scheme.

In the end, Keenan trounced his seven opponents, racking up 17,073 votes, the largest tally in the history of any aldermanic election in Chicago at the time. Hugh Rodham finished sixth, with 382 votes.

But Tony Rodham said his father wasn't disappointed with his defeat. "By the time the election was over," he noted, "the parking lot deal was dead, and Dad wasn't that involved anymore."

Keenan would go on to serve as the powerful assessor of Cook County in the mid- to late 1950s. A one-time political cartoonist, he found a way to use his artistic talents to his best advantage. "He sketched downtown buildings whose owners, desirous of favorable tax assessments, gladly bought those sketches for sums that were the envy of full-time artists everywhere," according to David K. Fremon, who wrote a history on Chicago's ward politics. "Such shakedowns earned Keenan a prison term for income-tax evasion."

For years afterward Rodham regaled anyone who would listen with stories about his run in the 1947 aldermanic election, and his Windy City political connections. One of Bill's mother's best friends, Marge Mitchell, for one, recalled that Rodham would spend hours boasting about those days when he visited his daughter and son-in-law in Little Rock. "He loved to sit in back of that governor's mansion under the trees. We'd go out there to smoke 'cause Hillary ain't gonna let you smoke. So he'd just sit back and tell those old tales about his days in Chicago, how he was old Mayor Daley's right-hand man. Hugh said he was just runnin' Chicago."

But Rodham's nephew Oscar Dowdy scoffed at such claims. "Uncle Hugh," he asserted good-naturedly, "was a great bullshitter. He wasn't close to Daley. He couldn't bullshit us because we were right there in Chicago. In fact, his talent falls right in line with his daughter, Hillary."

AND HILLARY MAKES THREE

IF A CHILD'S FUTURE COULD be determined by the date of conception by the mother, and the preoccupation of the father, then Hillary seemed destined to become a politician. On the same night Hugh Rodham lost the aldermanic election, Dorothy announced she was a month pregnant. After five years of holding off the inevitable, she had conceived during the heat of Hugh's campaign, and now she was about to become a mother.

Just as she had been in no rush to tie the knot, Dorothy perhaps had serious reservations about parenthood because of insecurities resulting from her hellish childhood.

A member of a big, close-knit family back in Scranton, Hugh had wanted her to start having little ones right away, and never could understand why she was hesitant. He would often point to her sister, Isabelle, who had suffered the same childhood traumas but already had a baby. But Dorothy—who saw herself as Isabelle's surrogate mother and protector—questioned her sister's judgment because Dowdy would never amount to anything more than a janitor.

However, on October 26, 1947, after a relatively easy pregnancy,

Dorothy, twenty-eight, delivered a chubby, happy, and healthy eight-and-a-half-pound girl at Edgewater Hospital, near the Rodhams' apartment. In the weeks before, the couple discussed possible names, and Dorothy chose Hillary Diane for its "exotic" sound.

While Hugh had adopted Chicago, he would always keep close ties to Scranton, and after Hillary's birth he and Dorothy drove back to the Rodham family homestead on Diamond Avenue for a celebration, and the infant's baptism at the Court Street Methodist Church. Later her brothers Hughie and Tony also were baptized there, though Hillary's baptismal record had somehow seemed to disappear by the late 1990s.

For Dorothy, the arrival of Hillary brought a disturbing sense of déjà vu. For the past ten years or so, working as an office girl and secretary, she had felt comparatively independent, free from the drudgery of housework and child care, which she'd been saddled with as a teenage domestic in California. Now she felt as if she were reliving the past: the feedings, the diaper changes, the crying, the cooking, and the cleaning. She'd been there, she'd done that, and she despised it.

As her son Tony Rodham, the last of her three children, who was born in 1954, acknowledged: "Our mother hated housework, she hated cooking. She hated it with a passion because in her younger days she used to have to do it all. She didn't want to do it. She had done enough. Any time she could get out she loved it because she didn't have to cook dinner. Her grandparents in California treated her like a slave. She would get all the housework, and she was responsible for her little sister, Isabelle."

And years later, after her daughter became first lady, Dorothy herself conceded that she loathed being anywhere near a kitchen. "I hated cooking then, and I hate it now. The family always ate everything I put before them. My attitude was if I was going to get in the kitchen and cook all that stuff, they were going to eat it."

In Hillary's first year, she almost died—not from her mother's cooking, but from a near-freak accident.

Dorothy had strapped her into a buggy and had taken her outside to be in the sun. As Dorothy chatted with her sister, Isabelle, and a few of the other young mothers from the Charlotte, four-year-old Oscar, who was playing nearby, happened to look over and saw that something was dreadfully wrong.

"Hillary had managed to wiggle herself around and her body was hanging out of the carriage—with the harness strap around her neck," he recalled. "I just grabbed her and shoved her back. Then there was this big commotion. Aunt Dorothy said, 'Oh, my God! What happened?' All the ladies got involved—my mother, Dorothy, another neighbor—to make sure Hillary was okay. Hillary has brought it up a few times that I saved her life."

By the time the Rodhams celebrated Hillary's second birthday, Dorothy was pregnant again, and on May 26, 1950, she gave birth to their first son, her husband's namesake, Hugh Edwin Rodham, who would always be known as "Hughie."

With only one bedroom and two children, the Rodhams decided it was time to move on, to fulfill the American dream, to get their slice of the pie.

PORTRAIT OF A MARRIAGE

THE RODHAMS INSPECTED MODEL HOMES in tacky new Levittown-style developments, but Max Rosenberg, who knew a good deal in real estate when he saw one, led them to a quiet community just northwest of the city limits called Park Ridge, which was earning the reputation as "The Queen of the Suburbs." Park Ridge had good schools, tree-lined streets, and each year the still bargain-priced houses were appreciating in value. Location, Rosenberg had taught Rodham, was the first rule of residential real estate investment.

In 1951, with some help from Rosenberg, Rodham bought a modestly priced, smallish, 1920s-era Georgian-style brown brick home with a narrow side yard at 235 Wisner Street, on the corner of Elm. The house that Hillary grew up in had a living room with an adjacent small sunroom, a dining room, a narrow kitchen with a cramped eating booth at one end, a small den that the Rodhams used as a TV room, and a miniscule powder room. Upstairs was a small tile bath, and three bedrooms—one for Hillary, one for her two brothers, and one for Hugh and Dorothy. There was a dark, musty basement, and a detached one-and-a-half-car garage. The Rodhams furnished the house mostly at Sears.

When they took possession, Park Ridge was a bastion of Catholic, Lutheran, and Methodist families. There were few, if any, Jews, and no blacks, except for those who came to clean for the more affluent families, which did not include the Rodhams. Their neighbors, for the most part, were white-collar workers, salesmen, small-business owners, and a few professionals. The men commuted to work in the city, while the wives stayed home and kept house, and the kids went to public and parochial schools. It was a safe, white-bread-and-mayonnaise community where everyone lived quiet, private lives.

Richard Voss, who was Hillary's age, lived across the street, and went through school with her, noted that he had never been inside the Rodham house. "In Park Ridge," he stated, "you knew your neighbors in the summer and come Halloween you never saw them again until Easter. Of the kids there, I don't think I was in five kids' houses. I knew Hughie and Tony, but we didn't have sleepovers like kids have today. Nobody did."

A member of the local Chamber of Commerce once observed that Park Ridgers fell into two political camps: Republicans and people who were more conservative. A classmate of Hillary's, Penny Pullen, who later became a Republican state representative, firmly believed that Park Ridge was "not a common man community," and that anyone like Hillary who grew up there was "given a sense of belonging to the elite."

Park Ridge remained a G.O.P. stronghold through the 1990s when fewer than one in four citizens voted for Bill Clinton in his first presidential election. And residents shouted down a suggestion that a portrait of the hometown first lady be hung in the Park Ridge library, though some photos of her were put up at her high school, and the intersection where she had lived was ceremoniously named "Rodham Corner."

In that quiet, all-American neighborhood, Hillary organized Olympic games, and she and her brothers, and neighborhood children held track and field events. The Rodham's next-door neighbor used a hose to freeze the backyard so Hillary and her brothers and friends could ice skate and play hockey. Unlike the other girls on the block who played house with their dolls, Hillary dressed up her black and white cat named Isis, after the Egyptian nature goddess.

The Rodhams were a competitive family. On Sundays, Hugh and

Dorothy would take Hillary and her brothers to a public tennis court and smash balls at one another, and the last man standing was the winner. "Our mother was pretty tough and you had to stand up on your own two feet," Tony Rodham maintained. "And there's something I live by today that she always told us—'Never start a fight, but if you are in one make sure you finish it.'" He emphasized that a much-publicized story about how Dorothy Rodham ordered four-year-old Hillary to confront a neighborhood bully was true. "This girl Susie used to pick on my sister unmercifully until Hillary stood up for herself," acknowledged Rodham, who was not yet born when the event occurred. "We were all taught that you've got to be able to defend yourself in all ways and at all times."

In the eating booth in Dorothy Rodham's kitchen, there were lively dinnertime political discussions, with each member of the family voicing their dissenting views: Hugh took the conservative Republican side, and Dorothy the Democratic. "Our mother was probably the only Democrat in Park Ridge," Rodham noted, "and probably a liberal Democrat. Dad never forced his politics on any of us. He allowed us to make up our own minds."

Aside from Hillary's school and library books, there were few other books in the house. Dorothy and Hugh weren't big readers, though they got the *Chicago Tribune*, which he picked up every morning at six o'clock at a neighborhood store after first putting on a pot of coffee.

A homebody and a penny-pincher to boot, Hugh rarely took the family out to movies or restaurants. A man of simple pleasures, he entertained the kids with card tricks and enjoyed a lively game of pinochle. In the evening, he was usually on the couch in the small den packing away chips and beer, watching television on an old black-and-white console that got three stations. He regularly watched *Sing Along with Mitch*, a popular musical variety show, starring bearded anti–rock 'n' roll record producer Mitch Miller. As the lyrics to vanilla Top 40 favorites flashed on the screen, Hugh at home in comfortable suburbia actually sang along, with little Hillary joining in.

But Rodham's all-time favorite TV character was someone much like himself: a big, blustery, avaricious blue-collar kind of guy, a bus driver named Ralph Kramden. Kramden and his pal, sewer worker Ed Norton, were always coming up with failed money-making schemes that caused friction with Kramden's practical wife, Alice. "Dad loved *The Honeymooners,* and he laughed like it was going out of style at that show," Tony Rodham reminisced. "Dad probably related to Kramden and Norton's business schemes. He just thought Jackie Gleason as Ralph Kramden was one of the funniest guys he ever watched. Dad had a great sense of humor. Mom would just kinda be hangin' out, doing whatever it was—and Dad would be watching TV."

Hillary's mother especially didn't see any humor in it when her husband bellowed, "One of these days, Dorothy, one of these days . . . Pow! Right in the kisser."

In *It Takes a Village,* Hillary remarked that "Most of the people I knew growing up had families remarkably like mine." But if that were true, Park Ridge would have been a rather grim place. Despite Hillary and Tony's glowing memories of the happy family homestead, the Rodham household was not a loving and warm place. Hugh Rodham was mostly hard-edged and nasty, and Dorothy was often dour and stern. Neighbors like Marjorie Voss, who lived across the street, remembered the Rodhams as "very private." While Voss shopped with Dorothy at the local Jewel Market and found her "pleasant," she didn't recall ever spending much time in the Rodham home. "Dorothy and I were neighbors, but we weren't buddy-buddy. After many, many years I didn't know anything intimate about them at all."

According to his nephew Oscar Dowdy, Hugh Rodham "was a nasty old bugger, and probably mean," a bully who seemed to derive pleasure from grabbing the hairs on the nape of the boy's neck, and yanking them so hard his eyes started to water. And when Dowdy had his own children, Hillary's father hadn't changed; he habitually pulled their pigtails and ringlets and made them cry, too. "It bothered me," Helen Dowdy acknowledged. "I didn't want to make waves so I just said, 'Now girls, Uncle Hugh didn't mean it.'" While he loved his aunt, Oscar Dowdy described her as "kind of cold, kind of standoffish. I'm a hugger and she couldn't really hug you, or if she did I didn't feel any warmth or sincerity. There was always some barrier. She was supportive and encouraging, but always at arm's length. She just had a difficult time being warm and truly affectionate."

Dorothy Rodham, though, looked and acted like the perfect housekeeper and mother figure, as Rosie O'Donnell, Hillary's friend and political supporter, observed on her Christmas show in December 1999. "She looks like a mom from Central Casting," O'Donnell told Hillary. "They cast the perfect mom for you. That's what it looks like. You call up a Hollywood casting agent and say I want the perfect mother. She's exactly it . . . [She's] got that American face, that bake-me-some-cookies kind of look."

"Well," Hillary firmly maintained, "she was a perfect mother." Having brought holiday cookies from the White House for Rosie and her audience, Hillary and her mother reminisced about all of the wonderful Christmases the Rodham family spent together in Park Ridge. "We used to do a lot of cookie baking, especially on Christmas Eve, and that was one of our traditions. . . . My brothers and I would compete to see who could make the biggest cookie . . . it was one of those typical things we went through every year."

But Oscar Dowdy contended that Hillary and Dorothy's memories of Rodham family childhood were a mix of fact and fiction. "Helen and I, we see Dorothy, or read an article, or see Hillary on *Rosie*, and they get into the family and how wholesome it was—and a lot of it is just so plastic. Hillary and Dorothy around the Christmas tree and baking cookies . . . oh, man! It just doesn't seem totally real. It's a lot of mythmaking." In fact, the one Christmas Eve tradition Dowdy clearly remembered at the Rodham household was when his Scrooge-like uncle Hugh sent Hillary's little brothers out into the Park Ridge cold to buy a leftover tree at a bargain price.

Tony Rodham, though, defensively blamed his father's penny-pinching on the fact that he had grown up "during the Depression when people lost all their money. He taught all of us the value of a dollar."

Helen Dowdy, a frequent visitor with her husband at the Rodhams', viewed Hugh and Dorothy as an odd couple in an icy marriage. "I just didn't feel there was any love there," she stressed sadly. "I don't think I ever once saw them touch each other, not even a hug, or a caring look. I hardly ever saw Dorothy and Hugh say a kind word to each other. It was always 'Get out of my way.' I never saw any loving feelings. I never saw the two of them together as a loving couple. Never.

"They must have cared for each other in some way. I don't think anybody can stay together that long if they didn't have some kind of caring for each other. But it was strange. From my vantage point their relationship wasn't based on love. And it didn't even seem like it was based on respect. I don't know what it was. Most of the time Hugh would be in another room, and Dorothy would be complaining about him, calling him 'an old fart.'

"There was constant tension. A lot of the bickering was over money. She'd say, 'He's such a tightwad. He's so damn cheap.' She was always saying how tight he was—that she wanted this, that she wanted that. It was constant."

Oscar Dowdy affirmed that in many ways Rodham was frugal to the extreme. "There was a time when I was in high school," he recalled, "when I worked for my uncle during the summer. I was about fourteen and he was paying me a dollar an hour and I asked him if I could get a little more and he said, 'Fuck you! I can go to Manpower for a buck ten.'" Rodham was known to turn off the heat at night in the winter to save on fuel bills, not caring if the family awoke freezing. Once, when Hillary complained that her shoes had holes in them, he demanded to know whether she'd done her chores before he considered buying her a new pair, and she was known to sometimes call him "Mr. Reality Check." Unlike the other children in the neighborhood, the Rodham kids didn't get allowances. Rodham's Depression-era philosophy was, "They eat and sleep for free. We're not going to pay them for it as well." The one luxury that Rodham permitted himself was a big car, usually a Cadillac, and that was because he suffered from a painful hip problem that grew worse with age; he needed the Caddy's legroom and comfort, plus he was able to write off the car as a business expense.

During the more than thirty-five years that the family lived in the house on Wisner, Rodham did the minimum amount of maintenance, with virtually no improvements or renovations. For years, Dorothy complained, but he ignored her pleas. In 1987, when the Rodhams put the house up for sale to move to Arkansas to be closer to Hillary, potential buyers fled in droves because of the horrible state of disrepair, and the place stayed on the market for months.

"The house was worn, and nothing had been done to it since the day they moved in," said Nancy Stuercke, the agent who handled the sale for the Rodhams. "The appliances were all very old, the linoleum in the kitchen was worn, the only change was an inexpensive vanity in the upstairs bathroom, something you'd buy at Kmart. The house still had 60-amp electrical service. It still had the original boiler. And even though Mr. Rodham had retired a number of years earlier from the drapery business, the basement was filled with bolts and bolts of rotting, smelly fabric. I told him to throw them all out but he said, 'Are you crazy? That's good fabric. It's worth money!' "

Because of the house's condition, Stuercke had tried to convince Rodham to drop his asking price from $275,000, but he was adamant. "I used to fondly call him my alligator," she said. "I'd say, 'Well, I think I'll go over there and wrestle with my alligator today over the price.' He always wanted to be very much in control. He had a set mind, and was stubborn. When I told him he couldn't get anywhere near his asking price he said in that gruff way of his, 'Don't these buyers have any guts these days? Tell 'em to come in and gimme an offer!' " At the same time, he did his best to nickel and dime Stuercke on the amount of her commission. "He tried to get me down as low as he could but I told him 5 percent was the lowest he was getting. He was chintzy. He was cheap."

During one of Stuercke's open houses, Bill and Hillary made a surprise visit from Arkansas. While Stuercke was thrilled to meet the governor and his wife, she was surprised at how little warmth she saw between the Clintons and the Rodhams when they greeted each other. "There was no hugging, no kissing," she recalled. "They were just cool with each other, not warm and demonstrative."

In fact, the only demonstration of affection she ever saw between Hugh and Dorothy was toward an old dog the Rodham boys had adopted at the SPCA some years earlier. The mutt, whom Hillary had named after Dr. Ernesto "Che" Guevara, the Central and South American revolutionary leader, was dying of cancer. Rodham had been furious when his sons had brought home the dog, complaining about the cost of care and feeding. But in the end Che had become *his* dog and everywhere Rodham went the dog followed obediently. "He was like a little bitty beagle, all skin and bones," recalled Stuercke. "I talked to Mrs. Rodham about maybe putting the dog to sleep, but she was horrified and said, 'Oh, no, we couldn't. We love that dog.' When I had an open house there I had to check the couch every time because that dog had a habit of pooping on it."

During Hillary and Bill's visit, the governor's security detail, concerned about strangers in the house, demanded that the agent take down her open house sign for the duration. "But Hillary said, 'No, leave it open.'" Hillary then took the realtor by the arm for a private chat and demanded to known why the house hadn't sold. "I said, 'Well, because your father priced it too high.' I could see Hillary was upset, and she said, 'I'll talk to my mom and she will handle it.' But Hillary warned me, 'Don't say anything to my father about this conversation. Let my mom handle it.'"

Hillary's brother Tony acknowledged years later that "it is very true" that their mother was able to manipulate her obstinate husband. "My father was, as all of us Rodhams are, very stuck in the way we want to do something. It's our way, or no way. But if my father would make a decision and it wasn't the real best decision to make, our mother could talk to him and explain to him and show him where it was kind of faulty—and nine times out of ten he would change it." A few days after her meeting with Hillary, the real estate agent received a call from Rodham who had agreed to drop his asking price for the house by twenty thousand dollars. "I don't think Dorothy was subservient to her husband," Stuercke observed. "I think she ended up getting whatever she wanted. My impression was that Dorothy was extremely intelligent—more than he. She wasn't like Hugh at all. I got the feeling Hillary was a real combination of the two of them—she has her mother's brains and her father's balls."

In the end, the house sold for $221,400 to a young couple who was forced to virtually gut and renovate the handyman's special. The one piece of furniture that the Rodhams left behind when they moved to a condo they had bought a few blocks from the Arkansas governor's mansion was Hillary's beloved piano. "Mr. Rodham brought someone in to give him an estimate on it, and when they told him it wasn't worth anything he said, 'Leave the goddamn thing.'"

THE BIG I AM

Hillary was about nine when her father, in his mid-forties, decided to go into the drapery business for himself. After selling curtains for some two decades, he knew the ins and outs of the game like the back of his hand, and was confident he could turn a good dollar running his own show.

"Dad sold a lot of material and one day some guy said to him, 'Why are you doing it for this company when you can do it for yourself?' So he opened his own business," said Tony Rodham, who was about two when his father went out on his own.

Over the years, however, it became an open secret within the Rodham family and among close friends that Hugh resorted to any trick in the book to cut a deal and make a sale. "Hugh was a wheeler-dealer, a shyster-type guy, always trying to screw somebody," Oscar Dowdy noted. "We once talked about him helping me get set up in business and we went out to dinner a few times. He told me, and this is pretty much verbatim, 'You're too fuckin' honest to be in business,' He could be sleazy—like saying 'You've got to be willing to pay for business.'"

In 1956, with some advice and counsel and probably financial backing from Max Rosenberg, Rodham started Rodrik Fabrics, taking with him a number of commercial accounts from his old employers.

"Our father was a drapery salesman—there was no more to it than that," said Tony Rodham. "He would sell to hotels and corporations. He was a one-man company. He'd get the orders. He'd send out the draperies to be made. He'd print the fabrics, and he'd hang the job. My brother, my sister, and my mother would help sometimes. The business never grew in terms of personnel. He was very happy the way he ran it. He did everything and he enjoyed doing everything. He liked to have control!" The only full-time help Rodham ever had was a black handyman by the name of Jim Atkins whom he found one morning hungover in a doorway. "Jim was the worker, vice president, and everything else below my dad," Tony Rodham explained. "He was whatever my dad wanted him to be."

For all but two of the fourteen years Rodham was in business, his company was located in two dingy rooms that reeked of tobacco and fabric dye in a North Chicago apartment building called the Broadmore, where his brother-in-law, Oscar Dowdy Sr., was the janitor, and had a small flat with Isabelle and their two sons. "Uncle Hugh's office was a sloppy mess," recalled Dowdy, who worked for him during the summer. "He chewed [Beechnut] tobacco and there were spit cans on the floor. But he didn't care if he hit the can or not. There was brown stuff all over the walls."

Despite the messy surroundings, and the family's frugal lifestyle, Rodham boasted that Rodrik Fabrics was a goldmine. "It was always my opinion that if he made a hundred thousand dollars a year, he'd say it was a million because that was the way he was," observed Donald Rodham, Hugh's first cousin. "Hugh was a blowhard. He was 'The Big I Am—I Am Hugh Rodham. I Am Important. I have a company and I could care less about anybody else.' If I got an opportunity I'd give him a zinger such as, 'Well, look at the big typhoon.' My mother would correct me and say 'You don't mean typhoon, you mean tycoon' and I said, 'I know exactly what I mean.' And Hugh would look at me and he knew what I was talking about.

"There was something of a clash between Hugh and me. I went for an engineering degree and he had that gym teacher degree, and I think what he felt was he had to continue to show that he was superior to me and he did that by bragging about his business. He always tried to lord it over me. He'd say, 'When you come out to Chicago, I'll show you around the town. I know all the fancy places. I know all the important people. If you want a good job, come and see me. I've got all these people working for me, selling all kinds of stuff.'"

Despite his vociferous claims of being a mogul, Rodham's estate was relatively small. After his death at eighty-two on April 7, 1993, he left everything to Dorothy, and specified that if she died his estate should be divided among his children and other relatives. Specifically, Chelsea Clinton was to receive her grandfather's shares in People's Energy Corporation (which Hugh had inherited from his brother Willard), and Dorothy's diamond engagement ring. Rodham's three-diamond ring was to be broken up and one diamond each was to go to Hillary, Hughie, and Tony. Hillary also was to get her mother's mink coat, and Hughie was to receive his father's silver presentation tray and pitcher (which he had inherited from his father). Rodham's interest in the inexpensive Arkansas condo was to be divided among his children, and Dorothy's pearl necklace was bequeathed to Hughie's wife, Maria Victoria Arias, a Cuban-born lawyer he had married in 1986.

"If Hugh had a significant estate he wouldn't have written the type of will he wrote," said Paul Lukes, the Chicago attorney who handled the Rodhams' wills and the closing on their home. "When there's a big estate people leave everything to a trust, and the trustee makes the division. But you don't say 'I give my woodworking tools to my son, and my '53 Chevy to my daughter.' Hillary was with a large law firm in Arkansas. If there were significant assets she would have advised him to get his affairs arranged, do some estate planning. But he didn't have a large estate."

DADDY'S PRINCESS

SOME PUBLISHED ACCOUNTS of Rodham family life have stated that Hillary was often the target of her father's wrath, that he had denigrated her intellectual abilities, withheld his love, competed with her, and even undermined her sexuality.

But family members contended just the opposite.

"Hillary was *always* Dad's princess," declared Tony Rodham. "All of that stuff that's been written about my sister and my father is total bullshit. How does a father undermine his daughter's sexuality — other than not wanting her to get laid? I can understand that. My father and mother both trusted her completely. She had freedom. That stuff that's been written makes me crazy, because it's totally false.

"My father adored my sister. Yeah, she came home one day with straight A's and my father looked at her and said 'It must be an easy school.' But that was the way he motivated people. He was tough and he wanted the best for his family, the best that he could do, and he wanted us to achieve everything that we could achieve. Everyone has different ways of motivating people and his was, 'If it's that easy, than you can do better than that.'

"His priorities were very simple. His job was to take care of his family and that's what he did. We lived in a nice house. We never really had a want for anything. We didn't get tremendous luxuries because that's the way my father was. Hey, when you made a dollar you put forty-nine cents away, and you could spend the fifty-one cents and that was it. We didn't have designer clothes as kids have now, but were clothed well, we ate well, and yeah, we had chores to do and if you didn't do them we caught hell for it. But that's how we all got taught responsibility."

Of his three children, family observers asserted, Rodham doted mostly on Hillary: he taught her how to read the stock tables in the *Chicago Tribune*, he devoted hours each weekend in the spring and summer to teach her how to swing a bat, he coached her in touch football, and he splurged on a piano that had a prominent place in the living room where he spent hours watching her practice. He thought of her as the perfect child. "I was a quick learner," Hillary acknowledged years later. "I didn't run afoul of my parents very often. They were strict about my respecting authority, and not just parental authority. My father's favorite saying was, 'You get in trouble at school, you get in trouble at home.'"

Oscar Dowdy believed that his cousin had won her father's unconditional love by overwhelming him with her intelligence and her driving ambition. At the same time, he believed, Hillary was the only one in the family who really knew how to manipulate Hugh Rodham in order to win his affection. "She was absolutely daddy's girl. Some of what has been written makes it sound like she was always struggling to satisfy her dad, but that's really a lot of bunk. I grew up with Hillary. I saw how loving and attentive Uncle Hugh was to her. He wasn't that way to the boys.

"He was proud as a peacock of her. Hillary knew how to get what she wanted out of him. She knew the right buttons to push. She knew how to sweet-talk him. She just knew how to deal with him. She was smart enough to know this is how I get what I want—and she certainly knew she was smart.

"Some children come into this world with God-given gifts," he continued, "and Hillary was born with uncanny, extreme intelligence. Her dad recognized it and worked with it and pushed her. Tony and Hughie were regular kids, but Hillary was not a regular kid. Oh, when we were little we played the kids' games—I was Tarzan, Hillary was Jane, and Hughie was Cheetah. But later Hillary was always in her room reading. She was a straight-A student. She got a lot of encouragement and a lot of nurturing from *everyone*, especially her father, and she expanded on it. On an intellectual basis, she was certainly smarter than the rest of the family, and she was very much aware of that."

Helen Dowdy agreed with their assessment. "Hillary was definitely always the apple of Hugh's eye, and she knew it. I never heard one cross word, or one reprimand. I wouldn't put anything past Hugh in terms of put-downs to anybody, but Hillary was his baby. He never went after her, never attacked her femininity, or her sexuality even back when she was not very attractive. He was just *so* proud of her because she had so much going for her. But the boys! Oh, boy! That was a different story. I mean it was like night and day."

Even from the street, Rodham's booming voice could be heard reprimanding or cursing his sons. "Especially in the summer when everybody's windows were open," recalled neighbor Marjorie Voss, "you could hear him yelling at the boys—not Hillary, not Dorothy—but Hughie and Tony." As Oscar Dowdy said, "Hillary got the love and Hughie got booted—that was pretty much it. Tony got his share, too, but Hughie seemed to get more of it. I think Hughie—well, both of them—but probably more so Hughie—was pretty envious of the attention Hillary got. Hillary was just very smart and earned her father's respect, and they wanted to get their father's respect.

"On Dorothy's part there was a bit of jealousy of Hillary, too, because Hillary was daddy's princess, and got his attention. Aunt Dorothy was always very, very defensive of Hughie because Hughie used to get the shaft from the old man—so it was a protective mother thing. Hughie wanted to emulate his dad."

Like his father, Hughie was a big boy who grew into a massive refrigerator of a man. Like his father, he would go to Penn State and graduate with a degree in health and physical education. Like his father, he would play football at college: in one game as quarterback he completed ten of eleven passes, and his father's comment was, "You should have completed the other one." Like Hillary, he would get a law degree. On his own, he joined the Peace Corps. Later, he would become an assistant public defender; he would try his hand as a radio talk-show host. And he would even take a shot at elective office, getting crushed by his opponent in the 1984 U.S. Senate race in Florida.

But it was Hillary who always got the gold ring from dad. "Hughie tried real hard to share the graces that Hillary had," Dowdy observed. "But it just wasn't there."

Tony Rodham, however, contended that his father treated *all* of his children with kindness and respect.

"Our father was a tough guy, yes he was. But he loved his children. He did the best he could for his kids. He hoped to train them in the right way. Hillary is where she is today because of the values and the upbringing my father and my mother gave her. He told her—he told all of us—'It's a tough world out there and if you want to succeed you've got to be the best at what you do.' And that's what was hammered into our heads. My sister is *very* good at what she does because that's how she was taught."

Beginning at Eugene Field Elementary School and through high school, Hillary was always considered the best in her class, always the teacher's pet. Her fifth-grade teacher was so enamored of her star pupil that she received permission to teach sixth grade just so she could have the serious, bespectacled, round-faced, chubby, smiling Rodham girl in her class again. "She could multiply and divide before most of us were adding," said classmate and longtime friend Judy Price Osgood. "She always was a little bit ahead of everybody." Outside of school, Hillary was a standout, too. In the Brownies and later in her Girl Scout troop, she won more merit badges and gold pins than any of her envious friends.

In September 1959, Hillary moved on to Maine East Junior High School where in ninth grade she came under the spell of a charismatic history teacher, Paul Carlson, who, like Hugh Rodham, was a staunch Republican, but also an extreme anti-Communist. Carlson had idolized Dwight Eisenhower and Joseph McCarthy, and still vehemently blamed President Harry Truman for firing General Douglas MacArthur as commander of the UN forces in South Korea almost a decade earlier.

Carlson was enthralled with Hillary, who he said "cut a very singular figure for herself. She spoke in a very clipped way. Her sentences were cut off at the period. Bing, bing, bing. She led in class discussions, and she wasn't afraid to give her point of view in a very strong voice."

The only time Hillary got into trouble in high school, however, was in Carlson's class. When the teacher used the extremist slogan "Better Dead than Red," a classmate whispered to Hillary that his personal preference would be to remain alive, which touched off a giggling fit in her. A fuming Carlson exploded and ordered his star pupil and her coconspirator out of his classroom. Hillary subsequently made up for her behavior with an impressive seventy-five-page term paper accompanied by two hundred index cards filled with sources, notes, and bibliography. By the end of Carlson's "History of Civilization" course, the teacher was convinced his prize student was a "hawk."

A few years after leaving Carlson's class Hillary read and reread Barry Goldwater's *The Conscience of a Conservative*, and, in her senior year, during the 1964 presidential campaign, she volunteered to be a "Goldwater Girl"—heading her school's membership committee of Students for Goldwater, recruiting classmates for Republican rallies, and checking voters' registrations under the supervision of local Republican leaders. One of the few supporters of Lyndon Johnson at school, Ellen Press Murdoch, recalled that she took "an incredible amount of heat [from Hillary] for being a bleeding-heart liberal."

The Reverend Don Jones, the new youth minister at the First Methodist Church of Park Ridge, was a far different archetype from Paul Carlson, but Hillary had become mesmerized by his avant-garde teachings and ideas, too. If Pat Boone or Tab Hunter had been intellectuals, Don Jones would have been their twin. With his white bucks, blond crew cut, blue eyes, the dreamy twenty-six-year-old divinity school graduate from the East Coast cruised the streets of bland Park Ridge in a fiery red Chevy Impala convertible. A month before precocious Hillary's fourteenth birthday she became active in Jones's aptly named "University of Life" program, which met on Sunday evenings. Hillary was enthralled with the young minister's raps on radical politics, far-out art, and hip poetry. One weekend Jones, who considered himself a liberal realist, took Hillary and her classmates on a field trip to Chicago's inner city where they met with a group of young black teens from the projects. Jones had them rap about art and violence—and the wide-eyed white girl from Park Ridge came away with a mix of new ideas. In the past, Hugh Rodham had driven the family through Chicago's black neighborhoods and made derisive remarks about how "they" lived. Because of Jones, Hillary now had a different perspective, but her midwestern conservatism was still firmly entrenched.

She jumped at an offer from Carlson to join "Main-ites in Motion," a non-school-related secret anti-Communist club he had formed. Carlson caused a furor, however, when he circulated anti-Communist flyers at Hillary's church, and accused Jones of brainwashing Hillary and the other members of his youth group. At the local library, meanwhile, Hillary attended lectures by hard-core conservatives arranged by Carlson.

Without Carlson's knowledge, she went with Jones's group to hear a talk by radical intellectual organizer Saul Alinsky—known, among other things, for staging "fart-ins" to protest corporate abuses. (She would later write her college thesis on Alinsky.) Hillary also went on another eye-opening field trip with Jones—to hear a speech at Chicago's Orchestra Hall by the Reverend Dr. Martin Luther King Jr., who was considered a troublemaker, and worse, by Park Ridge's extreme conservative element. Through her college years, Hillary kept in close contact with Jones, writing him intensely philosophical letters. In one, she admitted how *Catcher in the Rye*, which she had borrowed from Jones when she was fourteen, had sailed over her head. Years later, after she had become the first lady of Arkansas, she invited Jones to the governor's mansion to personally thank him for introducing her to Dr. King.

Hillary had landed on her feet running in high school. She was on the staff of the *Ghost Writer*—the sophomore newspaper; was a student council representative; a member of the cultural values committee, the brotherhood society, and the "It's Academic" quiz program team; and she chaired the committee in charge of elections.

But in terms of attracting boys, she always received failing grades. Hillary's first puppy love romance, with a boy named Jim Yrigoyen, ended before it ever really got off the ground when he mashed her face in slushy snow during typical boy-girl playfulness. "We were messing around in snowdrifts and I must have done it too hard, because when I got to school the next day, I found my dog tag which I'd given her to wear sitting on my desk," recalled Yrigoyen, who became a high school guidance counselor. A year later Hillary got her revenge again. Some neighborhood boys had been raiding her rabbit hutch in the backyard and she enlisted Yrigoyen to keep watch over the bunnies while she ran into the house. When she came outside, Hillary carefully counted the rabbits and found that one was missing. "She asked me, 'Were you a part of this?' I confessed and Hillary punched me in the nose."

School pals like Betsy Johnson Ebeling noted that Hillary was not "boy crazy," but recalled that in eighth grade she "had a crush on the cutest boy in the class, Don Wasley. He had blond hair, blue eyes, but he moved away. During the [1992 presidential] campaign, I joked that I was going to wear a T-shirt that said, 'Where's Don Wasley?'"

Her classmates, especially boys, thought she was conceited. In fact, according to Ebeling, "She was just very self-confident, very comfortable with herself." As a male classmate observed, "Hillary wasn't considered a great catch. The guys didn't think she was very good-looking. She had a dumpy figure and thick legs, and she wore these ugly, thick purple glasses and frumpy clothes. Ugh!"

Because of her gothiclike upbringing, Dorothy Rodham had no sense of, or interest in, fashion or style to pass on to her daughter. The severe Mrs. Rodham, in fact, once came to a gay party for Hillary dressed in a nun's habit. In sixth grade, Hillary had been forced to circulate petitions in school in an attempt to convince her mother to allow her to wear nylons to commencement; she lost and ended up wearing white anklets. In ninth grade, when other girls were starting to wear something tight, fashion-impaired Hillary was still attending class in her Girl Scout uniform. For one of the school dances, Dorothy had bought Hillary such a plain and prim chiffon gown that she told pals she was embarrassed to wear it, though she wouldn't have worn anything daring, either. Ironically, when Hillary was in her junior year of high school, she became a member of a powerful student committee that allowed her to review the school's ultraconservative dress code, which she staunchly supported.

Dorothy Rodham didn't raise her daughter to become "Miss Park Ridge." Her dream was for her to be the first woman on the U.S. Supreme Court, or at least that's what she claimed after Hillary became first lady. Meanwhile, Hillary's childhood fantasy was to become an astronaut, and she was shocked and disappointed when NASA responded to her letter seeking guidance by suggesting that flying into outer space was a man's job.

In the school newspaper, classmates had dubbed Hillary "Sister Frigidaire" because of her cold and aloof demeanor, and they jokingly predicted that after graduation she would enter a convent. Unlike other girls her age Hillary had no interest in anything feminine, according to Helen Dowdy, who was a year and a half older.

"Because we were kind of the same age group you would think it would be very easy for me to buy her gifts," Helen recalled. "It wasn't. She was like the hardest one to ever buy a gift for because I couldn't relate to anyone like Hillary. She was just *so* nerdy in every way. She had the hair just hanging, the big glasses, no makeup, no hairdo. Just plain-Jane nerd. She wasn't dating anyone—and had no interest. She was always upstairs with her books. We didn't spend much time one on one because Dorothy would always be there. Because of Dorothy Hillary never invited me up to her room. Dorothy wouldn't let you on the second floor because it was such a mess. The second floor was dark and cold. You'd walk over clothes strewn all over the place. Dorothy actually *kept* visitors from going upstairs. I think Dorothy kind of picked her battles and that wasn't one of them. That's how they wanted to live and that's how she let them live. Dorothy wasn't very domestic. She was always looking for something to satisfy *her*. In all those years, I was on the second floor of that house in Park Ridge maybe three times. And Hillary was always upstairs with her books. She was very to herself. It wasn't like 'I have to go study.' She *wanted* to study. That's where her head was.

"She never gossiped like girls do. She never shopped. She didn't talk about sex. She didn't talk about makeup, or clothes. It wasn't until she was in the governor's mansion that she and I would take walks and talk about stuff like that, but never back then."

At sixteen, Hillary had entered the political arena for the first time, and was elected vice president of her junior class. That same year she gave a poised, eloquent speech at an assembly of the entire school. But Hillary's dreams of becoming student council president faded when she was defeated in what she later claimed was a dirty, mud-slinging campaign waged by her two male opponents. The winner of the election observed years later, "Hillary today is just like she was thirty years ago."

Undeterred from public service by her defeat in the presidential election, Hillary served as a school ambassador when Maine East was merged with Maine South in her senior year because of overcrowding. The students at the new school were an ethnic mix—Poles, Italians, Slavs—resulting in rivalries among the groups. "Some corridors," Hillary remembered, "you couldn't walk down without feeling unsafe, uncomfortable." But others who had attended the school disagreed with her perception.

During her junior year Hillary was named a Merit Scholar, and she began sending out college applications. It wasn't long before she was inundated with invitations to recruitment teas organized by the local alumnae of the best schools in the country. Betsy Johnson Ebeling recalled that Hillary's father chauffeured them to the events in his metallic gold Cadillac, with a big wad of Beechnut in his cheek. "When we'd come to a stoplight, Hugh would open the door and spit," she said. "He was a curmudgeon, exasperating and exhilarating . . . he'd offer an opinion and wait for everybody to stomp on it. Hugh taught Hillary not to be afraid to speak her opinions."

Hillary had decided she wanted to attend an all-girls school and on the advice of two teachers had considered Smith and Radcliffe. But once she saw photos of one of the other famous Seven Sisters schools with its pastoral Gothic campus and bucolic view of a lake she was sold. One Sunday afternoon, while her father waited outside in his big car reading the newspaper and turning the sidewalk brown with tobacco juice, Hillary accepted an invitation from representatives of status-conscious, high-achieving Wellesley College to join the freshman class that fall.

In June 1965, she was named a Merit Scholar finalist, and won the Daughters of the American Revolution Citizenship Award, and the social studies award. The school newspaper had also interviewed her, and when she was asked about her ambitions, she curtly replied, "To marry a senator and settle down in Georgetown." (Years later, when asked by reporters about the remark, she snapped, "That was made up. I didn't say that!")

With Hugh and Dorothy Rodham sitting proudly in the first row, Hillary graduated in the top 5 percent of her class—fifteenth out of about a thousand—and was voted the most likely to succeed.

In early September, Rodham loaded his princess's suitcases into the Cadillac. With Hillary riding shotgun, and Dorothy in the back, they headed east. A whole new world awaited "Sister Frigidaire" at Wellesley, just outside Boston, where, her government teacher warned her, she'd become "a liberal and a Democrat." Aside from occasional vacation and holiday visits home, Hillary would never again live in conservative Park Ridge. "After we dropped her off," Dorothy Rodham recalled, "I just crawled in the backseat and cried for eight hundred miles."

Young William Jefferson Clinton; his half brother, Roger; and their mother, Virginia, in the innocent times of 1950s Arkansas. Years later Hillary blamed Bill's infidelity problems on the fact that his mother and grandmother had fought over him in his dysfunctional childhood.

CorbisSygma/Mike Stewart

The mid-fifties suburban blissfulness of the Rodhams often portrayed by Hillary belies relatives' assertions of an icy marriage and a chilly household. "I just didn't feel there was any love there," avows a family member. The future first lady displays her preternatural camera savvy while the dark personas of her parents, Dorothy and Hugh, and siblings, Hughie and Tony, are far more honest and revealing.

Della Murray, Hillary's maternal grandmother, who had an eerie likeness to a certain former White House intern, was married at fifteen and soon after gave birth to Hillary's mother. Her second marriage, to businessman Max Rosenberg, revealed during Hillary's senate campaign, sparked charges of pandering to New York's Jewish voters. Hillary's mother had a lifelong feud with Rosenberg that ignited slurs.

Courtesy of
Oscar Dowdy

Courtesy of
Oscar Dowdy

Courtesy of Oscar Dowdy

Courtesy of Oscar Dowdy

At eight years of age, Hillary's mother and her baby sister, Isabelle, were virtually abandoned by Della and her first husband, a fireman, and shipped off to emotionally abusive paternal grandparents in California. Shapely, vivacious Addie Rosenberg, Della and Max's daughter—and Dorothy Rodham's half sister—was a vampy lounge singer and dancer in whom Hillary confided intimate details about her college love life, while Dorothy Rodham was not fond of Addie. Like Hillary, Addie became a successful lawyer.

Hillary has never openly discussed her Rodham family political roots, such as her great-uncle George Beale Rodham, a Republican power broker in her father's hometown of Scranton, Pennsylvania, riddled at the time of the councilman's rule with patronage, gambling, and prostitution.

Dr. Russell Rodham, Hillary's father's youngest brother, was one of the bright, shining lights of the family, with a brilliant future in medicine. But his life spun out of control, and he suffered a horrible demise in virtual poverty at an early age.

The Rodham clan in Little Rock to celebrate Bill's second gubernatorial election. *Front row, left to right:* Hillary's straight-talking cousin Oscar Dowdy with Dorothy Rodham, and Dowdy's insightful wife, Helen, who was shocked by life in Hillary's Park Ridge home. *Back row, left to right:* The aging patriarch, Hugh Rodham, with son, Tony; Hugh's "princess," Hillary; Hughie and wife, Maria Rodham; and the boyish governor with dreams of the Oval Office dancing in his head.

Of all his women, the one Bill loved the most was his flamboyant and often outrageous mother, Virginia, who knew he was destined for greatness, and their joy together is clearly evident. The president soulfully mourns at Virginia's gravesite, morosely telling a friend after her burial, "I miss my mama."

Bright, driven, and ambitious, Hillary in high school was mesmerized by the teachings of a right-wing history instructor, but at the same time idolized a leftist, avant-garde, Methodist youth leader.

Hillary's controversial commencement address at Wellesley College catapulted her into the pages of *Life* magazine, but later *Life* editors spiked a story on Bill's governorship because of Hillary's dowdy looks.

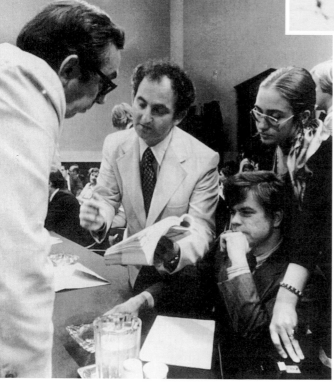

Presidential scandal and impeachment was in the air as Yale Law School grad Hillary, now seriously dating Bill, earns her bones working for the Senate Watergate Committee.

CorbisSygma/Arnie Sachs

Bill followed in the womanizing path of his political idol, JFK, whom
he met for the first time in the Rose Garden of the White House as a
representative of Boys' Nation, just four months before Dallas.

Wide World Photos

On the fast track: Bill, here with other officers, is president of the
sophomore class at Georgetown University, where he boasted about one
day sitting in the Oval Office.

The boyish Arkansas governor and the first lady dressed in her Gap finest relax in this candid moment on the grand staircase of the Little Rock Governor's Mansion.

The Arkansas governor and first lady pay an early visit to the White House, but their confident faces hide troubles in the marriage.

Chelsea has been a bonding factor in the Clintons' troubled union. When Chelsea was just a babe in arms, Bill sang her a lullaby with the lyrics "I want a divorce."

When Hillary learned of Bill's serious relationship with lovely Clinton congressional campaign aide Marla Crider—whose identity has never before become public—she went ballistic, even enlisting the Rodham men in an effort to end the romance. While Bill's mother held Hillary in disdain, Virginia had great affection for Marla and would have liked Bill to marry her.

Courtesy of Marla Crider

Finally, their mutual goal and curious pact is achieved! The Clintons take the White House and party at their first presidential inauguration.

Wide World Photos

"I NEVER HAD SEXUAL RELATIONS
WITH *THAT WOMAN*—MISS LEWINSKY.
I NEVER TOLD ANYONE TO LIE, NOT A
SINGLE TIME—NEVER. THESE
ALLEGATIONS ARE FALSE."

Corbis-Bettmann

White House spin control at its best (or worst), showing the first couple in a purported amorous mood as sex scandal explodes around them.

Wide World Photos

With Monica in the headlines, an anxious Chelsea walks between her warring parents as First Dog Buddy, in whom the president seeks private solace, leads the way across the White House lawn.

The strain of Monicagate manifests itself clearly on the grim faces of the first couple.

With scandal and impeachment seemingly behind him, a confident president mouths the words "I love you" to an impassive Hillary during Bill Clinton's last state of the union speech on January 27, 2000.

The president appears free as a bird as he contemplates his future, while a confident and concerned Hillary formally announces her first run for political office on February 6, 2000, declaring, "I know it's not always going to be an easy campaign. . . ."

Called an Illinois, Arkansas, and Washington, D.C., carpetbagger, Hillary establishes a new home base in Chappaqua, New York, for her controversial senate campaign, but questions remain as to whether the long-troubled union between the lame duck president and his first lady will survive.

FROM REPUBLICAN TO DEMOCRAT

IT WAS A TUMULTUOUS TIME IN AMERICA, the year Hillary matriculated at Wellesley. In Vietnam, where President Johnson had authorized a wider U.S. combat role, boys from Portland and Park Ridge and Paducah were killing and being killed. In Los Angeles racial tensions that had plagued the nation for years exploded in a bloodbath of rioting, arson, and looting in the "Negro" section of Watts. In racist Alabama, twenty-five thousand civil rights demonstrators, led by Martin Luther King, embarked on a fifty-mile walk for freedom from Selma, Alabama, to the state capitol in Montgomery, where King told the massive crowd, "We are on the move and no wave of racism will stop us!"

But the revolution abroad in the land had still not come to Wellesley's peaceful, century-old campus where Hillary and her classmates were confronted by high school–style dress codes and Victorian-era dating curfews. The historic goal of Wellesley was to turn out good wives and mothers whose mission was to "make a difference in the world." Their motto was, "Not to be served, but to serve."

"As soon as we got to campus there were all these girls doing maypole dances, sort of good-natured pom-pom girls, and I was appalled," recalled Pat Fry, from Philadelphia's Main Line, who became close friends with Hillary and was one of only three others in the class of some four hundred who would go on to Yale with her. "There wasn't much administration at that point in time. It was a characterless, unassertive group of people running Wellesley."

Beginning in her freshman year, however, Hillary's leadership abilities came into play. She fought to do away with the honors system, to establish a summer Outward Bound program, to reorganize the system for checking out books from the library, and she protested the college's policy of putting students together based on religion, race, and ethnic background. As Pat Fry noted, "Hillary just took to Wellesley like a duck to water. She just whipped us all into shape. There was a leadership vacuum there. Driven is not quite the right word for her, but Hillary was trying to get somewhere. She was always moving, always focused, but I don't believe there's a megalomania there." Despite her many causes, however, Hillary still was no radical. Cynical writers at the *Wellesley News*, unimpressed with what they viewed as her vanilla activism, coyly suggested that students should send to Hillary any ideas on "how to perk up school spirit."

Still a Goldwater Girl at heart, the articulate and confident political science major won easy election as president of the campus Young Republicans. However, her favorite reading material at the time was far from conservative: the monthly *motive*—an extreme magazine for young Methodists published by the church's university Christian movement—featured pieces about witch power, commune life, drug-induced hallucinations, and lesbianism.

While she was the daughter of a tobacco-chewing fabric salesman with no pedigree, Hillary had quickly installed herself and felt at ease in a circle of debutantes and wealthy girls from prominent families, a group that included Eleanor "Eldie" Acheson, the granddaughter of elder statesman Dean Acheson. Within that elite circle, she opened up about her political ambitions—expressing a desire to one day become class president, a wish that would be fulfilled to her amazement. She even expressed a desire to own a yellow Jaguar XKE convertible, the kind of car some of her moneyed classmates drove. In her numerous leadership roles, Hillary had developed a questionable pattern of giving her well-to-do pals key spots on committees, which had sparked an editorial rebuke from the *Wellesley News*. "The habit of appointing friends and members of the in-group should be halted immediately in order that knowing people in power does not become a prerequisite for officeholding."

During the summer between her sophomore and junior years, Hillary worked as a researcher and babysitter for a professor at Wellesley who was writing a book on the war in Vietnam, and by the time she returned to campus she was espousing strong antiwar sentiment for the first time. "She was off campus a lot," noted Pat Fry. "Hillary was campaigning for [antiwar presidential candidate Eugene] McCarthy. She was going to political functions and rallies in Boston."

As Tony Rodham observed, "At Wellesley College Hillary discovered that the Democrats were people more in line with what she truly believed in. In the family, we used to say Hillary was a Goldwater Girl and then she went to college and got an education and became a Democrat."

At Wellesley Hillary also discovered romance for the first time when she fell for Geoffrey Shields, a Harvard boy, who had also grown up in the suburbs of Chicago, albeit a wealthy community on the banks of Lake Michigan called Lake Forest. In high school, he had been a star football player and had excelled academically.

"We spent a lot of time with small groups of friends talking about political issues," recalled Shields, who became a lawyer. During their long chats, Shields saw Hillary's competitive side surface. He remembered her mantra as being, "You can't accomplish anything in government unless you win!" He said she was more interested in the process of achieving victory than in taking a philosophical position that could not lead anywhere.

Hillary dated Shields into her junior year, and their relationship became the subject of much campus gossip because she had become a celebrity of sorts. "Hillary was a big woman on campus, so the talk was— 'Hillary's dating this guy at Harvard,'" said Pat Fry. "Hillary was a part of our lives because she was our leader. Because she was a well-known figure, people would talk about her; it was like being in a company and everyone wanted to know whom the CEO was seeing. Wellesley was a pretty heterosexual campus. There was a sexual revolution but everyone took it seriously. People fucked a lot more, probably because the Pill and the IUD were available. When we first got there you had to be in at a certain hour, and it was a serious matter if you were a minute late. By senior year, there were guys in the dorms unbeknownst to the administration. It had totally changed."

By her senior year Hillary had become involved with another ambitious student, David Rupert, who was a government major and classmate of Bill's at Georgetown University. Hillary had met Rupert while she was working as a summer intern in Washington for the House Republican Conference, and Rupert for liberal New York Republican congressman Charles Goodell. Rupert said he felt their on-and-off relationship—which he acknowledged was sexual—ended because he never "stated a burning desire to be president. I believe that was a need for her in a partner."

While Hillary's love life was the subject of much campus gossip and speculation, she was extremely private about her romances, and few of the women in her close circle were aware of the depth—or lack thereof—of her relationships. "When her mother asked whether she was dating anyone," recalled a Wellesley chum, "Hillary always responded that she was too busy with her studies and activities." But, in fact, Hillary had been revealing her most intimate secrets to a woman whom Dorothy Rodham had long detested—Rodham's sexy and outrageous half sister, Addie Rosenberg, Della and Max's daughter.

"Hillary confided in Addie because she was certainly older, and wiser, and a whole lot more experienced with men," said Oscar Dowdy, Addie's nephew. "They were pretty close, and chuckled about some of the intimate things that went on in Hillary's love life. Addie told me that Hillary talked about two lovers while she was at Wellesley—David Rupert, and another guy before him. Hillary told Addie that Rupert was her first real serious relationship. Addie thought it was great for Hillary. She told me, 'You won't believe it, but Hillary has a human, sexual side. Hillary actually got laid. It's kind of exciting.'"

Thirteen years older than Hillary, Addie had always been a rebel. After graduating from Stevens College, in Columbus, Missouri, in 1954, with an associate degree in English, she had moved to southern California to break into show business, which infuriated her overbearing father. Max Rosenberg had had high hopes for his extremely bright daughter, and her decision caused a lengthy break in their relationship.

In Hollywood, petite, shapely, and vivacious Addie didn't make it in the movies, but instead became a vampy lounge singer and dancer who toured the country under the stage name of Addie Ross. For a time she had an act with another sexy showgirl, and there were suspicions within the family that Addie might have taken up exotic dancing. Early on she had brief marriage to a biker who rode a Harley, wore black leathers, and was in the vending machine business. Raised a Christian by her mother, Addie later converted to her father's Judaism after settling down and marrying a Jewish businessman.

While Hillary was enthralled with her madcap aunt, Hillary's mother had always held Addie in contempt. "Addie wasn't what Dorothy would have wanted her to be," observed Helen Dowdy. "She would embarrass Dorothy at times because she would say things that ladies don't say—the swearing, the storytelling about things that men talk about. She was wild. She was raunchy. She was loud. From what I saw she was an embarrassment to Dorothy. I remember one evening Addie had come to our house in the evening and she had spilled something on her dress. Somehow, miraculously, she had a little bikini in her car, and so she changed into it, and then wanted to go out to dinner. Oscar gave her a shirt and off they went. She was just wearing that skimpy string bikini underneath. But that was Adeline—don't look, but look. It's an understatement to say she was an exhibitionist, and I don't think Dorothy could quite cope with that."

By the time Hillary was at Yale, Addie had dropped her lounge act, gotten serious about life, and like Hillary had decided to become a lawyer. She finally got her degree in June 1979 at a small Church of the Brethren school called the University of La Verne College of Law, in suburban Los Angeles. Later, she established a small, successful corporate law practice in North Hollywood. Still, Dorothy looked down her nose at her. "We were sitting in the governor's mansion at Bill's second inauguration," said Helen Dowdy, "and it was just the immediate family, and Dorothy spotted her and said, 'Oh, dammit! Here comes that disgusting Adeline.' I didn't get it. Adeline was her half sister, but Adeline wasn't what Dorothy wanted her to be."

Dorothy Rodham's criticisms of Addie, however, had more to do with her strong feelings about her father, Max Rosenberg. "Dorothy's lifelong grudge against Max definitely carried over to Addie," Oscar Dowdy maintained. "Addie was more like Max than like Della. She had Max's mannerisms, his boldness, his business sense, his thirst for knowledge about stocks and the stock market, about what made the business world click. Dorothy was *never* close to Addie. Addie used to surprise me. She was a very strong woman, but she hungered for more closeness with Dorothy, with the whole Rodham family, and just was never was able to get it. Addie even went to Arkansas where she was a campaign worker for Bill, and she made financial contributions to all of Bill's campaigns. But in many cases the Rodhams, mainly Dorothy, didn't really make her feel very welcome. I used to be really upset at how they treated her, how ungracious they were to her. Grandfather Max probably wished Bill well, but I think because of Dorothy he was *never* included. And he was fed up with her treatment. Because of Dorothy, Max wasn't going to travel fifteen hundred miles to Arkansas to be insulted.

"As a child I felt that we were all part of the family and we all enjoyed each other's company. But I never picked up on Aunt Dorothy's hostility toward Max until my grandmother Della died when I was a teenager. And then Dorothy absolutely did not speak to my grandfather—I mean did not speak to him for years. Dorothy only kept up pretenses for Della, who wanted to keep peace in the family, at least on the surface. But once Della died, Max was poison to Dorothy.

"Getting into adulthood Hillary and Addie recognized they had a common ground, but I'm sure Dorothy voiced her disapproval. Addie was so mad because she and Hillary had some good times together and good conversations and were closer, and Addie was annoyed at the distance that was coming between them, most probably caused by Dorothy."

In the last years of her life, Adeline Elizabeth Ross Friedman suffered from diabetes. Shortly after she died in January 1999—a year to the day of her husband's passing—Hillary sent a note on White House stationary to family members and friends expressing her condolences.

"I have many memories of Addie from the time I was a little girl in Illinois through the last years when she helped campaign for Bill in California," Hillary wrote. "She was a unique character whose small size embodied a large spirit, a loud raucous laugh and a sack full of guts. As a young woman she loved to travel, perform and have a good time wherever she was. If there wasn't a party before she arrived anywhere, there was sure to be one before she left."

Except for the Dowdys, however, none of the Rodhams, or the Clintons, attended Addie's funeral.

Hillary made her ultimate mark at Wellesley in her senior year, the spring of 1969, when she successfully lobbied to become the first student ever to speak at commencement. Initially against the idea, college president Ruth Adams reluctantly gave her permission with the proviso that Hillary's remarks underscore the views of the entire class. She also demanded an advance copy of her text and a promise that Hillary not deviate from it.

The main speaker, whom Hillary had supported for election in 1966, was Senator Edward Brooke, a liberal black Republican from Massachusetts, who had aligned himself with President Nixon. The senator received an honorary degree from the college at commencement, and then went on to praise the students for their activism, but condemned what he called "coercive protest" by antiwar college radicals.

With Hugh Rodham in the audience along with such dignitaries as Dean Acheson and diplomat Paul Nitze, Hillary delivered her prepared remarks, but then swerved off the plotted course and gave an impassioned, extemporaneous rebuke of Brooke's comments. "We're not in the positions yet of leadership and power," Hillary declared, "but we do have that indispensable task of criticizing and constructive protest and I find myself reacting just briefly to some of the things that Senator Brooke said. . . . The challenge now is to practice politics as the art of making what appears to be impossible, possible."

Many in the staid audience were stunned, shocked and angered by her words of protest. Afterwards, Hillary was exhilarated and nervous at the same time, wondering whether she had gone too far by publicly attacking the most important black politician in the country.

However, her speech had caught the attention of the national press and she was secretly delighted with the exposure: the *Washington Post* termed her remarks a "mild rebuke," while *Life*—the *People* magazine of its time—featured her and two other college commencement speakers, including Ira Magaziner, who would years later work with Hillary on the health care debacle, as the cream of student activists. Some years down the road, though, *Life* would quietly spike a major feature story on the newly elected youngest governor in the nation—because his wife's looks didn't meet a top editor's beauty quotient requirements.

WHO'S TO BLAME FOR BILL

THE CIRCUMSTANCES SURROUNDING William Jefferson Clinton's birth were the stuff of true drama. Everyone in Hope, Arkansas, knew his young mother, twenty-three-year-old Virginia Cassidy Blythe, had been widowed only three months before by a freak accident—her husband, William Jefferson Blythe, on his way to pick up his wife and bring her back to their new Chicago home, had crashed and overturned his car on a dark road, stumbled out, then tripped and passed out face down in a drainage ditch, drowning in only a few inches of water.

Bill was delivered by Caesarian section in the early hours of August 19, 1946, in the Julia Chester Hospital in Hope. The waiting room was jammed with relatives. Wilma Booker, the surgical nurse in attendance, remembered going out to give them the news, only to be greeted by complaints. "They said, 'Wilma, it's hot as holy hell out here,'" she recalled.

He was a healthy, full-term infant, though his mother later claimed he had been induced a month early. Booker was proud to have been "the first one to smack him." Many years later she would be asked by one wag why she hadn't simply dropped him on the floor. "I said, there wasn't anything written on his butt," she said. "Look, I probably delivered a few convicts too over the years."

Hovering close from the beginning was Virginia's mother, Edith Grisham Cassidy, a correspondence-trained practical nurse, flamboyant, willful, determined to take charge. It was clear she was not about to leave Billy's care to her daughter. For the first three years of his life, she was the dominant parent, setting up schedules and adhering to them meticulously, giving him his first lessons in reading every morning, as he sat in his highchair, and hanging playing cards on the curtains to illustrate numbers. Virginia, living in her parents' home, was more in the position of a loving older sister, sneaking her baby away for long walks whenever she could manage it.

Virginia and her father, James Eldridge Cassidy, a warm, easygoing man, were used to dealing with her mother. On the whole, it was best to let her have her own way. She had a terrible temper, and had often used a switch to discipline her daughter; for years, Virginia had been forced to overhear her nightly harrangues against her husband, whom she constantly accused of infidelity. It gave Virginia a lifelong aversion to the idea of jealousy.

But whatever the differences of temperament that existed between Virginia and her mother, it was also true that Virginia, an only child, was treated like a princess by her parents. Her bedroom was nearly three times as large as the one they shared, filled with special blond furniture, vanities holding her endless supplies of makeup. When guests visited, they slept in a spare bed in her parents room, down the hall. No one shared Virginia's room.

She was a popular girl, always dramatically turned out, energetic and fun-loving, with a round face, dark brown hair, a pert challenge in her eyes. She'd met Bill Blythe while at nursing school in 1943 in Shreveport, Louisiana, when he came to the hospital with a young woman suffering an appendectomy attack. The two struck sparks at once—they left the hospital together, and married only two months later.

A wandering salesman from Sherman, Texas, Blythe had already chalked up three, possibly even four marriages (at least two half-siblings of Bill's would be discovered years later), and very likely was still legally married—but Virginia, madly in love, knew none of this. "All I knew of his life was what he had chosen to reveal to me," she said. After their wedding, Bill left to join the army, and Virginia went back to finish nursing school. Later she visited his family in Sherman. Bill, whom the family called W.J., had grown up on a farm, the sixth of nine children born to Willie Blythe and Lou Birchie Ayers. His father had died when he was a teenager, after which Bill had gone to work as a mechanic to help support the family, later becoming a traveling salesman.

Bill Blythe and Virginia were reunited after the war, in fall 1945. In his book *First in His Class*, and later, in a second book, *The Clinton Enigma*, Clinton biographer David Maraniss went to great lengths to point out discrepancies in Virginia's story—according to her the couple got back together in November, while army records pinpoint December 7 as Blythe's date of discharge. If in fact the two did not reconnect until December, this would mean Bill was a full-term eight-month baby—enough, Maraniss said, to cause rumors to spring up in Hope questioning his legitimacy.

In fact, full-term eight-month babies, while unusual, are far from unknown. It seems likely this particular line of questioning is no more than a red herring, and that Bill Blythe, the charming traveling salesman, was undoubtedly the father of the future president.

Virginia, never a passive type, decided quickly she would need to forge a better career for herself in order to care for her son. It is also likely she was chafing under the restrictions of living in her parents' home. She arranged to take a two-year speciality course as a nurse anesthesiologist in New Orleans, leaving little Billy with her parents.

She had already begun to see Roger Clinton, a fast-talking, hard-drinking man who ran the Buick dealership in Hope—a man her mother couldn't stand. A somewhat loose cannon as ever, at one point Edith even burned a jacket Roger had given Virginia.

Edith Cassidy kept strict control over little Billy the first three years of his life, organizing his daily schedule to such an extent he would later say it caused him to chafe against schedules the rest of his life; Bill had a reputation for being late, even as president. With Virginia away at school, Edith's position as primary parent was ensured, and she reveled in it. Virginia, needing to get on with her own life, obviously allowed it. It was only afterwards, when she came back home, that the conflict between the two women escalated, reaching a fever pitch when Virginia announced her intention to marry Roger Clinton, and take Billy with her. Furious, Edith tried to seek custody, to no avail.

The two women battled fiercely, each thinking they knew what was best for the boy. It was the sort of drama played out in many families. But unlike other minor family dramas, this one would suddenly become national news, a half century later.

In the September 1999 premier issue of *Talk* magazine, Hillary—fresh from the Monica Lewinsky scandal—gave an interview in which she blamed Bill's infidelity problems on the fact that his mother and his grandmother had fought over him in his childhood.

"He was so young, barely 4, when he was scarred by abuse. There was terrible conflict between his mother and his grandmother," she said. A psychologist once told her, she went on, that "for a boy being the middle of a conflict between two women is the worst possible situation. There is always the desire to please each one."

The comments took up only one short paragraph in a lengthy interview, but they were seized on by the sex scandal–hungry news media, and a near avalanche of ridicule followed.

"It is something like a birth defect, a grandma-inflicted psychosis that left him panting for almost any woman with a pulse," jibed *Washington Post* columnist Richard Cohen. Did Hillary, thundered Senator Mitch McConnell, a Republican from Kentucky, on CBS *Face the Nation*, excuse Nixon's Watergate crimes because he wet the bed as a youngster? The *Washington Post*'s Gene Weingarten submitted an open letter to his wife. His aunt Ethel had once laughed hysterically at his new moustache, he said—so "clearly, I shall now have to have indiscriminate sex with floozies."

A close associate of Virginia's echoed what many in Arkansas were saying privately after the interview appeared. "I'll tell you this, Hillary probably better be glad Virginia's gone. Virginia and Hillary never did hit it off. They used to put up a big front—oh yes, we get along, oh yes, we respect each other and so forth—but it wasn't true." It did not surprise Virginia's friend to see Hillary laying the blame for Bill's behavior at his mother's door.

Marge Mitchell, one of Virginia's dearest and oldest friends, just snickered. "I want to go on record as saying—that kiddo was never abused as a child," she said firmly.

"It's clearly ridiculous," said Dr. Stanley Renshon, a psychoanalyst and coordinator of a program on the psychology of political behavior at CUNY graduate school. "The idea that the conflict between two women is the root of it all—ridiculous. She can say it all she wants, and whoever the psychologist is [who said such a situation constituted severe abuse] should remain incognito, believe me. It sounds so dumb. Conflict between two generations is not unusual at all." Renshon, who wrote *High Hopes—The Clinton Presidency and the Politics of Ambition,* felt Bill's problems had more to do with an overwhelming sense of entitlement, which had only grown stronger over the years.

Immediately, the Clintons tried to quell the firestorm that was ignited by Hillary's interview, with Bill suggesting his wife's analysis was somewhat off base. "I have not made any excuses for what was inexcusable," Bill told White House reporters. He said he was loved despite a childhood with an alcoholic stepfather who was sometimes violent. "The most important thing is that every child needs to know growing up that he or she is the most important person in the world to someone. And I knew that."

Meanwhile, exploring her senate campaign in New York State, Hillary recanted somewhat, now declaring that she had not meant to suggest a tie between her husband's infidelities and any childhood abuse. "Everybody is responsible for their behavior and I am a very strong proponent and believer in personal responsibility," she said, "so I hope that people will take that message away from this." At the same time, Lucinda Franks, who interviewed Hillary for *Talk* asserted that the first lady's remarks had been misinterpreted.

Despite her mother's strenuous objections, Virginia married Roger Clinton on June 19, 1950. Neither Bill nor her parents were in attendance. The couple, along with Bill, moved to a small cottage in Hope. The relationship had been volatile from the start—at one point before they married, Virginia, little Bill in tow, trashed Roger's home after she discovered he had entertained another woman, hanging the woman's underwear out on the clothesline for all to see. Roger's drinking continued apace after the marriage, with Virginia herself doing her share of drinking, too. Not long after the wedding, Roger took a shot at her; she called the cops and he spent the night in jail.

When Roger announced in 1953 they were moving to Hot Springs, Virginia was pleased—she felt the distance might keep her parents from knowing about his drinking. But there were other reasons as well. Hot Springs had always been more her kind of town.

Hope, where Virginia had grown up and where Bill spent his first six years, was a town like many in Arkansas—small, decent, law-abiding, God-fearing. "A very, very small, Donna Reedish-type town," said Dr. Bill Schooley, a native, who would later serve as drama teacher at Hot Springs High School. "Everybody was very fashion conscious, very manner conscious. When students from Hope High School went to conventions, they stood out because of their dress, white gloves."

A pleasant town, a sleepy town, a town that prided itself on good behavior, Hope was known for its enormous watermelons, and little else. It was bland and inoffensive, the perfect hometown for an aspiring political candidate.

Hot Springs, on the other hand, was a whole other story.

Marty Elam Walker, who went to high school with Bill, remembered being interviewed by the dean of women when she applied for college in southwest Arkansas. "Well," said the dean, "I see you come from Sin City."

Walker was stunned. "Oh, no, ma'am, I'm from Hot Springs," she said innocently. It was her first clue as to how the rest of the state viewed her hometown.

A beautiful little resort, Hot Springs is nestled tightly within a national park, surrounded by small mountains. For much of its life, until late in the 1960s, it was a thriving center of illegal gambling—much like Scranton. People also came from across the country to bathe in the springs, which were widely believed to cure syphilis and gonorrhea. Business was brisk. As an accompaniment to the springs, various health cure scams flourished throughout the area.

"The dirty little secret was, we were the place you came to if you got venereal disease," said Clay Farrar, a local lawyer. "We had the largest free public health facility for treatment of venereal disease in the country. That's part of our dirty little past, not exactly something you put on your advertisings—if you have VD, come to Hot Springs."

Shirley Abbott, a native and author of an impressive memoir about growing up in Hot Springs, *The Bookmaker's Daughter—A Memory Unbound*, felt the town above all gave its residents a true working knowledge of politics. "You learned in your cradle that you could never know the truth or perhaps that there wasn't any such thing," she wrote. Hot Springs seemed to the casual observer a genteel town, low on crime, well managed, at the time she was growing up there, during the 1950s and '60s. Yet many town fathers were deeply involved in illegal operations, and gangsters held the reins. "After an upbringing here, New York City politics, or Watergate, or even the savings and loan scandal, could hardly come as a surprise," she wrote.

Melinda Barran, who served as mayor from 1989 to 1994, offered a far harsher judgment. "What you saw on the surface was an enormous amount of glitter, glitz, sophistication—and what was underneath was an enormous amount of sleaze, dirt, and fear and degradation," she said.

"There was a skeleton in every closet and practically every family spent a lot of time keeping them covered up." The skeletons, she said, consisted of "the way they lived and acted, the sources of their income, avoiding income taxes, gambling money, political influence, you scratch my back, not playing by the rules, breaking them all the time—Hot Springs was essentially the state whore, to be perfectly honest. That's what we were. A very high-class, very expensive, very beautiful whore. You'd like to take us to bed but you damn sure wouldn't want to marry us."

The fact that Bill came of age not in Hope but in Hot Springs has led some, like Barran, to feel the town left an indelible mark on him. Others disagree, vehemently. "Melinda [Barran] has always made the connection between the gambling past of Hot Springs and Bill's amorality or whatever," said Melinda Gassaway, executive editor of the *Hot Springs Sentinel Record*.

"I don't buy that. I grew up in that. Gambling was going on when I was a small child. It was pretty wide open even though it was illegal. A lot of us grew up here and haven't done anything outrageous, we've gone on to get an education, gone on to be productive citizens. I don't buy that at all."

Despite its manifold attractions—the racetrack, gambling casinos, hotels, and watering holes—not all Hot Springs citizens lived life in the fast lane, of course. "There really are two Hot Springs," said journalist Roy Reed, a native who wrote a biography of former longtime Arkansas governor, Orville Faubus. One group, the group Bill grew up around, the one Virginia and Roger were a part of, "went to the racetrack every day, drank a lot, lived a kind of a high life." The others were "kind of religious, churchgoing, never went to the races." There was a rigid demarcation line separating the two groups, who viewed each other with disdain and suspicion.

THE KID WANTS TO BE PRESIDENT

FOR VIRGINIA, HOT SPRINGS WAS a feisty, pragmatic, fun-loving town, capable of bouncing back in the face of tremendous odds—and as such, a perfect setting for someone who would show the same ability throughout her life. She settled in at once, made friends, forged a career as a nurse anesthesiologist, and quickly became a more or less permanent fixture at the racetrack, carefully scheduling her work so as not to conflict with the ponies. In 1956 she gave birth to Roger.

The fact that her husband was alcoholic, and frequently abusive to both her and the boys, was kept strictly off limits. Bill's childhood friends unanimously report being unaware of any problems in the home.

"People didn't call people alcoholics back then, not when they got up and went to work every day," said Rose Crane, who lived near Bill and attended Ramble Elementary School with him. "I think it's horribly unfair to take 1999 eyes and look back at a situation and rename it. I did not pick up it was an emotionally charged situation."

Virginia, though, in writing her book, left no doubt just what kind of situation it truly was. Roger drank constantly. When drunk he could be fiercely jealous—a jealousy she often seemed to go out of her way to incur, as a way of rattling his cage (Virginia was an incorrigible flirt). Often she would be forced to grab the boys and run out of the house, occasionally stashing them at the nearby Holiday Inn for the night. The atmosphere in the home was one of constant chaos and crisis.

Rose Crane saw none of this. Her memories are of a happy *Leave It to Beaver* childhood. "A million games of gin rummy, Clue, Monopoly, kick ball, shooting baskets—he had a hoop at his house, we had a hoop at ours."

She also remembers a German shepherd named Susie, who had a strong protective streak. "She was a Seeing Eye dropout. All of us were very carefully told by Virginia that because of Susie's training she was very serious about protecting Bill and so all bets were off if Susie became disturbed about something—everybody just quit. We loved her dearly but understood her job was to protect Bill and if it was uncomfortable for Susie, that was the place to stop."

Whether by design or chance, Bill was thus rather neatly shielded against the dangers of backyard roughhousing as a young kid. No one was likely to take a poke at him with Susie around. It was not unsymbolic of the way he was treated, growing up—he was special, a little prince, just as Virginia had been a princess in her time—just like her, he had the biggest bedroom in the house.

For the most part he wore the mantle well. He was a big boy, obviously bright, mature for his age, the sort of kid adults liked and trusted. He felt his responsibility strongly, as protector of his brother and mother. "Bill was father, brother, and son," Virginia attested in her book. He knew the real story of what went on in his house, his stepfather's drinking and temper—and knew, too, that it needed to be concealed from the outside world. Years later he would recount the tale of how at age fourteen he had finally confronted Roger, telling him he was to "never . . . ever . . . touch my mother again."

When Bill was sixteen, Virginia divorced Roger, only to remarry him four months later, out of pity. In the interim, she moved the family across town, to a house she had custom built. Somewhat chastened, Roger became a more shadowy figure after the remarriage. Ironically, it was during the brief divorce that Bill chose to legally change his name to Clinton, mainly for the sake of his little brother.

Much has been said, in the recent national analyze-Bill-Clinton parlor game craze, about alcoholic child syndrome. Yet there were other, more complicated threads operating in the home as well. Adolescent boys, psychiatrists have said, need to be able to throw themselves against a hard, unyielding wall that refuses to give. Only that way will they be able to rebel safely, recover, come to terms with the reality of authority, and move on. In most families it is the father—or a father figure, at times a coach—who provides the wall.

Roger Clinton was no wall. Confronted, he went down like a set of ten pins. On the surface, Bill suffered not at all; he went on to greater and greater success, rising eventually to the most lofty of heights.

But if the theory is true, he had missed a crucial stage of his development, the stage that reassures the adolescent that limits do exist, and will be enforced, and that one is not wandering alone in a lawless world. It may, of course, be sheer bunk, yet more than once, in interviews, friends have touched on it instinctively. Bill, they say, would have never gotten into so much trouble—if he'd only had a father.

But to the community, during those years, Bill appeared to lack for nothing; he struck most as an amazingly mature young man, clearly marked for special destiny. Ken Brown, who went through junior high and high school with him, remembered once actually saving a story on Bill that ran in the junior high school newspaper, in ninth grade.

"I saved it because I knew he was special," he said simply. The story reported Bill's election as to the junior high school student council, as vice president. "I'm not sure I knew he was going to be president back then, but I did come to that conclusion, not far down the road."

He tried to explain the impression Bill made. "He was a powerful presence, even in junior high. He was larger than most people, a big kid, and his head was bigger than most people—it grew to adult size earlier than most of us. He reached his adult height early, had broad shoulders. He didn't have to be odd or different in order to be a commanding presence. He was a regular guy, wore preppie clothes, not outlandish, kind of in mainstream, got in all the right school clubs, was drum major of the band.

"But he had a lot of confidence in himself. He was able to say what he wished, take whatever positions he wished—without feeling he was going to be intimidated or pushed around. A very respected kid, not just by teachers. He was respected by the students, too."

His clearest memory was of the time Bill got up in his eighth grade social studies class, a few years after the historic Central High School racial confrontation in Little Rock, to read a paper stating his belief in the necessity for integration. You could have heard a pin drop, Brown said. Very few, in that time and place, certainly no student, had the courage to speak out publically for integration. Yet Bill seemed able to do it with no trouble at all.

"Our group was known, by seventh and eighth grade, as the nigger lovers," said classmate Mauria Jackson Aspell. "Central High had happened. By high school we were all thought of as very liberal."

Rose Crane remembered having a conversation with Bill shortly after the Central High incident. They were both only eleven. "He asked me what I thought about it. I told him I didn't know, it certainly seemed to me to be a big mess. He told me he believed in equality. He said integration would be a long time coming but that it was the right thing."

Bill himself has said his belief in civil rights came directly from his grandfather, who always treated everyone the same and welcomed black families at his grocery store. According to many, Virginia had the same attitude.

"Bill was like an adult," said Carolyn Yeldell Staley, who became a close friend after he moved into the house next to hers, in high school. "He didn't set himself apart from friends, but he had an added dimension, like the godfather of the group. He was bigger, and so smart and talented and a leader."

Carolyn and Bill became instant friends, sharing among other things a great love of music—a pianist, she accompanied him playing the sax. "I got to be the girl in the boys' group," she said. Along with David Leopoulos, Ronnie Cecil, and Joe Newman, she hung out regularly at his house. "Virginia bent in half to make that home a place where her boys could bring their friends, enjoy themselves. Basically she gave us the house."

The daughter of a Baptist preacher, Carolyn drew the line at dancing. Once, at a party, she overheard someone ask Bill if she danced. Bill's response was immediate: "No, she doesn't, and my dad sells Buicks, and I don't drive Fords, either." She marveled that anyone could be that quick on his feet.

Hot Springs may have looked like Sin City to outsiders, but Bill and his friends, in high school, apparently led amazingly wholesome lives—playing touch football, going to movies, listening to records, playing card games, singing around the piano. There seems to have been almost a complete absence of any darker experimentation.

"We never thought of ourselves as goody-goody," said Staley. "But we didn't drive around, didn't drink, didn't smoke. We weren't surly and hoody."

As far as socializing, "Bill didn't really go out on dates that much then," she said. "He always thought he was fat. We were both tall and big. I'd say, 'You look good, Bill, there's nothing wrong.' It was only ten or fifteen pounds, but it made him feel mushy. He'd say, 'Oh, Carolyn, a duck can waddle. I don't want to waddle.'"

Still, Mauria Aspell remembered "a certain amount of boy-girl stuff, fun stuff, kissy face at parties—I was pretty boy crazy back then." Bill, in fact, had been her first kiss—playing spin the bottle in the sixth grade. Later there were "silly things, like trying to make each other jealous."

In general, at least with Bill's group, the class of '64 sounded like a shoo-in for the class of '54. Except for the music—especially Elvis.

Marge Mitchell, Virginia's nurse buddy, said Virginia had trained her boys never to call her at work unless it was a true emergency. Little Roger often broke the rule, but Bill never did. In fact, over all the years, she could only remember one time Bill called: the day "The King" died. Virginia, bursting into tears, agreed that this had been important enough.

Not everyone in Hot Springs High School was sure Bill would make his mark. "People say, did you ever have any idea he was bound for greatness?" said Warren Maus, a classmate. "You know, he was always sort of a chubby kid, always a little teacher's pet. I think he graduated, like, fourth in the class. But if you'd ask me to name ten people in my class who were really going to do something, really going to go somewhere, I probably wouldn't have named him.

"Basically he was always this sort of pudgy little guy, leader of the band. He was bright, well liked, he wasn't a geek, but certainly not a person I felt bound for greatness. He was just Billy." Occasionally, even today, Maus and another high school friend, Bobby Hanna, look at each other and shake their heads—"Imagine, Billy Clinton," they say. "Who would have ever figured?"

Even Mauria Aspell, his good friend, recalls what a shock it was to suddenly realize years later what Bill had become.

"He's one of the most charismatic people I've ever seen. And I don't know when that happened. I didn't see that in high school, I didn't see that in grade school, for sure. I liked him, he was fun, lots of fun; by the end of high school I loved him, he was my dear friend. But . . ." Even his speeches as governor didn't affect her particularly.

It wasn't until New Hampshire, during the first presidential campaign, that she suddenly saw something very different.

"I was sitting there with David Leopoulos, and Bill started talking and all of a sudden the crowd just stopped. He'd say something—and there would be this roar. And you felt it."

Amazed, she turned to Leopoulos. "When did he learn to do this?" she demanded.

"I dont think it was learned, I think he just unleashed it completely on a national scale and that's why I finally felt it," she mused. "It was weird, very weird. Someone you've known forever."

If there was a turning point in Bill's life, a point at which he knew he was headed for public office, it was undoubtedly the day he stood in the Rose Garden outside the White House, as a representative of Boys Nation, and shook John F. Kennedy's hand. The time was July 1963, the summer before his senior year. Bill was seventeen; the photograph shows an intense young man, mouth clenched, eyes fiercely focused on the president.

"In my mind, it was the seminal event in his life," said Maus. "It took him out of this atmosphere where he'd been this pudgy little band guy. He realized, I got elected to Boys Nation, hell, I can get elected." It made all the difference in the world. Rose Crane's mother, who taught high school English, later told her daughter that Bill had confided shortly afterwards that he was decided. He was going to go for public office instead of pursuing his music.

His strong sense of self-destiny, of course, had preceded the handshake—but it was the handshake that solidified the goal. After that, there would be no deviation. Over the next ten years, nearly everything he did—going to Georgetown University (the only college he applied to), getting elected to top class offices, working for Senator Fulbright, help-ing out in various political campaigns, winning a Rhodes scholarship to Oxford, working for McGovern, getting a Yale law degree, develop-ing and nurturing a network of men and women who could help when the time came, and finally, wooing and winning Hillary—would be a part of the plan.

Bill Clinton had made up his mind. He was going to be president.

HILLARY RODHAM VS. VIRGINIA KELLEY

A MODERN-DAY LOCHINVAR IN REVERSE, young Bill Clinton rode back to Arkansas out of the East just like he'd always told everyone he would, bringing it all back home, the ambition, the charisma, the energy, the drive that had been boiling in him since childhood, the political know-how he'd picked up from every local, state, and national campaign he'd worked in—and of course, the Rollodex he'd been compiling for nearly all his life. All broke out in brilliance, like the country boys say, the luster of his Georgetown/Oxford/Yale education shining in the sun.

Came back to save the state, as one newspaperman put it years later, not entirely cynically. After all, who better? He was young, educated, in love with politics, committed to helping his people, convinced he would make a difference. Home at last, he was ready to hit the ground running.

He came back alone—Hillary was headed for Washington to work with the Watergate committee, a fact he bragged about to everyone. She was, after all, the most brilliant woman he'd ever met; if she wanted, she could go anywhere. He just wasn't at all sure that any-

112

where meant Arkansas, at the moment. Or if it did (and this he didn't like admitting even to himself), whether she'd be able to fit in.

Their maiden voyage back to his home state had been something less than a resounding success. Nervous, perhaps, about Hillary's first meeting with his mother, he had first stopped off at the home of his friends Paul and Mary Lee Fray.

For years—privately and publically—the Frays would attempt to deconstruct exactly what happened that day. Figure out what went wrong. Beyond question, though, the chemistry between the four was way off.

Bill, with his usual ease, jumped instantly out of the car to hug his friends, introduced Hillary and apologized for their appearance— they'd been driving several days in an un-air-conditioned car. No problem, come in, have something to drink, the Frays urged. Bill bounded into the house.

Hillary, however, stayed in the car. She nodded politely to the couple when introduced, exchanged a few words, but refused to leave her seat.

"Maybe because I was pregnant? Because Paul was wearing shorts? Because we had a Corvette?" Mary Lee theorized wildly a quarter century later. "He had to have told her about us, that Paul was going to help him run for office. Did she not like what she heard?" For whatever reason, this was not how people behaved in Arkansas where hospitality had been raised to an art form.

Paul was put out. He was also stunned—this was Bill's true love? The woman he had told Paul he intended to marry? That hair, those glasses, that outfit. "I thought, my God, Bill Clinton, you son of a bitch—you could have any damn woman on the face of the earth, and you brought one that looks like the south end of a mule going north," he said. "That was my personal statement to myself."

Paul had promised Bill Clinton he would help him run for office the first day he met him, eight years before. "He was the smartest guy I'd ever met in my life who had common sense. I could assess immediately he had the ability to make things happen. When I first met him, I remember coming home and saying, Daddy—my daddy had worked for Truman—I think I met the guy today who's going to make a great difference in the state of Arkansas. He's not but nineteen but as I see it, he's going to Washington." Not that Paul had ever allowed himself to think higher than the Senate—this was Arkansas, after all.

Only a year or so older than Bill, Fray too was a dyed-in-the-blood political animal; he viewed everything through the lens of possible political effect. Seeing Hillary through the window of Bill's beat up Gremlin, hearing those flat Midwest vowels for the first time, his heart dropped; his first thought was that the boy had thrown a whammy into the works. "She had these whiskey-jigger-bottom glasses, thick lens, and she had on a prairie league dress, stuff of this nature. I said in my own mind, well, he's marrying him a hippie."

His concern was totally pragmatic. "I felt like since he was going to get into Arkansas politics, let's find somebody down here that (a) is amenable to the situation, (b) has money, (c) is going to have a likeness in her mind-set. She didn't fit that mold. She was not from here, was not going to mesh in unless she was totally prepared, and I didn't think she was wealthy.

"But I just felt like, hey, bottom-line, that's his choice, we'll have to live by it." He knew the two had a powerful connection, that Bill respected her advice above all others.

"My husband was looking for a beauty queen," said Mary Lee Fray. "That's what Bill had always dated. Someone who wore makeup, had her hair fixed—back then we wore stiff hair, black eyeliner, we'd line our lips with a pencil brush, wear heavy makeup." She also felt Paul expected Hillary to greet him with enthusiasm—"jump out of the car and give him a big hug."

Mary Lee had been looking forward to the visit for months. "Bill had been calling every day. I knew she wasn't going to be dangly earrings. I knew she was going to be different. I knew she was from Chicago." Still, the reality had come as a bit of a shock.

"I can remember standing around the car, saying 'Come on in, Hillary, I've got ice tea, fresh lemonade, fruit,'" she said. Hillary stayed where she was. It was clear things weren't going well, that she and Paul had not gotten off on the right foot. Bill by then was in the kitchen, helping himself, just like always. He seemed unfazed by Hillary's behavior.

Later, after they left, Mary Lee wrote to her mother. "I said, 'Mother, she's very plain, to the point you could call her homely. She would mix well in certain parts of Arkansas where they wear long clothes, no makeup. But Bill is madly in love with her. Make no mistake, this is the woman,'" she recalled.

But she couldn't help worrying a little about what Virginia Kelley's reaction would be.

"She didn't bother to clean up to go see her [future] mother-in-law. In the South you would have changed your clothes, washed your feet, your hair, been very meticulous going to see Mom. Especially Virginia, whose nails were in perfect shape, whose hairdo would be stiff, who would have cleaned the house all night, anticipating Hillary. Stayed up all night, cleaned it with a Q-tip if she had to." Watching them leave, Mary Lee felt a definite sense of foreboding.

Virginia Kelley has written quite openly about her initial reaction to Hillary in her book *Leading with My Heart*—Virginia, according to her friends, never uttered a dishonest word in her life. Mary Lee's qualms were well justified. Bill had apparently hoped, unrealistically, that the two most important women in his life would quickly see through their differences in style and realize how much they had in common—himself, of course, but also the fact that both were strong, independent, even fearless types. Over the years, they would indeed come to have a grudging respect for each other. But true warmth would never be part of the equation.

And the first visit home was the worst (Hillary and Virginia had met briefly when Virginia came to New Haven, with no particular reaction on either side). Part of it was Virginia's feeling that no woman was good enough for her beloved son, whom she adored zealously. ("It really was extraordinary, the way she talked about him," said one Arkansas Clinton-watcher, journalist John Brummet. "Everybody loves their kids, but with her, it was like she'd given birth to the messiah.") Virginia had met many of the women Bill had dated over the years, and her reaction had not always been unmixed delight. When he'd brought down Ann Markusen, a brilliant young woman he dated at Georgetown, who later became an economics professor, Virginia had taken an instant dislike to her, too.

"She told me, 'My God, he can't marry something like this,'" said Paul Fray. "I said, 'Well, why not, Mama?' I always called her Mama C. She said, 'Paul David, this ain't gonna work.' I said, 'Tell me why.' She said, 'Because I said it's not gonna work. I don't take to this one.'" Fray was sure she had managed to get rid of her. "Bill listened to his mama."

Virginia, said one woman who'd known her well, had always hoped

Bill would marry "a sweet cute attractive perky girl from Arkansas." Yet according to others, even some of those had not pleased her much either—including Sharon Evans, who was cute and perky enough to be crowned Miss Arkansas, but who she still felt was not quite right for her son.

But unquestionably, her antipathy to Hillary went far deeper. Both Virginia and Roger, Bill's teenage brother, were visibly shocked when she came through the door. It seems odd to think that such relatively minor traits—wearing no makeup, letting your hair hang loose in no particular style, dressing sloppily—could provoke such a response in the early 70s, but the South was (and is) a different country from the urban North. As one woman put it later, succinctly, "Hillary came down—and the entire state of Arkansas went 'uhh.'" Whatever else, her appearance marked her definitively to Arkansans as not one of us—a perception she would never shake.

"Your average Southern girl doesn't ever want to look bad if she can help it," journalist Gene Lyons explained. His own wife, Diane, had received a certain amount of reverse discrimination, going to college in the North, where many assumed that a good-looking, carefully groomed woman with a Southern accent had to be a lightweight. Virginia was a Southern girl to her rigidly painted eyebrows, to the carefully dyed skunk stripe in her hair. Her horrified reaction would not have been more immediate, visceral, or tribal, if Bill had brought home a Martian.

Bill could tell at once. As soon as Hillary left the room to unpack, he read his mother and brother the riot act. "I want you to know that I've had it up to here with beauty queens," he said. "I have to have somebody I can talk to. Do you understand that?" His eyes, Virginia noted, "bored through us like my mother's used to do." His reprimand did nothing to improve the atmosphere. Throughout that first, unsuccessful visit, Hillary remained "quiet, cool, unresponsive," Virginia unbending.

"Bill told me later that the reception had not been good," said Mary Lee Fray. "I said, 'Bill, this is the first time you've brought home the future missus. She's got to accept it—her little boy is leaving home.'"

But Bill knew it was more than just that. He told a friend, Virginia later learned, that he thought there was almost a kind of "cultural tension" between them (undoubtedly made up of equal parts region, generation, and Max Factor). Later, he spoke to his mother more sternly than he ever had in his life, telling her to pray for him this would work out. "Because I'll tell you this—for me it's Hillary or it's nobody." And Virginia did pray—she always wanted her sons to get what they wanted—even if she did spend her time between prayers grinding her teeth at the prospect of Hillary as a daughter-in-law.

There came a time, after Bill had returned to Arkansas for good, when he would take her to task once again, for her lack of respect and warmth towards Hillary. Brooding over this, she finally wrote Hillary a letter, opening her heart, asking for her forgiveness. Writing the letter allowed her to come to peace with the situation. Whether it had the same effect on Hillary is not known—because Hillary, whose meticulous attention to correspondence is legendary among her friends, never answered that particular letter, or referred to it in any way, according to Virginia's book.

Carolyn Yeldell Staley had also gotten phone calls from Bill at Yale about Hillary. "He told me he'd been hit by the proverbial bolt—*the* thunderbolt," she said. She was eager to meet her, but even though she was visiting her parents when he came, she would not get the chance for several years. Bill dropped over—but without Hillary. She had some reading she needed to catch up on, he told her.

It was natural for Bill to wonder if Hillary would ever consent to relocate to Arkansas, given that first visit. It had hardly been a smashing success.

But for himself, he was back home, after nine long years.

HIDDEN AGENDA

BILL NEEDED A HOME BASE, and Paul Fray is convinced he was the one who first came up with the idea that he should get a teaching post at the University of Arkansas law school at Fayetteville.

Fray urged him not to get mired in private practice. "I said, 'You need to call Wylie Davis (the law school dean) and tell him you want to go on faculty.'" There were several advantages—this would put him in the same district, the Third Congressional, that Senator William Fulbright had once represented, a district that also included his hometown, Hot Springs; plus, when it came time to run, he would have access to an unlimited supply of the most dedicated volunteer campaign workers in the world—college students.

Bill made the call, and began the interview process; everyone at the law school was impressed by him, though somewhat wary. Did this guy really mean to commit wholly to teaching? Or was it only a stepping-stone?

"The faculty was concerned he wouldn't stay," said Steve Clark, at that time the assistant dean, who met Bill for the first time when he picked him up at the airport in Fayetteville (later, he would serve as attorney general, while Bill was governor; later still, he would see his political career go down in flames, when it was revealed he had misused credit cards). They stopped for Mexican food—Bill had developed a taste for it when he'd worked on the McGovern campaign in Texas the year before—and discovered a number of connections; same age, similar backgrounds. Clark, in fact, came from an Arkansas town even smaller than Hope, Leachville, population fourteen hundred, over in the east, on the delta.

"He said, 'Man, I really want this job.' And I said, 'Well, you're going to have to tell them you're here to stay—that's their fear. They don't want you to be gone.'" As it happened, Bill made a great impression at the law school—"wasn't anybody who didn't like him," Clark said. In the end, he managed to convince the law school he would commit himself totally to the job. His word was good for nearly a whole semester.

Steve Clark didn't find out Bill intended to run for Congress until the following December of that year, 1973, at a law school conference in New Orleans, when one of Bill's friends asked ingenuously if he intended to get involved with the campaign. "I wasn't real pleased at the time," he said wryly. He soon came around, though, and got caught up in the fever.

Bill Clinton himself has said that his first political race—for the Third Congressional District seat—was the most enjoyable campaign of his life. Certainly, in many ways, it was the purest. Representative Barney Frank, of Massachusetts, once cracked that the only time he ever voted for a candidate without experiencing any qualms whatsoever was "the first time I ran for office. The second time, ehh," he grimaced, rocking his hand back and forth to signify wavering, "I had a few questions."

Along with his personality, his almost magical ability to connect with nearly everyone he met, Clinton had the singular moral advantage of the untested, this first time around. All the compromises, deals, scandals, dark secrets, hard questions, lay in the future. He was twenty-seven, unmarried, fresh out of school. Everyone thought he was a little nuts to think he could take on John Paul Hammerschmidt, the popular Republican who had held the seat forever—but then again, there was something bold and appealing about the idea of going up against such a huge target. If you made any inroad at all, it was bound to be noticed. And with all Nixon's problems, there could well be anti-Republican sentiment around to be tapped. For the most part, Arkansas was, and always had been, a Democratic state.

He took a kind of pure joy in the entire process—a joy that would possibly never be quite that unclouded ever again. Yet at the same time, a careful observer, viewing that campaign, could have picked up a multitude of signs of the future to come. It was all there, the potential, the talent—and the deadly fault lines. Seeds of greatness, seeds of ruin. The campaign of 1974 was a young man's race, full of the gusto and idealism of youth, and fraught with plenty of the mistakes youth tends to make as well. But as the child is father to the man, this first contest can also be seen as a single strand of Clinton political DNA, crammed full of information, in some ways an encoded history of the future—had anyone back then known how to read it.

There would be one big difference, however, between this first campaign and every other one he would wage over the next quarter century. Hillary was not around, not until very late in the game, August 1974, scarcely three months before the election. She was in touch constantly, often three times a day, by phone; she visited regularly. But she was *not* on the scene. So along with everything else, the campaign offers a unique chance to compare two worlds—Bill with Hillary, Bill without.

Once in Fayetteville, long before he had formally announced, Bill instantly began doing what he did best—forging connections. He made friends with David Matthews when he dropped into a local jewelry store to browse, shortly before the school year began. Matthews, who was starting law school that fall, was working at the counter. The two ended up talking for over an hour. A native of Benton County, near Fayetteville, Matthews had been active in the community and knew a lot of people. Bill left without buying a thing—but with another valuable contact in his pocket. Matthews would later serve as a driver during the campaign, and become a lifelong loyalist.

Bill met Brian Snow when he, too, showed up to teach that first semester at the law school. Snow had grown up in Fort Smith, Arkansas, gone to school at the university, then taken his law degree at Duke. An old Kennedy worker, Snow was itching to get involved in a campaign. He was instantly taken with Bill, who he thought was the most articulate person he'd ever met. And that memory! Not to mention his incredible network abilities—"He would write about twenty letters a day, handwritten letters to people all over the country, writers, journalists—a governor, someone at *Newsweek*—he had this range, this web of contacts," Snow marveled.

Ron Addington, who would serve as one of the first campaign managers (there would be several) was a graduate student in education at the university when he met Bill—he'd just gotten out of the army, where he'd been a captain, serving in public affairs, and was eager to work on a campaign. He was impressed with Bill's ideas, though not much with his appearance—long hair, sideburns, moccasin boots. He himself had long hair, but he knew enough to stuff it up under a wig when he went on Army Reserve drills, so he looked like a clean-cut guy. Bill's hair would continue to bother Addington the entire campaign; he looked on it as his personal responsibility. He knew there were some conservative types up in those hills, in northwest Arkansas, who would take one look and think, law school, hippie, forget it. Bill could never be convinced to use a wig, but Addington took to carrying a scissors around—anytime there were photographers on the scene, he'd get in there and snip off as much as he could. Not that it ever did much good.

It wasn't just the hair, of course. From the first, Addington had this sense of Bill as someone who badly needed others to exercise control in certain areas. As brilliant and articulate as he was, a born politician who could charm nearly everyone and who never forgot a face—he could nontheless go for weeks without paying his bills, could lose keys and test papers, and as far as driving went—well, even today there are those who believe that God in his wisdom purposely granted Bill Clinton the sort of life that would ensure he would never be at the wheel of a car.

Addington fell quickly into a seminursemaid role, nagging Bill to remember to do his law school work, hand in grades on time, pay bills. "They'd cut off the electricity at his house, he'd have to come over to my house, he couldn't even shave—the water was on a well and you needed electricity to run it." Once he ended up sleeping with Addington in his bed.

"Finally I said, 'Bill, give me all your bills.' We put them in a box and I assigned somebody in the campaign just to pay his bills every month."

As the campaign began to gear up, and the headquarters were opened in February, the volunteers began to gather. Doug Wallace, a senior at the university who was editor of the college newspaper, joined; Steve Smith, who'd met Bill when working for McGovern, came on board; several young women, including Marla Crider, got involved in manning the office.

The Frays showed up in March. Mary Lee Fray had tried her best to fight it. "We told Bill we had to have a budget, if we were going to come. I had a four-year-old and a newborn, we needed day care, diaper service, a nanny, pediatricians." Paul Fray had a good job, with health benefits, running the issuance side of the food stamp program for the state; he'd just been offered an even better salary to go with an oil company. Bill, on the other hand, was offering nothing.

"I said, we need ten thousand dollars. Bill about dropped his teeth. He said, 'Well, get the money off your dad! I'll call him myself!' I said, 'No way, you get the money,'" said Mary Lee.

In the end, though, it made no difference. Paul wasn't going to miss this one. He called a press conference, telling Mary Lee to attend; there he announced to the world (and incidentally, his wife) that he was resigning his job to go work in the campaign. Effective immediately. In fact, he told his wife, they were moving that evening.

That night they stuffed all their furniture into the U-Haul, including stove and refrigerator—the headquarters needed both—and left for Fayetteville. "We had planned to have a dinner party that night. The food was still in the oven," said Mary Lee, still sounding slightly shell-shocked twenty-five years later. It was still there when the stove was finally hooked up, two weeks later.

Bill's cavalier attitude towards money continued to drive her up the wall throughout the campaign. On the one hand, he didn't seem to care about it—"Greed is just not part of his nature," one old friend said—on the other hand, he seemed to expect others to provide what was needed. "Here, why don't you hock this!" Mary Lee once screamed, throwing her wedding ring at him—a gesture she regretted at once, since the ring was never found. (She suspected another staffer of pocketing it.)

By March, most of the major players had assembled; the campaign was in full swing. It was an intense, hothouse atmosphere, like every political campaign ever waged—yet even more, since nearly everyone was young and involved in their first real race. Passions rode high—and not all of them were political.

There were, for one thing, the hangers-on, the political groupies, who were ubiquitous. The candidate was exciting, good-looking, and appeared to be unattached—inevitably there was a rock-star effect. Women were drawn to him irresistibly. They showed up everywhere, pulled in like flies to honey, ants to a picnic. The guy was a literal babe-magnet.

Years later, Michael Medved would put the question to a Yale Law School buddy, who had gone on to work at the White House. "Am I confused? I don't remember Bill Clinton being a skirt-chaser back at Yale."

He hadn't been, his friend assured him. "But the thing was, he got down to Arkansas, he was running for office, and all of a sudden, all these women appeared. For the first time in his life he could have all the pussy he wanted."

There is some indication, though, that Bill was not unaware of the aphrodisiac effect of political power, even years before he ran for office. In her book, *On the Make: The Rise of Bill Clinton*, *Arkansas Gazette* political reporter Meredith Oakley says that Cliff Jackson, fellow Arkansan, fellow Oxford classmate, and longtime thorn in Clinton's side, remembered Bill once relating, with great gusto, an anecdote he'd heard when he worked for Fulbright—how a staffer, entering the Oval Office unannounced, had discovered Lyndon Johnson on the floor, energetically having his way with a young woman. Oakley's book was published, interestingly, in 1994—well before Bill's own White House sexual activity was daily fodder. Bill, Jackson told Oakley, had been mesmerized by the tale. "He thought it was so neat that LBJ could get away with something like that," Jackson said. Jackson also had a letter Bill wrote in which he referred to the story again—clearly, it had captured his imagination.

"He told me about that once in Oxford and then wrote it in a letter," Jackson confirmed. "We laughed, but there was something that came across—his attitude towards Johnson, how slick he was, that he could get away with that."

Paul Fray, too, had seen that side of Bill, long before. "Bill and I were riding in the car with Fulbright once, and he was quizzing Fulbright about Jack Kennedy and all his women. Fulbright got a little frustrated and told him, 'Bill, if you're going to idolize the womanizing side of Jack Kennedy, you're gonna end up turning out that way yourself. You don't need to be putting yourself in that kind of jeopardy.' I heard it myself, I was right there. Fulbright warned him, 'Don't idolize someone who does things that are wrong.' Bill shut his mouth; he'd been put in his place. But he, by God, didn't listen to the advice."

And Mandy Merck, a pal of his at Oxford, remembered Bill worrying aloud about Ted Kennedy's behavior at Chappaquidick. "He told me he thought senators, like all politicians at that time, regarded themselves as God's gift to women and behaved badly to them. He hoped, he said, he would never turn out like that."

No one goes into politics just to attract women. But certainly, the possibility had crossed Bill's mind more than once.

No one will ever know how many times Bill took advantage of his newfound allure during the 1974 race, though it is undoubtedly true that he did. "We'd be out on the campaign trail, he'd be with me, they'd be coming up, 'Bill, how you doing, how long you gonna be here,' asking the damn leading questions, and you knew what they were after," said Paul Fray. "I'd say, 'Billy, you need to take care of the problem or I'm gonna let somebody else handle it—I mean, the woman is ready to go!'" He himself had not exactly helped Bill hew to the path Fulbright had recommended, he admitted, unhappily.

"They'd write down their names, their phone numbers, their addresses on a napkin, whatever was handy, and hand it to him," said one office worker. "Just hand it to him, wherever he was."

Bill, at twenty-seven, was far more attractive than he had been as a teenager. In high school he'd been well liked, a good student, involved with the band and student government, a BMOC of sorts—but no athlete, no teen idol, certainly not the sort who mesmerizes cheerleaders.

At Oxford, too, Bill, though he'd had many friends, as always, had not cut much of a swath as sex object. "He was plump, he wore raggedy woolen sweaters, he had crap in his beard a good deal of the time," said Merck, who'd been a close friend, and who loved him dearly. "He wasn't real good-looking—overweight, bearded. I just thought of him as someone who was going into politics, and who was a plump, funny guy." Someone to joke around with—once, she recalled,

Bill had hugged her, saying, "Did you know I was the fastest fuck in the world?" When she asked what he meant, he chuckled—"You didn't feel that, did you?"

Actually, it was her impression that "very little happened to Bill at Oxford" that way—despite the fact that years later, writer Christopher Hitchens, in the throes of promoting his own book on Clinton, *No One Left to Lie To: The Triangulations of William Jefferson Clinton*, would declare to the press while on tour (without naming names) that she told him she and a friend had once had a threesome with Bill back then.

"An extreme exaggeration," Merck said, annoyed (the *Daily Mail* had figured out her name and were at her door at once). "It was just a story I told him about me and Bill and another woman getting drunk and kind of slightly naked on a rug together once. No intercourse took place. I think Bill ejaculated sort of spontaneously, but not into any-body. It was at most a little bit of fondling and sitting around drinking and talking, not unusual in our situation." A casual group grope, at least in her mind, nothing serious. They'd also played strip poker occa-sionally.

"I didn't screw him. I didn't give him a blow job. I wouldn't have felt bad if I had, but I didn't do it," Merck, now a professor in cultural studies, said firmly. "And I didn't engage in what I would call an orgy either. Mild petting. I told Hitchens about it and the fucker, if he's going around telling people that that was a threesome, it's a lie. There's a lot Hitchens could say to promote his book but I think that's really pushing it."

So for Bill, the experience of actually being pursued by droves of women was a brand new one. On the other hand, it had little effect on his relationship with Hillary, who was still his girlfriend, back there in Washington, still the one he thought he'd end up with.

There was, however, another situation. And this one did have at least the potential of changing things.

THE COLLEGE GIRL

MARLA CRIDER WAS A TWENTY-ONE-YEAR-OLD political science student at the university, a native of northwest Arkansas, born and bred. She had an appealing piquant face, green eyes, long brown hair, olive skin, a sharp intelligence, and an avid interest in politics. Doug Wallace hired her to work at headquarters early in the campaign, while Bill was off on the road. "Don't worry, you'll like him," he assured her. It was three weeks before she laid eyes on him.

When she did, the two of them hit it off at once; they spent hours talking that first day, comparing notes—they shared, it turned out, a great deal: the same basic Democratic ideals, the same desire to help, the same Arkansas roots, even the same birthday. Both were political junkies. Marla's uncle had served as sheriff, then county judge. "At age four, I was handing out cards at county fairs," she laughed. "It was in my blood."

Marla was deeply impressed by their first conversation. "I told my mother that night, 'Bill Clinton will someday be president.' I said, 'This is a determined man. He has set goals for himself, he is already savvy in international policy, working with Fulbright, going to Oxford.'

126

I just instinctively felt like the sky was the limit for him. Always, *always*. I never vacillated from that," she said.

A number of books on Clinton—starting with David Maraniss's 1995 biography—have mentioned a "college girl" who was romantically involved with Clinton during his first campaign, and supposedly had to be pushed out the door whenever Hillary showed up. No one, however, had ever managed to find her, even to identify her, though not for lack of trying. And no one had ever heard her side of the story until now.

"In twenty-five years, I've never talked about this," said Marla. "And I'm so grateful to my friends for never mentioning my name." Every time a new book comes out, she flips through it to the section on the first campaign. No one's gotten it right yet. "For the record," she said dryly, "No one ever pushed me out the door, not ever." But worse things did happen.

Almost everyone in the office was involved with someone; it was that sort of fevered atmosphere—the truth is that politics often makes for bedfellows, period. A number of marriages either faltered or went down for good during the campaign. Pat Weber, who was helping with public relations, left her husband for David Ivey, whom she later married; another couple came close to breaking up when the husband got seriously involved with an office worker.

And Marla and Bill began seeing each other. It started casually, very naturally—late night suppers, long talks in the office. She knew, of course, he had a girlfriend named Hillary, and even asked him point-blank if he were engaged to her yet. Bill said no. "If she chose to come back, I would probably pursue the relationship," he told her. "But we're not engaged." She could accept that—he was unattached, free to see someone else, at least that's what he told her, and she believed him.

Marla's uncle, Bruce Crider, who had been sheriff, then county judge, was "sort of the godfather, the patriarch of county politics" in the area. Even though he had been out of office for four years, he was still the man to see; Bill had made a point to get his blessing early on in the campaign.

According to Paul Fray, Bruce Crider was not pleased when his young niece got involved with Bill. Fray was at a restaurant with Marla the night Crider stormed in, furious, to confront her. Fray quickly moved a couple of tables away to give them room.

"He tore into her ass with both feet," Paul said. "He said, 'You are going to stop this relationship with this candidate, because it is coming back to haunt me in my race. Everybody's talking about what kind of a sorry no-account niece I've got, to be with this son of a bitch.' He preached at her for twenty minutes, running her down."

After he'd left, Paul went back to the table. "I said, 'We've got to talk this over. That's your kin—that guy is going to be telling everybody, 'Don't vote for Bill Clinton, he's messing with my niece.' We can't have that." Marla, said Paul, refused to listen. "She blew me away. She said, 'It's not his business.'"

Paul took it up with Bill the next day. "I knew damn well she wasn't going to tell him. I said, 'Billy, Bruce is bent out of shape about this.' I said, 'Man, you gotta do something.'" Bill waved him off. "He said, 'Well, it's gonna be her decision.' I said, 'Bullshit. It's gonna be, by God, our decision.'" But he could tell he wasn't getting through.

"She was definitely his type, though," Paul said later. "Dark hair, round face. She fit the mold; there've been others, too, like that. They all look a little bit like his mother." Years later, when he and his wife saw Monica Lewinsky on televison for the first time, they turned to each other at once. "Marla," they both said, instantly. (Today, twenty-five years later, Marla is quite slim, with short, frosted hair, and looks nothing like Monica.)

Marla herself does not recall the incident with her uncle that Fray relates. She was aware, though, that another of Bill's handlers, Ron Addington, had spoken to him about the relationship.

"Ron thought his job was to manage the candidate. Bill told him to mind his own business. He said, 'I'm not married, she's not married, leave us alone.' Ron didn't like that," she said.

It made sense to her, though. What was the problem with two unmarried people seeing each other? Why was it anyone's business but their own?

Somebody else, however, thought it was very much her business too.

Hillary seemed to know about their relationship almost from the beginning—Marla was convinced some of Hillary's friends from the law school in Fayetteville must have clued her in—and to see it as a true threat. There were a number of incidents that seemed to underline this. The day of the runoff for the Democratic primary, Hillary showed up at the office unexpectedly, having flown down from Washington. Bill had already asked Marla to come with him to Fort Smith that night, where he had a TV appearance, when Hillary appeared; of course, he had to renege. Later that night, triumphant, Bill and Hillary came back to the office.

"Everyone was cheering," Marla recalled. "And I had a glass of wine in my hand. She comes in behind him. Strolls up to me, takes the glass of wine out of my hand, says, 'Hmm, wine'—takes a drink of it, gives it back to me and says, staring me down, 'I'll have to get some of that.'

"It was her way of letting me know—like a cat—marking its territory," Marla observed. "Everybody in there just turned and looked, like what the hell was that about? And Hillary just had this kind of half smirk on her face and she strolled on off."

Another time, a pair of socks prompted an odd interchange. Marla, Bill, and several others were sitting at a table discussing his schedule. Hillary, down for another visit, walked into the room.

"And she said, 'Marla?' This was in front of everyone. I said, 'Yes, Hillary?' We were always very formal with each other."

"We're trying to get some of Bill's clothes together for him to make this overnight trip," continued Hillary. "And we can't seem to find any of his socks. I knew *you* would know where they were."

Bill was furious. "Would you two take this outside?" he said tightly.

"He was red, that pulsating red," Marla recalled. She got up, quickly found the overnight bag, dug out a pair of socks and returned, handing them over.

"Thanks—somehow I knew you'd know that," Hillary said, with poisonous sweetness.

Later, Bill apologized to Marla. "He just looked at me and said, 'I am so sorry.' Basically he said, 'This is my fault. I have allowed this to happen.' It was apparent, he said, this was going to have to be dealt with."

The incidents amazed Marla—here was this strong, intellectual woman, with her brilliant mind, her Yale law degree, clearly superior, the Watergate committee behind her, reduced to acting like a jealous shrew—over a college kid?

It was sometime later that Marla went to Bill's house and found the letter from Hillary open on his desk. The letter that talked about "the plans we've made, the goal we've set"; the letter that insisted his feelings for her, Marla, would pass—"let me remind you it always does." She stood over it a long time, confused, unsure. What, exactly, was going on here?

She knew she could never ask him directly about it. But a few days later, alone with him in the car, driving him home, she managed to bring it up obliquely. It had been several days since Hillary had returned to Washington. She had not called.

"I need to ask you something," Marla told him. "You and Hillary, what's the deal? She hasn't called lately."

Bill shrugged. "We're just trying to make sure we're both doing what we want to do, what we need to do with our lives," he said.

"Are you in love with her?" Marla asked.

"Yeah, I am," he said. "But I don't know if all this is right. I don't want to mess her career up, and I don't know if she can fit in here. That's important to me, and I just don't know if she can do it."

"What is it about her?" asked Marla.

"She challenges me, every moment of every day, intellectually," Bill told her. "She makes me a better person. She gets me started, kicks my butt, and makes me do the things I've got to do."

Marla stared at him, uncomprehending—he sounded like he was talking about a drill sergeant. "And you're going to build a marriage off of this?" she said dubiously.

Everybody at the campaign had been trying to understand this relationship. "Everybody at headquarters. I knew his mother didn't understand it. Nobody did." Now it seemed he didn't really know himself.

Marla shifted gears. "Have you ever truly been in love?" she asked him. "You know, where your heart hurts and you can't eat and all that?"

Bill was quiet for a moment. "Well," he said finally, "Maybe my problem is I've had those feelings too often."

Marla fell silent. What he seemed to be saying was that he loved them all, that maybe he'd never really felt true love, so he had nothing to compare it to. "It was like he just kind of equally loved everybody," she mused.

And here was this strong, forceful person, Hillary, telling him she knew best what was right for him. Using her lawyer's skill to prove she was what he needed, overriding objections.

"I've had people tell me who've heard her in a courtroom that when she gets in front of a jury, she is one of the most persuasive people they've ever heard in their lives. And that's what she would do to him. That is how she would talk to him. She had an ability to persuade him, argue her case, as an attorney persuades a jury. He was the jury, she was the attorney," Marla said, looking back.

But the idea of a relationship where the most important thing was the game plan, the goal, the political objective—and normal, human, emotional feelings were secondary, set off to the side, considered less important, well, it was not, she believed, something most people could even conceive of, much less want. "If you had heard how she played him, how they played each other, her idea of a courtship, the things I happened to be a part of, or recipient of—it wasn't a normal healthy relationship in my opinion." It seemed odd, bizarre; it seemed, more than anything else, very lonely.

Both Paul Fray and Marla witnessed incidents in which Hillary apparently attempted to pay Bill back in kind during those months. Paul overheard Bill on the phone, talking to Hillary. "She told him she'd gone out with some guy in Washington and slept with him, on and on and on. Billy broke down and told her, 'Well, damn you, why are you doing me this way?' He was really torn up about it."

Marla was in the office. "Some friend of theirs, a banker, from New York, was coming down that night. Bill was going off somewhere. Bill said, 'Where's David going to stay?' And Hillary said, 'At the house.' He said, 'At my house? But you're staying there, it's a one bedroom house.' And she said, 'Oh, I'm sure we'll stay up talking all night.'" There were, Marla felt, lines being drawn in the sand. "It was, 'Okay, if you're gonna do this, then I'm gonna play it my way.'"

Bill, Marla knew, could have a jealous side himself—even though it rarely showed itself. She herself had been the recipient. One time she and her friend Mark Stodola, another campaign worker, went to a party in Bentonville. Marla had left her car back at headquarters. The next day, Mark picked her up at her house early in the morning so they could attend a speech Bill was giving—he always liked staffers to be around when he gave a speech.

They sat in the back. Bill got up to take the podium, looking out over the audience. Spotting them, his face turned bright red. "I said to Mark, what is wrong with him?" said Marla. Afterwards, they went up to the front, to ask if there was anything he wanted them to do. He pointed directly at her. "I'll see YOU back at headquarters," he ordered, sternly.

Mark dropped her back there, and she waited for Bill to arrive. "What is the matter with you?" she demanded, when he walked in.

Bill shook his head. "Some things are better left unsaid," he told her.

"This is so unlike you, not to say what's on your mind," Marla said.

Bill wheeled around. "Did you have to go home with him and sleep with him?" he yelled. "I cannot believe you would do that to me!"

Marla cracked up—Mark was just a buddy, the idea was ludicrous. "I don't see a damn thing funny," Bill grumbled. "This upsets me."

Nothing happened, he just gave me a ride, she assured him. She eyed him cooly. "Are you upset because you're jealous of me, or is it you're afraid I'm not going to be focused on the campaign?" she said.

Bill, still angry, didn't bother to answer. It was a side of him she'd never seen before. Actually, she thought it made him seem more human.

Hillary may have tried to arouse Bill's jealousy on occasion, but she had other weapons in her arsenal as well. Among them were the university friends she and Bill had made together. Unlike the campaign workers, most of whom were wary of her, if not downright hostile, this group had grown fond of her, felt she was one of them. Once at a campaign staff party, held at the Shelton's house (George Shelton was a local banker, involved in the campaign), Marla was confronted by Bill's law school colleague, Brian Snow. He was slightly drunk, and very angry. Pushing his face into hers, he demanded loudly, "Why don't you get the hell out of this campaign? You're trying to interfere with Bill and Hillary!"

"I was embarassed and stunned," Marla said. "I just sort of turned around and walked away—I was not about to get into anything." Several people came up to comfort her. Steve Clark gave her a hug. "He said, 'He had no right to do that, you have been here since early on.' He was very supportive."

Snow does not remember the scene, but admitted it could have happened, easily.

"Back in those days I could've said something like that. I was very protective of Bill," he said. He chuckled. "It's like when I question witnesses. Could I have done that? Yes. Would I have done that? Yes. Do I remember doing that? I do not.

"It could've happened, though, because I cared about him and I cared about Hillary. It would have fit, in that I could've been aware of something going on that I didn't think was in his best interests or Hillary's, and I've never been shy about speaking out. I mean, I wanted him to be able to achieve what he needed to . . ." he trailed off. The memory, though, had gone. "Those were my drinking days," he said.

Steve Clark also pulled a blank. "I don't remember that," he said, amused. "It could have happened, but I've slept too many nights since then to recall.

"I'm not questioning it, though," he said. "I have a lot of respect for Marla. If she said that, I bet she was right."

Whether Hillary ever heard about that particular incident is not known. But it's clear that at some point, she realized her friends were not going to be of sufficient help in getting Bill back on the right track. She would have to turn to the people she trusted most—her family.

Sometime in the early summer, a dusty black Cadillac with Illinois plates pulled up to the door of the headquarters, and two men got out—an overweight older man with a bad limp, and a young man who closely resembled him: Hugh and Hughie Rodham. Hillary had called in the troops.

Marla never doubted it for a second—Hillary had sent them down from Chicago, with instructions to run her off. Practically the minute they barged in, Hughie made a beeline for her.

"Hillary had assigned him to me. He walks in and immediately, 'You must be Marla.' Here we go. His assignment was to occupy all of my time that I would allow him to occupy. I'm positive of it. We became kind of friends and all, but it was hysterical. He was asking me questions, 'Where did you grow up? Tell me about your family'—like he was supposed to report."

Paul Fray agreed. "Hughie Rodham went after that girl with both barrels," he said. "Hillary sent him to do the bidding for her, to get her ass gone. He was putting a rush on that girl something hard."

At one point, Marla complained to Paul. "She came to me and said, 'I want you to get that son of a bitch off me.' I said, 'I'm not in the business of managing affairs, what's the problem?' She said, 'He's over here every thirty minutes, I can't run him off.'

"I said, 'I wonder who's creating the problem?' She said, 'What do you mean? I said, 'I'm asking you to assess who sent him over.'

"She said, 'I know who sent him, his damn sister.'"

Even Marla couldn't imagine that Hillary had told her brother specifically to get rid of her in so many words; that would have been too crude. "He knew he was supposed to. But Hillary's good. She probably said, 'Hughie, when you get down there, you may want to get to know . . .' She has a way of manipulating things to take place without people realizing."

Hugh Rodham, Hillary's father, said very little to Marla. But he managed to make his presence known. "He scared me. A very intimidating man. He'd just sit at headquarters and stare at me. I'd say, 'Mr. Rodham, you going to hang up signs today?' Yep. No smile, just 'yep.'" Even after Hughie went back to Chicago, Hugh hung around, even showing up at staff parties, keeping his eyes on her. "Hughie was gone, but there was still representation there," said Marla.

"It amazes me," she said, looking back at that odd time. "Even then, the pattern of her lack of trust in him was set. It wasn't just me. There were others she was suspicious of. But that pattern was set long before they got married.

"And she still decided the most important thing was that political partnership, that goal they'd set, rather than taking care of their personal life, or being confident, or having a trustworthy relationship. I'm just amazed, as a woman, at her thought process. To be so smart and allow that to happen . . . to go for politics over personal life and love and happiness.

"They had all these rules, but he kept breaking them." She shook her head. "And he's still breaking them."

Years later Tony Rodham disputed that the men in the family had been sent to Arkansas to end Marla and Bill's relationship. "That's totally false," he contended. "We went down there because Hillary asked us to go down and help her boyfriend get elected to Congress. People like to spread rumors and make stuff up. We went at Hillary's request—and we did *everything*."

In practice, their help mainly consisted of nailing up posters. At first Hugh Sr. did make an attempt to get out in the country, shoot the fat with a few people. "He'd go to gas stations and get out and talk to these guys, he'd tell them he had a future son-in-law who was running for Congress and they'd say, 'Fine, we're gonna vote for Hammerschmidt, thank you anyway,'" said Paul. "He didn't have too much of an approach."

Paul didn't take to him. "He wasn't a friendly person at all, hell no. Real rough. A typical Yankee, if he can't call the terms, he don't want to play."

Campaign workers tried to help by rubbing mud over the Caddie's Illinois license plates, to obscure its origins, but it didn't do much good, Paul thought. A Yankee to the bone, Rodham radiated his alien roots the minute he got out of the car. "He finally recognized he wasn't going to be worth shit talking to anybody, so he just went ahead and started nailing up signs," Paul said. He spent much of the summer going fishing.

Ron Addington disagreed—he thought Rodham had actually managed to connect with some of the rural types. "He would go, sit around and spit tobacco, talk to those cattle guys, did a lot of that. He got along with a lot of people out in the countryside, surprising how much he did. He was a good old man, real straight shooting, very smart, not well educated, just a street smart wise old man, chewed tobacco, had a big limp."

While not everyone was fond of Hugh, or Hughie, Tony Rodham, when he came, was popular with all. "Just a good kid, best personality in the world," Addington said. He impressed everyone with having the makings of a good old boy. One night Tony had a few drinks and got a little rowdy and was picked up by the police. Addington had to go down and get him released, but that only seemed to increase everyone's affection for the young man.

"In Arkansas one of the things they do is go to 'sale barns' where they sell cows and horses and pigs," Tony Rodham said years later. "My father used to go up and sit up in the top row. You gotta remember he was a Republican at this time. So he would talk to the old farmers, and his line always used to be that if he could, he would vote for Bill Clinton, and nobody understood what he meant. They always assumed here's this good ol' boy sittin' there chewin' tobacco, talkin' about votin' for Bill Clinton. . . . But he got a lot of votes for Clinton."

As the campaign continued, it was not just Bill's relationship with Marla—and possibly others—that gave Hillary cause for concern. It seemed to her, in Washington, connected only by phone, that the entire headquarters was slipping badly, veering out of control. Too many girls, too much fooling around, too little attention to business— the whole office seemed disorganized, on the brink of chaos.

But most of those in headquarters thought the campaign was going fine—if occasionally a little rough around the edges, perhaps. Steve Smith, who'd become more involved after the school year ended (he'd been a graduate student at Northwestern), didn't think the chaos was "any worse than any other campaign I've been in," he said. "Any campaign I've ever been involved in has been crazy. Why would people get involved in politics if they were sane?"

No one in the campaign had had much experience, including Clinton, true. But it had worked out pretty well even so, he thought— adequate media coverage, a knowledgeable candidate. They had to do a lot of scrambling for funds, of course—but how was that different from any other campaign? And Bill was unflagging.

Addington agreed. "He'd be up at six in the morning, go to some kind of breakfast meeting, go to law school, teach two or three classes, hit the trail in the car with somebody, get back about 3:30 in the morning, get two hours sleep, get up and go again the next day," he said, marveling. He took catnaps in the car.

As far as his staff went, "even though most of the people were new to the game, I think most of them made up the difference because of their enthusiasm and willingness to work endless hours," Addington said. In general, "we were a pretty well-organized group."

And when it came to fundraising, everyone agreed Bill had the magic touch. 'He can raise money like nobody's business," said Marla. "He could go into poverty-stricken areas of Arkansas and come back with more campaign checks than anybody I've ever seen in my life. He literally would go door to door, coffeeshop to coffeeshop."

"There's not a son of a bitch alive in this country that can raise money like he can. Nobody can," said Paul Fray. "I'll venture to say

he'll go down in history as the finest man, as it relates to conning somebody out of dollars. He just can. He knows what to say, when to say,
how to say it."

He also had a special technique—something the staff called the "glad-
to-meet-you letters." Every campaign stop he made, he had an assistant
write down the names of everyone he'd met. Back in the office, staffers
would immediately compose letters to each one; Bill would sign them,
add a note at the bottom, and it would be in the mail the following day.
Thousands went out. Invariably, Bill was able to remember something
specific and personal about every person he'd met.

So most felt sure the campaign was on a roll, that headquarters was
operating smoothly. But that wasn't how Hillary saw it.

Much has been made of Hillary's decision to join Bill in Arkansas,
after Nixon's resignation in early August 1974. This was, many have
been certain, the final triumph of love, against all odds—Arkansas, his
mother, the fact she'd be giving up all chance for a high-powered East
Coast job, maybe forever. Certainly, love had something to do with it.

But as always, love involved the dream, the ultimate goal. And her
decision to come down was fueled in no small part by her absolute
conviction that only she could whip Bill's campaign into shape. That
without her, it could founder badly. That she needed to get down there
fast and take over the reins, exercise firm control over both the office
and the candidate—or all might be lost.

Still, she had doubts—not that she was needed, badly, but about
her ability to acclimate herself to a small, rural Southern state, a state,
as she was to say later, she didn't think her parents could even find on a
map. She talked them out with a few people.

Terry Guzman, whose husband, Ray, was a law professor in Fayetteville, had gone to work at the Watergate committee in January, after
Bill had recommended her ("the only person from the University of
Arkansas law school—everyone else was from Yale, Stanford, University of Chicago."). She remembers having long discussions with Hillary
about what she would face, going down there.

"I was very honest about the fact that it would be an opportunity to do
a lot of really terrific things—because it's such a small state, it's very easy
to be a big fish. But that it was going to be difficult," she said. "Hillary was

a strong lady, and that was going to take some getting used to. I was really frank, and I think she appreciated that." It was, said Guzman, the only time she ever saw Hillary "dither" about anything.

Guzman was a native of Arkansas, yet even she had had trouble getting hired as a lawyer—there had only been two women in her law school graduating class the year before. Gender was the big problem; she and Hillary didn't discuss regional differences, or Southern attitudes towards appearance, though she knew Hillary had "no interest in anything to do with clothes, looks—she dressed very seventies militant." Guzman herself had "too much Southern" in her to do that. At one point during the impeachment inquiry, she appeared on nationwide television to read a report. Within minutes of getting back to the office, she heard from both her mother and her aunt—they had not, however, called to congratulate her. "What possessed you to wear that dress?" they both shrieked. That, Guzman knew, was the South. But it wasn't the sort of thing you talked about to Hillary.

"She didn't talk a whole lot about feelings. She talked about what she wanted to do, but *not* feelings. Hillary's very controlled. Very, very, very private. I worked with her day and night for nine months, and I still would not say that I knew her. Just very closemouthed about everything." She was, though, "clearly" in love with Bill, she thought. When he visited her in Washington, Hillary was "clearly thrilled to see him. There was a lot of affection there. They were remarkable friends." It was no surprise to her when Hillary decided to go.

"It was kind of a hard choice to make," said John Laibovitz, another lawyer who worked on the Watergate committee. "Arkansas wasn't the kind of society she was used to, and in a sense she was putting herself in a subservient position, at least in terms of appearances." He thought Hillary was a strong-willed, forceful person, very mature for her age, someone who knew her own mind. "In my view, it was a conscious decision when she decided to go to Fayetteville, that she was hooking on with this guy, that was the way to go."

Bill, whom he met when he came up to visit Hillary, had not impressed Laibovitz much. "It was a little bizarre. He was twenty-seven, but already an old-time pol. That's how he struck me when I met him—that he already had all the moves of all the politicians you could think of. Coming out of the sixties, that was a little disconcerting, that all the promise of the sixties generation, the idealism, could come to this—good old politics, glad-handing, slap on the back, remembering everybody." Hillary did not strike him as a political type at all.

"But she was obviously very enamored of him, very proud, probably a better term.

"And Hillary was off to Fayetteville."

THE HILLARY SURPRISE

HILLARY DROVE DOWN TO ARKANSAS accompanied by her friend Sara Ehrman, whose condo she'd been staying at in Washington, while another friend, Alan Stone, an Arkansas native, did the driving. She'd met both when working for the McGovern campaign. Stone tried to ease her mind about where she was going, telling her the South wasn't so bad, while Ehrman, a native New Yorker, argued against the decision the entire trip, telling Hillary she was making a big mistake.

The campaign headquarters staff were all quite aware of Hillary already, of course—they had seen her when she came down for visits, and fielded daily phone calls from her when she checked up on Bill. Ron Addington had talked to her several times the very first day he met Bill, in fact. "Bill handed me the phone and said, 'This is my girlfriend—she and I have been doing this stuff together a long time and whatever she tells you, you need to do, she knows what's going on,'" he said. His reaction, he said, was "Well, yes, ma'am."

In the past, Hillary had popped in for weekend visits and left quickly; other than a few hissy interchanges with the woman she considered her rival, she was not seen as any kind of a threat.

But now she was here for good.

"The Hillary surprise," Marla termed it. No one in the office had any idea she was coming to stay, let alone that she clearly intended to take over when she did. Bill had said nothing to anyone, opting to deal with the situation by total avoidance.

Hillary alienated many on staff almost at once, with her abrupt manner, her take-no-prisoners style, her barely concealed contempt for what she considered their sloppy work ethic.

"There were few people she tolerated in that office," said Marla. "She was very dictatorial. She literally came in and just turned everything around, changed everything. She didn't know how to deal with Southerners. We are very easygoing, laid-back, which drove her nuts."

Basically, Hillary gave every sign of sharing the ancient Northern assumption that anyone who talks like that can't possibly be smart—unless, of course, they had proved they were on her own territory, the all-important academic front. "She couldn't help herself," said Marla. "I think she thought if they weren't with the law school or teaching at the university, she just was not as likely to converse or ask them to take on roles or responsibilities."

Instead, Hillary came down on the staff like a wolf on the fold. She immediately, in Addington's words, began "kicking ass and taking names."

"We'd been having a good time," said Marla. "There was a good feeling, good synergy, we liked what we were doing, believed in the cause. People came in, we made them feel good. And we got things accomplished.

"She would get furious if there was any frivolity. *Furious.* It was like— 'Have you forgotten what our goal is?' She unraveled. It was almost like she was angry the whole time." Almost at once, the fun began to drain out of the campaign, at least in the office. A number of volunteers cleared out.

"None of those kids really liked her," said Paul Fray. "She would come in, want to run the show, tell everybody what they were supposed to be doing. They'd come and ask me, 'Hey, do I have to do this?' I'd say, 'Let me show you what to do.' That led to a lot of friction between us."

Addington put it simply: "When Hillary arrived in August, it was sort of like—'Well, you guys don't know what the hell you're doing—I'm gonna straighten this place out.'

"Thing is—we had gotten him to where he'd gotten to. Of course, she had been there several times before; it wasn't like this was first time we'd ever met her. But she came to take the place over. And did. People lost enthusiasm. You can't kick people in the ass and not pay them anything, too. They were getting kicked in the ass, they were being told, 'You'll do this and you'll do that,' and it was like, 'The hell I will.' A lot of people, especially a lot of volunteer people, just walked away."

Bill, Addington thought, wasn't really aware of all the conflict in the office—he was on the road so much. Everyone on the scene felt the tension, though. "The girls just couldn't stand her, giving orders all the time," said Addington.

If Hillary had a hard time relating to the office staff—nearly all of whom were college seniors at the very least—it was not surprising that her few forays out into the field of rural Arkansas were virtual disasters.

Early on—but never again—Bill allowed her to accompany him on a campaign trip, to a tiny rural town named St. Paul. Late that afternoon, Marla, working the phones back in the office, got a call. The man asked to speak to Paul Fray, who was out. The caller was blunt. "Bill Clinton was just here with some woman," he said. "You need to tell Paul to tell him, 'Don't ever bring her back over here ever again.'" When Marla asked what the problem was, he said, "She's not our kind of people, she just don't get it," said the caller firmly.

When Paul returned, Marla passed the message on. He sighed. "I tried to tell him," he said.

"St. Paul was so small, so country, they had to pump sunlight out there," said Marla. "You're talking very small town, very don't-bring-your-Washington, D.C.-lawyer-friend-here-with-a-Yankee-accent. It was her tone, the way she was dressed, all of it."

Regional prejudice was alive and thriving in 1974. Hillary didn't look, talk, or act like a Southern woman; nor did she intend to change one iota to adapt to the new environment. She had marched into Arkansas with the same confident, self-assured, no-nonsense manner that had worked so brilliantly for her at Wellesley, Yale, and the Watergate committee, but in Arkansas Hillary laid an egg. The angry caller had been right—Hillary didn't get it, and didn't want to. Accommodation to circumstances was not, had never been, a part of her character.

There is, as nearly every Arkansan is at pains to point out when discussing Hillary, a Southern way of doing things and a Northern way. Steve Clark offered an example:

"I used to have a lady who headed my litigation section in the attorney general's office, big tall striking blonde. I'd send her out to litigate cases and they'd say, 'Why, darling, you're just the cutest thing, I almost feel guilty to have to file a case against you,' and she'd just smile and say, 'Why, I'll just have to do my little heart's best.' And then she'd nail their damn foot to the floor, let them bleed to death.

"Hillary was not that style. She'd say, 'Know what? I appreciate your condescending attitude, you old mossback, but guess what, buddy, when this is over you'll be the one slain and I'll be the victor.'" For many, it was too much to take.

Clark eventually, especially after the campaign was over, came to respect and like her a great deal, even to the point of teasing her that she needed a new middle name if she ever wanted to fit in—Hillary Sue, he thought, would do the job nicely. But he understood the problem. "You have to remember, there's only two and a half million people in this state. Everybody knows everybody, who's married to whom. And that's not Chicago, not New Haven, not the world she came from. It's a good old boy state, and she wasn't a good old boy. She wasn't Hillary Sue. She'd been a pioneer, a role model, she was very plainspoken and some people wanted quiet, shy, demure."

She crossed swords with everyone in the office, including Bill. But for Bill, fighting with Hillary, at least over strategy, was part of the game. Both seemed to derive a certain enjoyment from their battles. Ron Addington remembered one well.

"The three of us were in the car. We were headed to Eureka Springs. They were discussing some campaign strategy and it got louder and louder. Then they were screaming at each other at the top of their lungs. I don't remember the specifics but I do know it was not personal. It was about the campaign, a decision that had to be made.

"She was in the backseat, hitting on the seat. He was in the front, either hitting on the dashboard, or he'd turn around and scream at her. And I'm driving, you know? We pull up to a stoplight and she gets out and slams the door, the light turns green and he says, 'Go on! Go on! Just leave her!'" Addington dutifully pulled away as Hillary headed back to headquarters on foot.

When they returned "it was like nothing had ever happened," Addington said. Bill had had a nap in the car, and woken up totally calm. "Dr. Jekyll and Mr. Hyde," said Addington. The entire fight had rolled off both of them. That, though, just happened to be the fight he remembered. "If I really sat and thought about it, I could probably remember fifteen or twenty more," he said.

Marla once got a call from Paul Fray, out on the road with Bill and Hillary. "Call them and tell them we'll be late," he said wearily. "I'm trying to separate a blowout, out here." It was clear, to everyone, that this was how the two related. But others did not get quite the same pleasure out of fighting with Hillary.

Paul and she had been at loggerheads practically from the first moment they had laid eyes on each other out in front of Paul's house. Paul by now was the designated campaign manager (Addington had dropped back, nervous about his graduate school standing).

The two locked horns daily, sometimes hourly. "She would ask me a question and I would say, 'Why do you ask? Don't you understand what the principle is involved?' And she'd get very upset, think I was being condescending towards her," Fray said.

Hillary, arguing her points, tended to refer back to the one campaign she had participated in before, the McGovern campaign, in Texas. Paul called her on it every time. "You lost in Texas, Hillary—remember?" he would taunt. "You didn't win down there."

Hillary, when upset, did not pull her punches—she'd let loose with a string of invectives, turning the air blue, going, as one said, straight for the jugular—much like her father did back in Park Ridge. "She gets foul fast. They've both got as short a fuse as you've ever been around," said Fray, who had a temper himself. "He's got that emotional volatility about him and she does, too. They'll both explode. He'll come back later and say, 'Hey, I really didn't mean that.' She does not. She keeps it burning"—just like her mother who had held a lifelong grudge against Max Rosenberg.

Bill's temper, too, had been well on display throughout the campaign. Brian Snow, who had an office down the hall from him at the law school, was astounded when Bill walked in one day and immediately started roaring at him. "Apparently my wife had said something that offended him, something about how she would vote for a woman candidate against him, or why was he running against Hammer-schmidt—it seemed pretty inconsequential. And why take it out on me? But he got really mad, his face turned all red."

Minutes later, the storm had blown over without a trace. Many over the years would make the same observation Paul had. Bill blew, then got over it; Hillary did not. "The better friend and the fiercer enemy," Steve Clark said.

Still, Clark for one thought their separate talents worked well together, her strengths complementing his, adding up to a formidable whole. "His gregarious nature, quick mind, ability to use his people skills, her organizational and analytical skills. She's probably best at identifying the problem, defining it, proposing ways to resolve it. That's not his strength and he doesn't want it to be. You know, you write the play, I'll do the performance.

"She was more the architect, he the builder. She's the planner, he's the contractor on site, relating to everyone. She was the one saying, this is where you want to go and this is the way to get there. She's the one that has that skill, to say, okay, let's figure out what we want, I'm gonna draw this map."

Yet others perceived a somewhat disturbing trend, once Hillary came on board. It was almost as if he was starting to doubt his instincts, his basic intuition. He began what would become a lifetime habit of rounding up opinions from every available source before making a move.

"She almost caused him to second-guess his own instincts, start asking other people what they think. I would hear her say, are you sure about that? I think you ought to call so-and-so and check with them. I then started seeing a pattern where he would not make an important decision on something without checking with four, six, eight people. Then he and Hillary would make the final decision. I watched that," said Marla. It chilled her because Bill Clinton's native gut feelings had been the best in the world, Marla felt.

"When I first met him he had absolutely wonderful instincts about people, about people's response to issues, the issues affecting America. He was middle-America and could basically relate to all that. He should have used the instincts God gave him. Instead—and I do blame Hillary to a large degree—she would convince him he needed to surround himself with all the spin doctors, the sycophants."

And of course, given Hillary's natural tendency to trust only those with academic pedigrees, they were invariably the ones whose advice she urged him to seek. "When you start asking the academic community what they would do, it's certainly going to change from what the average Joe American thinks," observed Marla. She watched Bill, late in the campaign, begin to distance himself just a bit from his roots—a disquieting process.

"If he had trusted his gut instincts more over the years, I don't think he would have gotten into nearly so much trouble." She was thinking not so much of the latter-day scandals as of some of the endless political compromises Clinton had made in his career—"giving away the ranch when he didn't have to," as journalist Max Brantley put it.

Once ensconced in Arkansas, Hillary clearly appeared ready to hang in for the long haul. Yet Marla was still not sure she was Bill's permanent choice for a life mate. "I was watching him, his attitude, his body language, listening to his words, and I think there was probably a point in '74 when it was probably going to be—cut bait, go. I wasn't convinced it would pan out. But God give her credit—Hillary hung in."

Bill himself has been quoted as saying about Hillary that he "tried to run her off" at one point but she was determined to stay; Mary Lee Fray has offered the opinion that Hillary had come down to fight for her man. All these views perpetuate the common notion that it was Hillary who knew her own mind, Hillary who held the reins, Hillary who refused to quit on the relationship. They also rather neatly reflect the myth that the entire relationship unfolded along the lines of generic all-American romantic comedy—boy meets girl (cute), they encounter problems and part briefly, they reunite forever. House lights up.

In fact, of course, the reality was less one-sided and a great deal more complicated. No romantic comedy yet written has ever presented a scenario in which boy and girl meet, cute or otherwise, and decide they will together take over the most powerful office in the free world. The reality involved the game plan, and here Hillary held all the cards. She was convinced she was the only one in the world who could get him where he wanted to go—and he believed her. Hillary won out over her competition in Arkansas just as she would continue to win, down through the years, if winning meant that she and Bill would be yoked together permanently. He would stray—monthly, weekly, even at times hourly, but never leave; she would—metaphorically, but genuinely and eternally—have him by the short hairs.

Not to say that there wasn't plenty of real emotion on both sides, then and later; love, affection, companionship, true warmth. Hillary's jealousy would be well noted over the years, time and again—she was capable of falling into a sulk over even minor flirtations—culminating with her unmistakable fury, visible to all, when she learned the truth about Monica Lewinsky, "the first time in my life," as Bill confided sadly to a friend, "I can honestly say that somebody hates my guts." But as always, the personal fury would be laced with another anger—the knowledge that he was straying not just from her, but also from the plan; violating not just the marriage, but the pact. As ever, the two were inseparable.

Many in Arkansas sensed that the bond between them was complex, not immediately understood. Brian Snow was taken aback when he first met Hillary, after she came down. "Bill had been telling me about her, just raving about her, how much he cared about her, how bright she was, how she was just wonderful. I guess I was expecting Sharon Stone to walk in the door. When you've been built up to that point, you kind of expect Miss America."

Years later, during the 1992 presidential campaign, he wrote an article about the Clintons, describing his first reaction to Hillary. "I said when I first met her I was kind of surprised because I viewed her as being homely. I mean she had the whole Wellesley look, wasn't combing her hair, big thick glasses, didn't wear makeup. But I also wrote, that was her choice, she wanted that look, and now she's chosen to be pretty and she's very pretty."

A few months afterwards, he ran into Hillary at a campaign dinner. She eyed him with distaste. "You know, I want to tell you something," she said icily. "I've never thought of myself as being homely."

"I felt like I'd been stuck with a knife," he said. He fell all over himself, apologizing. But later, he puzzled over the interchange. Why did it matter to her? "I'd always figured she didn't care, she was so bright and talented—why would it bother her for somebody to say she looked homely at one stage in her life?"

The two of them had seemed an unusual combination, he'd thought at first. "Here was Bill, six two or three, a good-looking guy, people thought he looked like Elvis, and Hillary with the Wellesley look. It was hard for me to picture them physically together. But as I began to see what they wanted to do in life, I saw them as a perfect match. Bill made it very clear, he was going to be president."

Not long after Hillary's arrival, Marla's mother got an anonymous phone call, warning her that her daughter had become involved with Bill Clinton. Marla had never shared the details of her relationship with her parents. She was twenty-one, it was her first serious involvement, and she had wanted to keep it private. Now her mother was deeply upset. "She would have never told my father, he had a heart condition, he would've killed us both," said Marla. Instead she waited until they were alone to talk to her daughter.

"I came in and my mother was very quiet and she said, "I know." I said, "You know what?" She said, "I know about you and Bill."

The informer—Marla was never able to determine whether it was a man or a woman—had told her mother that they felt she should know her daughter was getting herself into a lot of trouble, that she needed to talk her out of spending any more time with Bill, or with the campaign.

"I said, "Mother, I like this guy. We enjoy each other's company.'"

"This hurts me," her mother said. "I'm concerned about you. Can he really treat you right if his goal is Washington, D.C.? Do you really think you're gonna go up there with him if he wins?"

"Maybe," said Marla—Bill had talked about taking some of the staff with him; she was good at what she did. It was possible.

"But doesn't he have this other woman, from Washington?" said her mother. Marla said yes. "So, wouldn't you assume you're just being used?" her mother pressed.

"Mom, I really don't know," responded Marla. "I know what he says. I know we enjoy each other—I don't know if I would put that label on it."

"Marla," said her mother, firmly, "You are being used. You need to think more of yourself than that."

"We both shed some tears," Marla remembered. "She basically thought he should not have gotten involved with me. She was looking at the whole picture—trying to protect me from what she called the cruelty of politics." By unspoken mutual consent, they never discussed it again. It would be many years, however, before Marla's mother became a Clinton follower. "It was after I was married, and safe," Marla said, amused. "Then it was, 'Oh, I just love that Bill Clinton.' I would laugh—'What's different now, Mom?'"

Marla's mother never received another phone call, but Marla herself felt sure she was being followed at times when she left the office. At her apartment, she received a number of hang-up calls. The situation made her increasingly uneasy. A good friend, who also worked at the office, grew concerned.

"She'd say, 'I'm working on the campaign but I'm not sure the son of a bitch is worth the risk you're taking—I like his politics but I don't know if I like him as a man.'"

Marla never knew who was responsible for the anonymous calls, but she was very aware of Hillary's wrath, and uncomfortable with it. To some extent the entire office had become divided—with most of the staffers, well aware of Bill's relationship with Marla, rooting for it to succeed. The entire scene had become tense, unpleasant, a minefield. "I was young, inexperienced in this sort of give and take. I didn't know how I was supposed to respond. He wrote me a note that said, 'I know that there are things about us I should really be sorry about, but I'm not. I care about you. I am grateful that you have been here with me during this time.'" He was, she thought, trying to apologize for some of the turmoil.

Eventually, Marla came to realize her relationship with Bill would never go anywhere, that his pact with Hillary was too strong. She also realized she had let herself become too emotionally involved with this man, and needed to protect herself. He, it was fairly clear to her, might have been perfectly happy to have their relationship continue in some amorphous, undefined manner as long as possible. If anyone was going to end it, it would have to be her. They had a final meeting, in which she told him she was leaving the campaign. "It was very adult, very aboveboard," she said. Bill was sad but understanding. "He said, 'You need to take care of yourself.' He also said, 'You just don't know how much you mean to me.'" (Years later his final conversations with Monica Lewinsky were much the same.)

It ended; their paths diverged forever—as much, anyway, as the paths of two native Arkansans can ever diverge. Marla left the state for a time, but eventually came back home, living first in Little Rock, then Hot Springs.

She looks back on that time with a mixture of amusement, nostalgia, and wistfulness. It was only a matter of months—yet she feels sure they were important months, that the glimpse she had into the complexity of Bill and Hillary Clinton's relationship was a valid one.

"It was a period of time when he was not married, even though they had an understanding, she made that perfectly clear. I'm not so sure those weren't some of the first real feelings he'd had, but then we got the game plan enacted and we've seen what it's been since then. So— how lonely has he been? How lonely has she been? Do they love each other? I think maybe the only way they know how. But I think for a short period of time, early on, maybe, he may have been willing to love in a different way."

It was a time, she felt, when his potential for true emotional involvement was still alive. "I have never said I felt I had anything to do with that. But it was still a period of time when he could have taken a different road.

"We'll never know."

Marla had come to know and love Virginia Kelley during the 1974 campaign, and the two of them had always seemed to share a special bond. Some, like Paul Fray, felt they resembled each other—the dark hair, round cheeks, sharply defined mouth. She had never said a word about their relationship to her, but "Mama knew lots," she believed.

Once, years later, just before the 1992 presidential election, she ran into Virginia for the first time in months, on the street in Hot Springs. Virginia hugged her, kissing her on the forehead like she always did when she saw her. Marla congratulated her—"Wow, I guess you're just about to get your boy there," she said.

Virginia beamed. It had taken a lot of folks a lot of time and effort, but it looked like it was finally going to happen, she said. "But you know all about that—you were right there, at the very beginning," she said.

Marla said yes, she knew. And then Virginia did an odd thing. She put her arms around her again, pulled her close, and whispered in her ear. "Oh, Marla," she said, and there was no mistaking the yearning in her voice. "What if, what if, what if."

HILLARY USES THE "J" WORD

Hillary had distinct notions of what Bill should and should-n't do, whom he should see, whom he should avoid. One person she was totally opposed to him having any contact with at all was the for-mer governor, Orville Faubus, best remembered for his most nefarious moment—the time he stood at the school door of Little Rock Central High School, September 1957, in a last-ditch attempt to block integra-tion—an empty, symbolic gesture, since President Eisenhower had already called out the National Guard to make sure the law would be obeyed.

Faubus, whose father had given him the middle name Eugene after his socialist hero Eugene Debs, had actually been considered somewhat of a progressive, a Huey Long type, while in office, and was still respected by many in Arkansas as a consummate politician who'd made a crucial, even inexplicable, error. Outside the state, of course, it was a different matter—the only thing anyone knew about Faubus was Central High, and he was viewed as a typical Southern racist, a ludicrous little man who'd attempted to obstruct the path of history. Hillary was adamantly against the idea of Bill having anything to do with him whatsoever.

Actually, though, Bill had already met with Faubus, long before Hillary came down, early on in the campaign. Brian Snow was shocked when he told him. "I said, 'Bill, what in the devil are you going to go see Faubus for?' And he said, 'He's one of the great campaigners and a smart guy.' I don't think I would've wanted to see Faubus myself, I had some memories of Central High. But Bill said, 'You know, it was really helpful, he had a lot of insightful things to say.' He said Faubus had been in touch with campaigning in Arkansas as well as anybody he'd ever seen. And Bill had a political philosophy that was miles apart from Faubus."

David Matthews, the law student who served as one of the drivers during the campaign, said Bill occasionally shared bits of Faubus political wisdom with him on their trips. "He said Faubus had told him, 'Never turn down food when somebody offers you food in their home — it's an insult.'" Another piece of advice Faubus had passed on, he said, was, "Always be late to a meeting — because then everyone notices you." As hoards would have a chance to witness over the years, Bill Clinton might at times change his positions, his views, his tactics, even his testimony under oath — but he would never fail to follow those two rules to the letter.

It is not known if he discussed any of the Faubus homilies with Hillary, though. She had a distaste for old pols like her father and her great-uncle, George Rodham, the Scanton councilman, who offended her then lofty political sensitivity. Whereas Bill had such a genuine love for the game, it spilled out into real affection for nearly all the players.

Similarly, Hillary could not stomach Paul Fray, who struck her as rough-edged old-time politician all the way, someone not averse to working the gray areas. The rancor between them escalated during the last months of the campaign, finally reaching its zenith at the very end.

The race for the Third Congressional District ended on a sour note. All losing campaigns are bittersweet, but by all accounts, this one's denoument was particularly unpleasant.

"The night we lost was probably the longest night of my life," said Addington, who had taken a recess from graduate school so he could be in on the finale. "I was in Fort Smith, where the bulk of votes were being counted, so I was back and forth on the phone to Fayetteville."

At around 10:30, Hillary called to say they'd had a report that some of their votes were being stolen in Fort Smith. "She wanted me to do something about it. I said, 'What in the hell do you want me to do about it? What can I do?' "

Hillary said, "I want you to call the U.S. attorney, get his ass out of bed and have him meet us down there in one hour."

Addington did as told. He and the attorney sat waiting at the Fort Smith headquarters until midnight, when it occurred to Addington that maybe Hillary had meant for them to go to the courthouse. She had—when they arrived, Hillary, Bill, and Paul Fray were all there already, their tempers not noticeably improved by Addington's delay. They exchanged a few sharp words, then the entire group stood around for two more hours, while the votes were counted.

"Hillary said, they're stealing the votes! And the attorney said, well, how can we prove it?" Addington spotted an older guy sitting at the Republican table, "someone who had sucked up to us during the campaign, I thought he was one of our supporters." Now it seemed likely he'd been a spy. It all seemed suspicious; Addington, like the others, was sure there were stolen votes among those being counted that night. "That's just me saying that. I don't have proof. But I am sure it happened. It still happens even today—black boxes get bought. We would have won, if it hadn't been for that."

Helpless, totally frustrated, each of the group reacted in different ways. "Fray was cussing and cussing," said Addington. "Bill was just stone-faced. Hillary kept saying, 'Do something, do something, do something.' It was a big crowd, couple of hundred people, and we're just standing there like a bunch of ding dummies, watching ourselves get beat."

By three A.M., it was all over: Clinton had lost by a mere six thousand votes. He, Hillary, and Fray went back to Fayetteville in their cars; Addington went home to nurse his sorrow in silence. The others, though, particularly Hillary and Paul, were cut from a different cloth. When in doubt, slug it out.

The minute Paul walked into the back room at the Fayetteville headquarters that night, Hillary hit him between the eyes. She was angrier than Paul had ever seen her.

"You fucking Jew bastard!" she screamed.

Hillary had cursed him out plenty of times before. But this was the first time she had used a religious slur, and it hit hard. It was not something he would ever forget. "I promise you it happened. It created a chasm I never really overcame," he said.

Paul Fray was actually a Baptist—later on he would train for the seminary at Ouachita Baptist University. But his father was Jewish, the son of immigrants, and Paul was very proud of his roots. "You don't talk about my forefathers. I come from Cohens (the high priests, in Jewish law). My dad used to tell me, 'Son, do you realize what we are, what tribe we're from? You need to understand, that's your heritage.' "

His immediate reaction, of course, was to explode back. "'You can't talk to me like that.' I let her know that in no uncertain terms." Bill Clinton, Mary Lee, and campaign worker Neil McDonald were also in the room at the time. Both Mary Lee Fray and Neil McDonald confirmed Paul Fray's account.

"Yeah, it happened," acknowledged McDonald years later. "Heat of the moment and all that. You have to realize where Hillary's from. And Paul does have some Jewish in his background."

The fight raged on, with McDonald posted at the door to keep out any curious staffers. According to various reports, a few ashtrays were heaved, the blue language flew, as Paul and Hillary blamed each other for everything that had gone wrong in the campaign. Mary Lee, defending her husband, brought up some of the problems with Bill and women; Bill for the most part was quiet, letting Hillary handle the combat.

In the end, exhausted, everyone filed out quietly—there was nothing more to say. The chance of any further working relationship between the Frays and the Clintons had pretty much been reduced to ashes.

But Hillary's attack on Paul's Judaism would continue to reverberate. There had been too many witnesses for it not to get out.

"I never asked Bill point-blank about that statement back then, because it really wounded the shit out of me," said Paul. "He thought it was one of those things, you blow off, go on. I've heard him say, 'If anything was wrong, forgotten and forgiven, no big deal, heat of the moment. A pretty violent exchange occurred—so what.'"

But for Paul, the cut went too deep to forget. "Hillary can be a sweet girl, but she knows damn well that has wounded me for years. I'll go to my grave with it."

One nasty epithet, slung in anger, hardly defines a person. And Hillary has always had a tendency, when enraged, to go for the gut.

"Hillary always knows what buttons to push," said one person who knew them both well. "There aren't many things in life she does that aren't calculated. Everything is thought out. She looks at the enemy and decides which kind of weapon to use. Do I use intellect and talk this through? Or do I get down, use the sort of weapon they understand? And with Paul, it's temper and words. So she was doing exactly what he understood."

Unfortunately, this was neither the first nor the last time Hillary would use such a slur. Bill Becker, the local head of labor (since passed away), sought Paul out to ask him about it shortly afterwards. "He said, 'How could that damn woman be that stupid?'" recalled Paul. "I said, 'Well, I think it's a question of her having a little bit of a problem.'"

State trooper Larry Patterson—who along with trooper Roger Perry went public in 1994 with stories of Bill's sexual escapades in the governor's mansion—later also reported in a taped interview produced by a conservative group that he heard both the Clintons tell ethnic jokes and use ethnic slurs. Oddly enough, they had a habit of slinging these slurs at each other, he said—"Jew bastard," "Jew motherfucker" being the most common ones used.

Paul, struggling to understand, thought Hillary's anti-Semitic slur might have something to do with her father, who had worked in fabrics his entire life, and had undoubtedly had dealings with Jews in the garment industry, particularly early on when he worked briefly in New York. "I think he was possibly ostracized by them, that he didn't feel he'd been treated fairly by them," he said. A blunt-spoken man, Hugh Rodham would have voiced his sentiments freely, Paul speculated; Hillary, he thought, may have grown up hearing such comments.

Hugh Rodham's mother, Hannah Rodham, was known for her own violent antipathy to both Catholics and Jews. Hillary's uncle Russell Rodham once told a Catholic friend at college his mother would have a fit if she knew they were rooming together. There is no question Hillary's father himself grew up hearing ethnic slurs in the home.

Paul also thought perhaps a vein of anti-Jewish sentiment might have sprung from the time in the early 60s when Harry Weinberg, a tough, wildly successful corporate raider long before the term was generally known, took over the Scranton Lace Company, where Hugh's father and other relatives had worked their entire lives. Paul believed Weinberg's takeover had ruined the company.

"Harry was a bastard, but a lot of us are bastards," said Paul. "It doesn't mean your religious preference should be held against you.

"If that woman's going to cuss everybody of a Jewish lineage, once she gets around them and has a little friction, then she has a real problem. Those are the only deductions I can make as to the reason," Paul said.

In fact, there was a much more likely reason behind Hillary's epithet, which involved not the Rodhams, but her mother Dorothy's family, and the fact that Hillary's maternal grandmother had remarried a Jew, Max Rosenberg. Several biographies and untold magazine and newspaper profiles on the first lady had failed to turn it up. Dr. Jean Houston, who advised Hillary on her book *It Takes a Village*, and who spent hours discussing cultural roots with her, remembered sharing a tale about her own single Jewish relative, a half-Cherokee; Hillary laughed but did not return the confidence.

When the news broke about Hillary's Jewish connection in the midst of her blossoming New York senate campaign, the press outdid itself. "Oy Vey, Hillary's Almost Jewish!" bannered the *New York Post*. Playwright Wendy Wasserstein contributed a modest parody to the *New Yorker*, about her own long-concealed "shiksa" roots. A column by Andrea Peyser bore the headline "The First Shiksa wants to be a yenta? Oy." Few doubted the revelation was anything more than "another clumsy ploy by the First Lady's ham-handed New York advisors," as a *New York Observer* editorial put it, adding that it was "awfully heartwarming to see how Mrs. Clinton uses dead relatives to score political points."

"Now the First Lady ventures forward into the land of the no-longer-living (and no-longer-available-for-comment) to give us a story about sort-of-Jewish roots. Given that she comes from Illinois, where the dead regularly cast ballots in tight elections, perhaps her political grave-robbing is to be expected," the editorial said acidly.

One *New York Post* reader, Edward Hochman, suggested it was time to recycle Joseph Welch's famous charge to Joseph McCarthy: "Have you no sense of decency, sir? At long last, have you left no sense of decency?" Another, Donna Mazzucca, declared heatedly that Hillary was "insulting the Jewish community's intelligence" with this ploy. ("We are not idiots; we see through her transparent, politically inspired juggling act.")

Most found the whole thing amusing, with a few pro-Hillary political types insisting stoutly—and predictably—it was all to the good, that this connection made her practically an honorary member of the tribe. "Jews will now feel she is one of their own," enthused New York political consultant Hank Sheinkopf. "People will feel that she's more like them and they'll be more likely to listen to what she has to say." At the very least, he added later, "like chicken soup, it can't hurt."

And by the end of the year, Hillary's own staff felt relaxed enough to poke fun at the entire issue. At a Christmas party thrown for Hillary and her inner circle, held in the Washington home of chief of staff Melanne Verveer, some eighty attendees caroled a parody of "The Twelve Days of Christmas," called "The Twelve Days of Chappaqua" (the site of Hillary's just-purchased New York residence). "On the third day in Chappaqua, New York gave to me—three new Jewish relatives," they sang cheerfully. The first lady, according to reports, "laughed heartily."

But there was that darker side to the story, which has until now gone unreported—Hillary's mother's grudge against Rosenberg, who, she felt, had reneged on a promise to send her to college sixty-two years earlier.

Dorothy never forgave Max, and did her best to keep Hillary removed from him, according to Oscar Dowdy. Hillary's cousin also asserted that Dorothy's anger often spilled out around the rest of the family, at times in the form of anti-Semitic slurs. Dowdy himself said he had been an eyewitness to such outbursts.

"Aunt Dorothy would say, 'Oh, all those damn Jews are so cheap,' and 'That Jew has to watch every dime,' that kind of thing," said Dowdy. Dorothy Rodham's mother, Della, herself would often call her husband Max "you cheap Jew bastard," when angry, Dowdy said. "They certainly had their share of arguments. Grandpa Max was very proud of Hillary, and recognized that she was very bright, an exceptional person, but the closeness was at arm's length, because of Dorothy. Dorothy had kind of poisoned Hillary's mind about Max."

Hugh, on the other hand, got along well with Max, whom he respected for his business acumen. But Hugh, known for his abrasive humor, was not above a few below-the-belt jibes. When convicted spies Julius and Ethel Rosenberg were sentenced to die in the electric chair, Hugh jeered, "Watch out, Max. You're a Rosenberg. They're going to fry all you people," a Rodham family observer recalled. "Hugh teased people like that. You weren't sure how serious he was. I guess it was mean-spirited, but Max didn't take him seriously."

At one point some years back, Dowdy insisted everyone come together—Max and Dorothy—for a Thanksgiving dinner, and they did. But the rift was not mended. "I don't think they said a word to each other. Max felt bad about it. I don't think he understood."

The crux of the problem, Dowdy felt, was "money, money, money. The whole Rodham clan seemed to think Max was very wealthy. He was pretty wealthy but I think they thought he was a whole lot wealthier than he was. I don't think they ever felt like they were getting a fair shake. They expected more. More presents at holidays, things like that."

Dorothy was also "infuriated" when Max was remarried two years after Della died—to a Jewish woman from the Chicago suburbs. (The marriage collapsed a few years later, as did a later marriage, in California, to a gentile woman). Max's mother for her part had never accepted Della, who had remained a Christian, attending a Presbyterian church regularly. "Della wasn't very religious, but I do remember her saying her prayers every night," said Dowdy. "Max had no problems with it. He would drive her to church."

Dorothy Rodham could hold a grudge, Dowdy said. "It seems like she can't get along in life unless she's really pissed at someone," he said. Helen Dowdy corroborated his description, though she has many warm memories of Dorothy, who she said was always immensely kind to her children. "It's sad, but Dorothy's always mad at somebody. And it tends to last forever. Dorothy doesn't get over it; she doesn't deal with it."

In recent years, according to the Dowdys, Dorothy Rodham's animus focused on Oscar, who had been extremely close to Rosenberg. Again, money seemed to be at the root of Dorothy's anger—Oscar inherited a fairly large amount when Rosenberg's daughter and Dorothy's half sister, Addie, died, leaving an estate valued at about $3.5 million. A good portion of that money had been left to Addie by her father, who had declared himself indigent for tax reasons before his death. Besides Dowdy, Addie left sizable sums to a number of charities—but she didn't forget the Rodhams. She bequeathed $10,000 each to Hillary and her two brothers,

Hughie and Tony. Dorothy personally visited Addie in the California Hospital where she lay dying to pick up the $30,000 check, but none of the Rodhams attended her funeral. "Dorothy said she was there for a week or so toward the end visiting Addie and felt like she had said her goodbyes," Helen Dowdy said.

Dorothy's resentment had passed from Max to Addie to Oscar, agreed the Dowdys.

"The way I see it, Hillary is Dorothy's daughter," observed Oscar Dowdy. "Dorothy passes on this attitude and feeling, and Hillary accepts it. It's unfortunate. People are taught prejudice. The apple doesn't fall far from the tree.

"To me, Hillary and Dorothy have a lot of likenesses. They can both turn you on or turn you off. I don't think they take anybody's feelings into consideration. What's good for them is good—nothing else matters."

Hillary's brother, Tony Rodham, said the revelation about the family's Jewish connection had not come as any big surprise. "We knew about Rosenberg," he said. "We were all aware. It was no big deal. In our family, with my brother, myself, my sister, my mother, my father, we're not Jewish in any way shape or form," he said firmly.

The Jewish community in Arkansas is a tight one, even more so than in other areas; in the 1970s it was even tighter. Slurs traveled fast. A year or so after Hillary's attack on Fray in the campaign headquarters, Paul was having lunch with Bill at the Belvedere country club in Hot Springs, just before his campaign for attorney general got underway. A high school classmate of Bill's—a Jewish guy—came up to their table. After a few words of greeting, he confronted Bill directly.

"He said, 'What is wrong with Hillary?'" Paul recalled.

Bill asked what he meant. "He said, 'Well, I heard what she said about him'—pointing at me," said Paul. "'How could you have ever gotten involved with someone who'd say something like that?'" Everyone who knew him knew of Bill's utterly genuine acceptance of all people, across the spectrum of race, religion, sexual preference. It was, many felt, the most admirable part of his character.

"I just sort of bowed my head, like hey, man, you don't need to be talking about this crap, something that happened in the past, no big damn deal," said Paul. "I thought it had blown over—because I thought nobody but people in the damn room knew about that. But word got out. It just went out of the damn headquarters like a rocket."

Bill, the great conciliator, attempted to soothe his former classmate, telling him it had been a momentary thing, nobody had been hurt, it was all over and done with. "He was doing his best to cover his ass," said Paul.

The minute the man left, Bill turned to Paul angrily.

"He said, 'What the hell, did you say something about this?' I said, 'No, I haven't said a damn thing about it.'" Bill, still sore, shook his head. The assault had taken him by surprise. "He was always a pushy guy," he said, referring to the Jewish classmate, ready to drop the subject.

As ever, though, Paul insisted on sizing up the situation through the all-important political lens.

"It's going to come back to haunt her, unless you figure out a way to get it straightened out," he warned Bill. "If she stays in the background, I don't think you've got a problem."

Hillary, of course, would not stay in the background. Still, it would be many years before she would find herself in a situation where she, not Bill, would need to woo Jewish voters, and in one of the most unforgiving arenas in the country, New York.

Anti-Semitic comments tend to have long lives, particularly in politics. It has taken Jesse Jackson years, a great deal of work, and many fulsome apologies, to pull out from under the shadow of one ill-advised muttered sentence, his famous "Hymietown" slur.

In the year Hillary announced her intentions to run for the Senate, Paul received several calls on the subject of her angry slur years earlier. "I've had a lot of guys calling me from New York, asking if there's any truth to the story," he said. "They wanted to substantiate the rumor. I said, 'Do what you gotta do, if you want to give me a lie detector exam, I'll sit for it. You want to give me truth serum, come on. It happened.' One guy said, 'How in hell is she gonna carry the Jewish vote when all that shit comes out?' I said, 'I don't know. I wish her luck.'"

A political pragmatist like Paul, of course, is well aware it is not the slur itself that interests the callers, so much as its possible use as a crowbar to be wielded against Hillary at the polls. To some people, particularly those in Zionist organizations, Hillary became an enemy long before she entered the campaign for the Senate—when she spoke out favorably about the possibility of a Palestinian state. For these people, nothing she has done since to assuage Jewish voters, or to woo them, has had much effect; to them, her fate was sealed in that moment. "That one little statement," one man told Paul, "is going to cut her head off." Paul's story is simply grist for the mill.

"The boys across the water," as Paul calls the Mossad, Israel's intelligence unit, "are aware of [Hillary's anti-Semitic comments]." This may ring of conspiracy theory to some, but in fact, Israeli intelligence has always made it their business know everything they can about political leaders and their relationship to Jews. To them it is a matter of survival. They were aware of Madeleine Albright's Jewish background, for instance, long before the rest of the world—even before she was herself, according to her.

Bill, too, is aware of the problem, Paul is sure, and always has been. He has no doubt the two of them have probably had some tense discussions on the subject. "Hey, he has some major flaws, and she has some major flaws," Paul said equably. Bill's, of course, are far better known to the world. But considering Hillary's reputation as a devout Methodist, someone whose politics are infused with a strong spiritual sense of mission, who could not bear for her husband to even sit down with a known racist like Orville Faubus, it could well be that hers are the more surprising.

UNIVERSITY LIFE

THE CAMPAIGN OVER AT LAST, Bill and Hillary had time to relax, spend time with mutual friends in Fayetteville—the Henrys, the Blairs, Richard Atkinson among others. Not that Bill was ready to let the campaign go, exactly; he spent hours going over it, obsessively, discussing it endlessly, trying to figure out exactly what he could have done differently. Generally, he did this before an audience—Bill was not the type to ruminate privately.

Brian Snow recalled one night. "We were socializing, Bill, Hillary and my wife. And Bill got started and he was telling us all about numbers—this county and that county, he just went on and on and on and finally Hillary said, 'Bill, shut up! We've had all we can take.' "

Both were now teaching at the law school, where, just as at Yale, Hillary was impressing colleagues more than Bill with her dedication, focus, and strict attention to detail. He was undoubtedly the more popular teacher with students, though, with his warm, easy, relaxed manner. Snow had been amazed, watching him earlier in the year with his constitutional law class. "He would come in from that campaign, he would have been up all night, and he would walk in—bleary-eyed, in rumpled clothes. I'd say, 'You're gonna teach? How are you gonna do that?'"

Bill would just shrug, unworried. "He'd say, 'Man, I've been talking all my life, I'm just gonna go in there and talk.' I would go in and listen to him, and they were excellent presentations. He had a superb command of his subject."

"There was a total contrast with respect to teaching styles," said Ray Guzman, another law professor. "It reflected their personalities. Hillary was generally considered to be a tough, no-nonsense professor—a formidable professor who held students' fingers to the fire. Bill was more laid-back, more pleasant, the conversations in his classes were more open. Hillary was probably considered by most faculty members the, quote, better teacher."

"The old joke was that Bill never gave anything less than a C because he was afraid of losing a vote. His grades were extremely high, always. Whereas if somebody didn't perform in Hillary's class, I have absolutely no doubt she wouldn't think twice about giving the student an extremely low grade."

Hillary's take-charge attitude toward Bill was visible from the start. At one point, word got out that Wylie Davis, the dean, had decided to ask Bill to take on a particular extra assignment. Hillary, a newcomer, a first-year assistant professor, immediately marched into his office to insist the assignment be given to her instead—Bill, she told Davis, had too many other things he was involved in.

"Even then, she was, if not covering him, at least trying to see he didn't get spread too thin," said Guzman. It was, he thought, unusual, to say the least—this was, after all, still just a girlfriend. Not a wife, not a fiancée.

Bill's biggest gaffe as law professor—losing all the test papers for his criminal law class—would of course be remembered forever around the school (especially since he would years later cross paths once again with one of the students in that class—Judge Susan Webber Wright, who would fine him ninety thousand dollars and hold him in contempt for his "false and evasive" testimony in the Paula Jones case).

At the time it happened, Bill went to see Wylie Davis, telling him the exams had been either lost or stolen. Davis regarded him with suspicion. "Professor, the notion that anybody would steal those examinations is mind-boggling," he said frostily.

"Eventually they turned up but it was too late. I believe they were underneath the seat of his car," said Guzman.

Hillary showed a softer, or at any rate, more appealing side to her law school colleagues than she had to campaign staffers. Max Brantley, then a political reporter for the *Arkansas Gazette*, saw her often that year when he visited his wife-to-be, then on the law faculty. "Hillary in unguarded moments is in my view a whole lot more fun than a lot of the world thinks she is," he said. "She has a loud, don't want to say bray, but it's a loud laugh, and it's real. When the business at hand is business she's dead serious about it. When the business at hand is fun, she's a lot of fun. But I don't think many people get to see her in unguarded moments."

Bill and Hillary kept the competitive edge up, even when socializing. Their favorite downtime activities involved games—charades, volleyball, softball, hearts, spades, Trivial Pursuit, Botticelli, board games. "They were high energy, high motion," said Brantley. "They enjoyed intellectual games and contests, and were very competitive. Bill more so than Hillary even, to the point of getting silly. Bill would get mad sometimes if he didn't win. She wasn't quite at this level about these games that didn't have anything riding on them. He'd shout at people on his team, shout at Hillary. She'd just get an exasperated look about her, and not pay it much mind."

Steve Clark, assistant dean, would often take a break to walk with her down to the local Jet Set Inn, two blocks from the law school, to pick up an ice cream cone. "She was the kind of person you did that with. We'd laugh and giggle—she was fun to be with, very clever and witty," he said.

He was impressed with her hard work as a teacher. "She spent a lot of time concerned with individual students, very dedicated. She was also involved in getting the legal clinic off the ground, which meant a lot of hours." The legal clinic, manned by students, mostly served indigent clients. "Hillary was very caring, very committed to the work," Clark said.

She was also the only person he'd ever met who he thought would make a good member of the U.S. Supreme Court. "She clearly had the skills. I told her that once." Hillary had just smiled, happy with the compliment.

Clark would eventually run up against Hillary's sharper side, though. It came a few years later, when Bill was attorney general, and Clark was considering getting into politics himself. He took her to a local restaurant in Little Rock so he could run the idea by her.

"I bought her a glass of wine, and I said, 'You know, if your husband runs for governor or senator, I think I'm going to run for attorney general,'" Clark said.

Hillary leaned across the table. "Well, then do me a favor," she said, brightly. Clark asked what she wanted.

"You need to lose a little weight," she said. "Because it's a little embarassing to ask people to vote for my little fat friend Steve."

Clark, taken unawares, was stunned. "I think I said something like, 'Well, don't hold back.'"

Others, too, would notice it more and more over the years—Hillary could sting like a killer bee. She could be the warmest, kindest, most concerned friend in the world, always remembering to ask about family, to write the notes, make the calls, do the right thing. But she could also—sometimes at the most unexpected moments—release a sudden bolt of venom, even with friends. And rarely be aware of the effect.

Terry Guzman, who worked with her on the Watergate committee, remembered visiting the Clintons at the White House one summer with her husband. Ray Guzman had just spent several weeks at the beach, and sported a dark tan. "He walks in—he's been teaching thirty years, he's a nationally known bar review speaker—and Hillary said, 'Oh, Ray, you've got such a good tan! I understand you've invested in a pizza parlor.'"

Embarrassed, uncomfortable, Guzman said nothing.

"He was angry. Why'd she say that? She could zing him even then. She can be witty, but she can also be real acerbic," Terry Guzman said. "It's got a two-edged sword to it, her wit. Just observations that are real cutting at times. They can be funny, but you'd never be quite sure.

"She does not brook fools, and she's got a great bullshit detector. She can cut through someone's bullshit faster than anybody I've ever seen. I think that may be part of where her reputation for being standoffish comes from. She doesn't like to waste her time, doesn't like somebody to even think they can get away with something. It can be kind of off-putting at times."

Brian Snow found himself getting a new view of Hillary late in 1974, when he and the Clintons went to New Orleans for a national law school conference. To him, Bill Clinton was the warmest guy in the world, "just a lot of fun; he could charm the devil out of everyone." Hillary, on the other hand, was "much more withdrawn, much more serious . . . somewhat aloof."

But somehow he and Hillary clicked on that trip, for the first time. One day they spent hours walking the streets of the French Quarter, talking and laughing, while Bill was off doing something else. "She was very engaging, very friendly—a good sense of humor, too, which I prize."

At one point, a street denizen, reeling, collapsed right in front of them. "He was apparently totally intoxicated. I didn't know if he was dying, or what," said Snow. "All this stuff was coming out of his mouth—it was kind of an ugly scene."

He turned to Hillary. "One of us should probably do mouth to mouth," he said. "Who's going to do it?"

"Not me—you're going to do it," said Hillary, adamantly.

"Fortunately for us the police came by at that point," said Snow. "They called for paramedics, who took care of it." After they'd left, he turned to her again.

"Hillary, this deprived us of the chance to save someone's life," he said.

"Oh, no, it didn't," she said, laughing. "It deprived *you* of a chance to save someone's life."

"I saw a whole different side of her that day," Snow mused. "But I didn't see it very often."

MARRIAGE FROM HELL

Bill and Hillary Clinton were married October 11, 1975. Once again, the story put out by the Clintons over the years has the distinct flavor of having come from a Universal publicist, circa mid-fifties. Bill, in other words, proposed cute, too. One day Hillary saw a house she liked, near the campus in Fayetteville, and commented on it. The next time Bill picked her up at the airport, after she had been off visiting friends up north, he told her, coyly, "Well, I bought that house you liked. I guess that means you have to marry me." Violins up.

Others, more cynical perhaps, think something more than a sudden burst of romantic passion may have been at work.

Sometime in 1975, Ron Addington, by then teaching at a college in Arkadelphia, started getting calls from Fayetteville. "People thought I was still the person who could influence him," he said. All the calls were about one thing: the fact that Bill and Hillary were living in sin.

"The calls came from a lot of our own inner circle people, loyal friends, campaign type friends," said Addington. "They were worried and scared to tell him. They'd seen him blow up at me a hundred times, they knew I could take it. They said, 'You need to tell him people are talking.'"

Addington realized he had to pass it on since Bill was already thinking about the upcoming race for attorney general.

It turned into the biggest fight they'd ever had. "I said, people are talking about you and Hillary living together. Boy, he got mad, started shouting—kill the messenger, you know."

"It's none of their goddamn business! She's got her apartment, I got mine!" Bill fumed.

"But everybody knows you all are really in the same apartment," said Addington.

"What the hell you want me to do?" Bill yelled.

Addington said, "If you want to run for anything else, you better get married."

Bill was quiet for a minute. "You think so?" he said.

"Yeah, I do," said Addington. "Get married."

"So they got married," said Addington, who had no doubt this was the spur. "It had to be brought to his attention. He thought that nobody cared."

The fact that their living together might be an issue had been brought to his attention before, of course—even before Bill ran for Congress.

"Hillary came down to take the bar," said Mary Lee Fray. "And we talked about the issue of them living together. She wanted to put the same address as Bill's on the bar application form. Paul was jumping up and down—and Hillary said, 'You mean no one lives together here? No one has sex before marriage?'

"And Paul said, in Arkansas it's not accepted to run for office when you live with someone. I think she thought we were trying to be dishonest, trying to judge her. I said, 'Put another address down, like your parents, just don't have the same address as Bill.' It was the eye of the church—I don't think she realized how important the church was in Arkansas politics back then."

It was not that Hillary wasn't the one for Bill—she had always been the one, Marla Crider notwithstanding. But both of them had qualms about marriage. It has been said, of course, that Hillary's concerns had to do with living in Arkansas, dealing with his mother, shelving her own ambitions. But it seems more likely both of them had exactly the same qualms—and that they had to do with Bill's Achilles heel, which was located unfortunately nowhere near his foot. Neither of them had any reason to think he would, or could, be faithful.

Bill Clinton had always been powerfully drawn to women—as a second grader, he had waved from the window of his mother's car at his crush of the moment, Mauria Jackson, saying softly, "Goodbye, my white flower." Later, there had been many more crushes—at high school, in college, at Oxford. Some, surely, had been full-blown affairs. Certainly the keen interest was always there.

Yet before his return to Arkansas, no one had ever mistaken Bill Clinton for a womanizer. The manic rush of the campaign, the sudden crowd of lusty, adoring groupies—even the sense, perhaps, that he was back home after years of schooling, years of doing the right thing, of being the pluperfect golden boy, and entitled, finally, to reap a few rewards—all had combined to unleash something deep within, and this was one genie that would not be going back in the bottle any time soon. Maybe the oddest thing about the scope of Bill Clinton's sexual proclivities was the way they did not truly begin to expand until he was close to thirty—a time when many are turning away from the idea of multiple partners. It's tempting to wonder whether a more satisfactory teenage sex life might have changed history; as it was, Bill Clinton would be frozen in time forever as a perpetual horny adolescent, eventually becoming the best-known one in the world. In this, as in so many ways, he reflected the attitude—if not the actual activities—of many American males in his age group, those whose teen years predated the sexual revolution. Other societies, with more open attitudes towards teenage sex, have often noted with amusement that Americans tend to view sex through a giggly, prurient scrim—the scrim of frustrated adolescence.

Mauria Jackson Aspell, who grew from being his special white flower into a close lifelong friend, witnessed some of his indecisiveness.

"Should he get married, should he not? And I said, 'Do you love her?' And he said, 'Yeah, I love her.' I figured he couldn't stand the idea of settling down. He said how brilliant she was, that he felt like she was a real match for him, that he loved spending time with her. The decision wasn't, was she the one. It was whether to marry or not."

He knew the problem, and she knew the problem. But the game plan—the pact—won out.

Once decided, the wedding was swiftly, even hastily arranged—"I don't think they looked on it as all that big a deal. They had too many other more important things on their mind," said Hillary's cousin, Oscar Dowdy. The plans called for a small ceremony at their house, followed by a large reception at the Henrys, attended, according to one source, by "every political connection in the state of Arkansas."

"There had to be around four, five hundred people there," said Addington.

Bill actually waited until the morning of the wedding, before letting his mother know Hillary was keeping the Rodham name. Virginia had driven up from Hot Springs with her friends, Bill and Marge Mitchell, and Patti Howe (later Criner), a longtime friend of Bill's.

"Bill called and said, 'I got to talk to you all,'" said Marge Mitchell. "That meant he had something on his mind. We didn't know what, but we were ready for it. That was his warning—'I just need to talk to you all, I'll talk to you at breakfast.'"

Sitting with them at the Holiday Inn over breakfast the morning of his wedding, Bill delivered the bombshell. "I thought Sister [Virginia] was going to have a fit," said Mitchell. "Bill just looked at me and said, 'Disappear.' I did."

"All I could focus on was the roar that filled my head," Virginia later said in her autobiography. "My tears started to flow. Marge later told me she almost cried too." Part of her reaction, she added, had been pure shock—"I had never even conceived of such a thing." It had to be, she thought darkly, some new import from Chicago.

Because at that time, in Arkansas, people didn't do such things—particularly people planning on a political life. Virginia was devastated. Still, with her usual verve, she managed to pull herself together. She and Mitchell did their best to ready the house for the two o'clock wedding, stopping on the way over to pick up flowers.

Bill and Hillary's house looked totally unprepared for a wedding. "As far as we knew they hadn't really made a whole lot of plans about this. They still had paint buckets lying around, it was crazy," said Mitchell. "Sister looked at me, I looked at her and said, 'This house will not be ready in time. I guarantee you it won't.'"

The two of them swiftly decorated the bay window with mums—"We figured they could stand there for the ceremony." Mitchell attempted to put pots of mums outside, too, but ran into a problem.

Hillary had placed a few Halloween pumpkins on the porch; every time Mitchell moved the pumpkins out of the way to set up the mums, Hillary stubbornly put them back in their original place. Finally, after the third time, Mitchell collared her. "Those mums are staying," she ordered. Hillary recognized a will as strong as her own, and gave up the fight.

Mitchell, who says she got along with Hillary from that point on, later came to understand why she'd kept her name. "She was just ahead of her time." Hugh Rodham, whom she got to know later, led her to believe there was another reason as well, she said. "It was because the Rodham name was so well known in the East, it would be helpful in her law practice." It was simply more Hugh Rodham bombast, of course; there had never been a lawyer in the Rodham family before Hillary, and the Rodham name had only a scintilla of cache in blue-collar Scranton.

The private ceremony went off without a hitch, with one exception. When the Methodist minister performing the service, Victor Nixon, asked who was prepared to give this woman in marriage, Hillary's father was unable to utter a single word. "When he said, you know, who gives this woman, my husband stood there, stood there, and the minister finally kind of said, 'You can step back now,'" said Dorothy Rodham years later "He didn't want to give up."

After a few moments of silence, the ceremony resumed. Rodham's ambivalence about his daughter's choice of husband was well known— Bill himself had described his initial reaction to him as "toleration, not acceptance." Robert Clarke, a childhood friend, remembered running into Hugh in Scranton later that year. "Well, my daughter's married to a politician," he'd said, so dismissively that Clarke had not even asked for his name. He was in "absolute shock" when Bill ran for president and he realized for the first time he was the one Hillary had married.

"My parents actually liked Bill," Hillary declared, appearing on TV in late 1999, accompanied by her mother. Dorothy corrected her. "After a while," she said. Hillary concurred. "Yeah, after a while."

Virginia wasn't the only one upset that day about Hillary's name decision. When the Frays arrived at the reception, Bill made it a point to inform them, too. Paul went ballistic. "I went, 'Oh, here we go.' You promised not to cuss," said Mary Lee Fray.

Bill was very curt. "He said, 'You don't really know Hillary, you're going to have to accept Hillary, I'm married to her.'" He turned to Mary Lee. "Shut him up," he said. "Now."

"He was always saying that to me about Paul," said Mary Lee.

"The kids had new clothes, we'd brought pewter water glasses for a present, when we left the house Paul intended to be nice," she said sadly. "But when he was told she was going to stay Hillary Rodham—in politics, in Arkansas, that just doesn't work."

And of course, in time even Hillary would come to realize Virginia Kelley and the Frays had been absolutely right. Five years later she would reverse her decision and formally become Hillary Rodham Clinton (though not to the extent of changing her name legally).

Bill and Hillary, in keeping with their rather slapdash approach to their nuptials (Hillary had picked up an off-the-rack dress the day before the event), had neglected to plan for any kind of a honeymoon. It was Dorothy Rodham who orchestrated it, arranging for all six of them—Bill, Hillary, Hugh, Hughie, Tony, and herself—to travel together to Acapulco. The Clintons thus became one of the very few couples in history to go on a honeymoon arranged by, not to mention accompanied by, a mother-in-law.

"The honeymoon wasn't important to them," maintained Oscar Dowdy. "It wasn't going to be a romantic occasion. I'm sure neither one of them were that excited about it." Tony and Hughie, of course, "would jump at any opportunity to get a free ride," he said. "That's the way they were."

The odd arrangement did give Bill a chance to get a better sense of his in-laws. At Hugh Rodham's closed-to-the-media funeral in 1993, Bill remembered in his eulogy being pulled over by Mexican police while on the trip—he had somehow forgotten to bring his driver's license. Hugh told him to sit still, he'd take care of it, and jumped out of the car to deal with the officers.

"Bill said all he could see was Hugh waving his arms, doing all the talking. Then he walked back to the car, got in, and said, 'drive away,'" said Rodham pal Robert Clarke, who attended the funeral. "Typical Hugh," he added. "He knew how to take command of a situation."

Left unexplained (and curious only to those who had ever been in similar straits) was how he could have possibly pulled off such a trick, speaking no Spanish whatsoever—unless, of course, one of the waving hands had been clutching a wad of bills. Acapulco is nowhere near the border, and Mexican police in general are notoriously reluctant to admit they understand English. Still, apocryphal or not, the tale captured Hugh's essence—hearing it, Clarke and his brother exchanged nods. That was Hugh Rodham, all right.

Bill launched his campaign for the office of attorney general two months after his wedding. He rounded up many of the people who'd worked on his congressional campaign—Paul Fray being one of the few who did not make the cut. Ron Addington, teaching at Henderson University in Arkadelphia, handled public affairs from his office.

"Bill would call every day, I'd take down quotes, type up a press release and get it in the mail by five oclock," he said. "Every damn day. I was doing it on state time, too. I could get fired now, doing stuff like that from my office, but in those days you could get away with crap like that," he said.

Addington had managed to get through the congressional campaign without any major rifts with Hillary. This time, he would not be so lucky.

"I'd gotten a bunch of labels printed, got college kids to stick them on the envelopes, and went down and bought a bunch of stamps. I paid for them and sent the bill in to get reimbursed," he said.

The next day he got a call from Hillary, who was hopping mad.

"Who authorized you to buy stamps!" she howled. "You don't have the authority to spend campaign money!"

Addington was furious. "I'm doing this down here free, I don't have time to get approval from you for a goddamn roll of stamps," he hollered back.

"I'm going to come down there and pick up those envelopes myself!" she threatened.

"You just bring your ass over here and get 'em," said Addington, hanging up on her.

For him, it was the last straw. He continued to put out press releases for a few more weeks—"never got reimbursed, either"—but he'd had it with Hillary for good.

"That was her style. That's just an example of the way she treated everybody." He has a vague memory of mentioning it to Bill. "He said something like 'Oh, just overlook her.'" But Addington had soured. When the campaign headquarters opened in Little Rock, shortly afterwards, he took up his press releases, labels, and envelopes and handed the whole pile over. For better or worse, Hillary had managed to alienate him forever.

"It's the way she treats people. And she's done that all the way through," he said. "I have friends who are state troopers and they've told me some godawful stories, when she was first lady in the governor's mansion—the way she treated the troopers, the staff. She was awful. Usually being appointed to the governor's staff is a plum job. They considered it punishment. They had to put up with her. They had to put up with him, too, having to hide his activities, being out all night long, no routine or family life. But the real reason they just did not want to be there was because of Hillary.

"She just has a way of not treating people civil. I don't know what it is. Her old daddy would probably tell her, 'You're doing wrong, you're not treating people right.' Her mother's not that way, she's mannerly, prim, proper." Addington, of course, had no way of knowing about Dorothy's own approach to anger, or Hugh's.

"A lot of people say—even my students, in my classes—'Wouldn't it have been awful if he hadn't married her? He wouldn't even be president.'" It drives him nuts. "I say, 'Bullshit!' He probably would have been president sooner. If he'd just had a smart, attractive wife. He would have succeeded, no matter who. She probably has done more to hurt him than to help him."

Many in Arkansas agreed—though Bill's friends knew better than to say it to his face. But when it came to Hillary's style, her abrupt way of dealing with people, her refusal, at least for many years, to change, to soften her approach, to make any kind of attempt to be charming, Bill—who was certainly aware, he was acutely sensitive to all human interactions—seemed at all times blissfully unconcerned. Over the years the point would be made continually—she was his Bobby Kennedy, his hatchet man, she was the one who could handle the nasty situations, and who actually seemed to get a real kick out of charging into the fray. With her deflecting the fire, he could continue to be beloved.

It's not a situation unknown in politics. But even more important, perhaps, it's not uncommon in marriages, either (though generally, the sexes are reversed)—the sweetest person in the world who ends up with a bully, the charming hostess paired with the antisocial lout. With onlookers rarely wondering whether this may not have been a direct choice, conscious or not, on the part of the seemingly nicer person—fueled by a deep need to express (if only obliquely) quite another side of their own character.

And of course, it's not an unknown dynamic with parents and children, either—the soft-spoken mother who raises a fiery pit bull. One of the most often told tales of Hillary's childhood is the one about the time she came home, crying because a tough neighborhood girl had taken her on. Dorothy insisted she go back out and deck her; Hillary obeyed. There is no question that Dorothy wanted to raise her daughter to be a fighter. Most observers have looked to blustery Hugh as the natural progenitor of Hillary's confrontational style; yet Dorothy, so much more decorous and mannerly, perennially egging her on from the shadows, may have had even more to do with it.

Bill may have waved off Hillary's anger with Addington, for expecting to be compensated for expenses, but for the most part, he took her opinions about people very seriously. Hillary trusted few people, and made sure Bill knew it.

Journalist John Brummet, a political columnist and author of the book *High Wire—The Education of Bill Clinton* recalled one instance clearly, when Bill was governor. "We were talking about a woman journalist who'd really been tough on him. And he said Hillary had told him never to be alone with her, because what she really wanted was either him, or to compromise him in some way. That had never occurred to me, or to him. But he said, 'Hillary knows this kind of thing.'

"That's largely the dynamic of the relationship—almost a good-cop bad-cop marriage. He'll be your buddy; she's over in the corner staring you down and later is going to tell him you're no good."

Brummet found her "cold and aloof and unapproachable," a sentiment he shared rather widely. One day, accompanying Bill on a state trip, he was horrified when Bill sat down in the seat next to him and asked him point-blank why he didn't like his wife.

"He said, 'Staff people tell me you don't like Hillary; I want to talk to you about it." Brummet attempted to slide further down in his seat. "I said, 'Ohhh, I don't want to talk about that." But Bill was insistent.

He then launched into an attempt to explain Hillary—or perhaps, his choice of Hillary. "He said, 'Here's why—she's a remarkable person, she's so smart, she can figure things out and she's the smartest person I've ever known.'" He knew not everyone was enamored of her, but he thought it was basically a problem of "a Midwestern girl and a Southern guy."

He was factual, he was logical, making his case. But what struck Brummet the most was his tone. There was a complete absence of passion, or love.

THAT OLD CLINTON MAGIC

Launched on his first statewide race for the office of attorney general, Bill continued to amaze people with his skill as a campaigner. He had been honing it all his life, of course, from childhood on, but there was a nearly magical cast to it, the sort of thing that can't be taught or analyzed. "The great seducer," many would eventually call him. One on one, in a home, a hall, on the rope line, the man could not be beat.

David Matthews remembered attending one of his first appearances in the campaign. There were three candidates in the Democratic race that year. The first speaker, John Clayton, talked about his aims, what he intended to do in office, and was well received. The second, George Jernigan, also spoke about his programs, why he wanted to win, and was also roundly applauded. Then Bill got up.

Unlike the others, he didn't say a word about the current race for attorney general. Instead, he talked about how much he appreciated all the help he'd received from people in the Arkansas River Valley during his congressional run. He named families he'd met along the way, talked about the communities he'd visited, mentioned the towns,

177

the little things he remembered about each. Simple memories—the peach pie he'd been served in one town; the church barbecue he had attended in another. His voice was quiet, conversational.

Then he concluded: "Regardless of whether I win this race or any other future race, I will never ever forget the love with which you received me, the warmth with which you took me into your homes, the food you served me, the watchful care you gave over me," he said. "I want you to know I'll remember it the rest of my life."

And the crowd erupted into a standing ovation. Jernigan, shaking his head, knew right then it was all over, he told Matthews later. Bill Clinton was going to be the next attorney general of Arkansas.

"He just thanked them for what they'd done. It was brilliant. It made the hair on the back of your neck stand up," said Matthews. To him, it would stand as the best political speech he'd ever heard—up to the point that Bill gave his crucial "last dog dies" speech in New Hampshire in 1992.

"He speaks differently, depending on who he's talking to," said John Brummet. "He'll talk to a civic club in Little Rock with an insider business man's sophistication. Then get him at a general store and it's not just that he'll slap you on the back, he's suddenly talking the way those people talk. His accent, his inflections, his expressions—it all changes."

Brummet himself would never forget one particular moment which seemed for him to crystalize Clinton's astounding abilities.

"We were in this small town, a rural Arkansas town, walking the sidewalks. He always tried to keep a good old boy with him, some gray-haired fellow, to sort of give him some credibility with the country folk. This guy pulls up at a stoplight, with three or four barking dogs in his pickup. He rolls down the window, 'Hey, Bill Clinton!'

"And Clinton—what impressed me was—he did it all so fluidly, in one motion. He waved at the guy, started toward him, and as he started, he said to his campaign aide, 'This good old boy, what kind of dogs are those?' And he said, 'Well, they're bird dogs.' 'How old are they?' 'About three.' So he runs to the guy and says, 'Hey, those are good-looking bird dogs, what are they, about three?' The guy says, 'No, they're two.' But he goes home and tells everyone, 'Boy, Bill Clinton knows his bird dogs.' "

Journalists emerged starry-eyed from their first interview with Bill—a glow that remained even when they discovered he had actually said very little of substance.

Few were immune. "I'm like everybody with Bill," said Max Brantley. "I saw in him what I wanted to see—Ivy League educated, Oxford educated, save the South liberal." What he didn't see, until later on, was "the consensus builder/compromiser/politics above just about all else."

In the years to come, it would be no suprise that many writers—Hillary chronicler Gail Sheehy among them—would argue that Hillary continued to stay with Bill in part because he kept seducing her. After all, it was one of the things he did best as a politician—didn't it make sense for him to use his powers at home, too? And many would feel they had witnessed such scenes themselves. Joe Klein's originally anonymous book *Primary Colors* presented one prototypical incident, which read (and played, in the movie) like absolute truth—his Bill character is late for a meeting in New Hampshire during the 1992 primary because he has taken a break to bed down with a willing librarian. His wife is angry, and clearly suspicious, too, when she finally meets his plane. She erupts stingingly—and "Bill," rather than argue the point, throws his arms around her, an affectionate bear, crooning a song, jollying her out of it.

There is no question it was a scene that was undoubtedly repeated over and over in their lives together—Bill, caught, would wheedle and charm Hillary out of her anger. "He used to call her Hige," Paul Fray said. He at times even cooed in baby talk. "He was just so much fun," Hillary herself has said.

But Hillary had her agenda, too—and her own seductive powers, though not the sort, perhaps, that would work as well on campaign crowds, or possibly any audience, other than Bill himself. She had convinced him at an early age that he *needed* her to succeed. And while he would stray, constantly, obsessively, repeatedly, he would at the same time continue to cling, almost like a small child. She was his talisman against failure, his insurance card, his beacon, and with the exception of a few brief points in his life, he would never seriously consider giving her up. They would remain locked together.

Those who interpret their alliance only along the most traditional, soap opera lines—he the cheating scoundrel, she the private, aggrieved wife—or alternatively, she the cold, unforgiving harridan, he the love-starved puppy forced to go outside the home—are missing a good deal of the picture. It was Bill, in some ways, who was the needy one in their relationship; Hillary, in some ways, who held the important cards. For in spite of all appearances, his most consuming need, the one he married for, was not sex at all—though it turned out, as it usually does, that sex refused to stay out of the picture.

"He's always deferred to her judgment," said Ernie Dumas, a long-time political journalist at the *Arkansas Gazette* and Clinton watcher, now teaching at the University of Arkansas at Conway. As Bill was installed as attorney general—then, two short years later, as governor— Dumas, who had several friends on his staff, watched the process unfold. To some observers, it appeared that Hillary, now working at the Rose law firm in Little Rock, had little to do with the day-to-day operations of office those first years. Dumas knew better.

"She didn't have that much visible role in policy making that first term—except the staff apparently saw it all the time," he said. "They'd have these sessions, and decide okay, this is what we need to do, and Bill would say yes, yes. Then the next morning he'd come in and say, 'Hillary says that's wrong. We shouldn't do that.' He always sided with Hillary. If Hillary said something, that was the way it was going to be, because Hillary said it and she was smarter than they were. He bought everything. They might have had a shouting match at home about it, but Hillary's notions would carry the day. Undo what everybody else had done.

"He had this great faith in her political wisdom. And it was misplaced. I don't think she knew much, don't think she ever knew much. Her judgments were generally wrong, as far as I could tell. But he won in spite of them. She would want to do stuff that Steve Smith [one of his top aides that first gubernatorial term] thought was precisely the wrong thing to do politically—but she'd persuade Bill it was the right thing."

One incident tickled him. "If he really wanted to nail you, he would cite Hillary. When he was head of the National Governors Conference, they passed this welfare reform bill in Congress, and he'd gone up to testify and gotten all this glowing praise—this young governor from Arkansas who'd come up and presented this thing, and gotten it passed.

"I had been following it, written a great deal about it—and basically the bill was written by the American Public Welfare Association. I said that in this editorial, and he'd seen it."

The next time Dumas ran into him, Bill was "kind of tight-lipped, trying to smile. He said, 'You know, Hillary says I get recognition on this welfare thing everywhere in the country except in my own newspaper. You don't give me any credit.'

"I said, 'Well, Governor, whatever credit you deserve, but it was the plan of the American Public Welfare Association.'

"But the thing was, he was citing Hillary. That'll show you. *Hillary says,*" Dumas chuckled.

BILL, GENNIFER, AND JUANITA

AS THE CLINTONS SETTLED into Little Rock, which would be their home for the next sixteen years—twelve of those years to be spent in the governor's mansion—their personal lives became more and more separate, diffused. Fayetteville had been a small academic community. In Little Rock, there was more room to expand. Hillary had her job at the Rose law firm, Bill was attorney general, and then, almost overnight, governor—at thirty-two, the youngest governor in the country.

No one can know how many women he would become involved with over the next decade and a half. He would later confide to Monica Lewinsky that the number had run into the hundreds, and there is no reason to doubt him. By most reports, Bill tended to have several long-term affairs running simultaneously, buttressed by incessant one-night stands. But at least two women from those early years would later come back to haunt him: Gennifer Flowers and Juanita Broaddrick. One would come close to derailing his bid for the presidency; the other would only surface openly around the time of his impeachment, to add a final, sordid grace note to the story.

In the wide world of illicit sexual relations, barring a revealing photograph (like the one showing Gary Hart holding a nubile Donna Rice on his lap aboard the *Monkey Business*, which effectively scotched his presidential candidacy) or a telling stain that can be analyzed for DNA information (which led, of course, to Bill's impeachment), it is often all but impossible to separate truth from lies. People in our society, as one observer has commented, do not tend to witness other people having sex. In addition, people tend to lie about extramarital sex—all people, not just politicians.

Gennifer Flowers's tale appeared to be full of holes and inaccuracies, all of which the Clinton machine landed on with full force. She referred to a hotel that had not existed at the time; she insisted their affair had lasted twelve full years. She maintained in her book, *Passion and Betrayal*, that she had first met Bill while working at KARK-TV, in 1975—though Mary Lee Fray insists she introduced the two long before.

These and other errors made it relatively easy for Bill's supporters to believe (or at least claim) she was making the whole thing up—right up to the point when he finally admitted under oath that he had slept with her, though only once, back in the 1970s.

Just like Dolly Kyle Browning, who would surface later, attempting to one-up everyone with claims of a thirty-year-affair, Flowers painted her relationship with Bill for the most part in soft, pastel tones, appropriate for a *Harlequin* romance.

"These women," said journalist Max Brantley wearily, "have misinterpreted seven or eight boffs. I don't misbelieve he had relations with them but if they thought he cared about them, it's sad."

In her book Flowers describes their affair in florid tones—the two engaged in slightly kinky high jinks, which included phone sex, rubbing food on each other (generally common refrigerator staples like milk and ketchup), and the occasional bondage; once, she even made up his face, using her own cosmetics, she alleged. They named their private parts, she reported—hers was "the precious," his was "Willard" (the name of Hugh Rodham's brother); it had, she averred, a Willard-like personality (Willard, the brother, was big and fat). Bill angled repeatedly for a threesome; Flowers was not up for it. She is vitriolic about Hillary, describing her as "a fat frump with big thick glasses, an ugly dress and a big fat butt." Bill, she says, referred to her as "Hilla the Hun" and "Sarge." They rarely discussed her, though, because "our time was too precious." Once, when her band was playing at the governor's mansion, Bill attempted to lure her into the men's room for a quickie; Flowers demurred.

It was, in other words, a fairly typical backroom affair, of the sort that recalls Lenny Bruce's famous bit—"Men of my generation never cheated on their wives. Because I'm sure, to a wife, cheating implies hugging and kissing and loving someone else." Under this definition, Bill Clinton probably rarely cheated on Hillary in any real sense, and Hillary knew it. Marla Crider had been a *real* threat to their relationship. But Gennifer Flowers was not. She was, of course, a steadily burning irritant, as were they all. Flowers was positive she was aware — at one point, she ran into Hillary at a Democratic fundraiser. Hillary stared daggers at her, and Flowers was sure there would be a confrontation, but there wasn't.

Arkansas state troopers Larry Patterson and Roger Perry, who served in Bill's security detail, told the conservative magazine *American Spectator* and the *Los Angeles Times* in 1994 that the Flowers affair had gone on several years while Bill was governor. Patterson recalled driving Bill to Flowers's apartment on many occasions, and waiting outside in the parking lot for up to two hours. Sometime around 1991, when Bill was gearing up for his presidential run, Flowers began calling the mansion constantly, according to the troopers. Not long after, she was given a modest post as administrative assistant at the Arkansas Board of Review appeal tribunal, a job she lost soon after going public with her tale in the *Star*.

To the press, to the Clinton machine, Gennifer Flowers was the almost prototypical bimbo, a blond sexpot hawking her tale in the tabloids—who were, for quite a while, the only ones who would touch the story. Juanita Broaddrick, however, was a whole different matter. Her own tale first broke into the world in the austere (and rabidly anti-Clinton) pages of the *Wall Street Journal*; she was handled if anything with even more gentility than had been shown Kathleen Willey, the woman who accused Bill of making a lunge for her in the Oval Office.

The *Journal* piece, by Dorothy Rabinowitz, came close to fawning—Broaddrick was "a woman of accomplishment, prosperous, successful in her field, serious; a woman seeking no profit, no book, no lawsuit." Moreover she had a "sunny disposition," and was "the kind people like and warm to." The message was clear: this was no Gennifer Flowers or Paula

Jones, no part-time singer or lowly office clerk. Rabinowitz alluded to Broaddrick's wealth numerous times, even going so far as to list her live-stock—thirty cows, five horses, and a mule—as if affluence alone was the final proof of credibility.

Still, her story was disturbing. According to Broaddrick, she met Bill Clinton in 1978, when as attorney general, making his first bid for governor, he had stopped by her successful nursing home. He invited Broaddrick, a campaign worker, to visit headquarters when she visited Little Rock.

Not long after she came to town to attend a seminar and called him. He convinced her they should meet in her hotel room. There, after a brief discussion in which she told him she was married, and also seriously involved with another man, he, according to her, forced himself on her, holding her down and biting her lip. He then quickly adjusted his clothes, donned sunglasses, and left—suggesting on the way out she get some ice for her lip. A friend attending the seminar with her backed up her story—she said a shaken Broaddrick, with a swollen lip, had told her about it later that day. Broaddrick had also shared the story with others, including the man she was involved with, whom she would later marry.

In 1984, when her nursing home had been named the best in the state, she received an official letter of congratulations from the governor—at the bottom was a handwritten note. "I admire you very much," it said. Five years later, Broaddrick ran into Clinton himself in a hotel corridor, while attending a nursing home convention. He said he wanted to apologize, saying he was a changed man. She backed away. A few months later, she heard he was running for president.

In 1997 Broaddrick, deposed in the Paula Jones case, had filed an affidavit denying any sexual contact with Clinton. A year later, faced with the independent prosecutor's office, she had changed her story, fearing, she said the consequences of lying to the feds; she appeared in their report as Jane Doe No.5. She then decided—for reasons that remain obscure—to share the whole sorry mess with NBC's Lisa Meyers, in a taped interview the network sat on for weeks, finally airing it on *Dateline*, February 22, three days after the *Wall Street Journal* article appeared.

By the time Broaddrick's story became public, the entire country was thoroughly sick of the entire business—having weathered the impeachment trial, the Starr Report, the constant stream of tawdry revelations. The reaction was subdued. Who kept quiet about a sexual assault for twenty-one years? On the other hand, who accused the state attorney general of such a crime? Who was naive enough to let a man come to her hotel room, talk openly about an extramarital affair, then expect nothing to happen?

Many believed, in the words of one law school professor and former colleague, that "if that was rape, I participated in plenty of rapes back in the seventies." The times had been different; date-rape was an unknown concept. Broaddrick was not the first woman to remember an unpleasant sexual encounter years later and conclude in retrospect it had been felonious. In the wake of the Clarence Thomas–Anita Hill hearings, women across the country had spent the last few years reviewing, often relabeling, their sexual histories.

Max Brantley wrestled with the question. "To put it crudely, I'm pretty sure he screwed her. What can I say, like everybody else, why would she be lying? I wouldn't venture a word in print in which I expressed skepticism about her account. Only two people know. There's such a lack of bad motivation, I don't want to question her.

"But all of that said, it was the seventies. People weren't as educated about correct means of sexual engagement. She was a married woman who was having an extramarital sexual affair, she called him up, agreed to meet him in her hotel room privately. Everybody always said no once. You tried again, they'd say no, and that was yes. As she said herself, this has been something in the room between my husband and me ever since. I think she was afraid he didn't fully believe it was an unwanted advance. Over time a woman who has a good marriage and a happy life and something she regrets might have reintepreted a half-hearted no as something more.

"At least, that's an alternative theory."

"SLICK WILLIE," HILLARY, AND CHELSEA

BILL HAD SLID from the attorney general slot into the governorship easily. Because the Clintons were so young, the first gubernatorial campaign and election had garnered relatively wide media attention. As a result, an old friend of Bill's, writer Martha Saxton, had gotten the green light from *Life* magazine to do an intimate fly-on-the-wall profile, with pictures by her photojournalist husband, Enrico Ferorelli, of the inauguration and the happy couple's first days in the governor's mansion.

"It was to be Hillary and Bill at home, them having breakfast the first morning in the mansion, Bill with his mother—we were there for three or four days to do something intelligent and serious," Ferorelli said years later. Naturally, he acknowledged, the Clintons were excited—to be in *Life* was still considered major national exposure, though, by then, the magazine, which had gone from weekly to monthly, was in a steep editorial and circulation nosedive.

But the words and pictures never made it into print, disappointing the Clintons, and infuriating Saxton and Ferorelli.

According to the photographer, the feature was killed by then-executive editor Eleanor Graves, wife of Ralph Graves, powerful editorial director of Time, Inc. "I was told," the shooter said, "that Eleanor killed it because—and these are the exact words—'Hillary's as ugly as a dog.'"

A chuckling Graves claimed she had no memory of the story, or of having spiked it. "You know," she added, "we say a lot of things that are confidential when we're laying out a story. We don't expect them to go around the world. Indeed, Hillary may have looked like a dog—I say 'may' because I have no memory of it. But what I've seen of her of that era she was no beauty."

Graves suggested talking to Phil Kunhardt, *Life*'s managing editor back then, with whom she often made editorial decisions. But he went blank on the subject, too. "If they say that's what happened, I guess that's what happened, but I have no memory of it. However, Hillary looked pretty mousy back then. John Loengard was the picture editor, he would have made the assignment."

Loengard, in fact, did remember the spiked file. "I don't remember Hillary looking goofy, and I don't remember Hillary being Sandra Dee. Photogenically, it was not an interesting story like a Jack and Jackie who were two *very* photogenic people with very photogenic props doing very photogenic things," he said. "Eleanor [Graves] was more prone to discuss the looks of people, she made such judgments often—but that didn't kill stories. The pictures were nice, but not terribly interesting. It wasn't compelling."

Whatever happened in the hallowed halls of *Life*, the editor's feelings about Hillary's looks had, in fact, reflected the views of many of the citizens of Arkansas who considered her quite unattractive.

Bill's first term was not terribly smooth. More than one observer has compared it to his first two years in the presidency.

"I've said that in my classes," said Addington. "Basically, I equate the first term of his presidency to the first term of his governorship. Because he just didn't understand that you've got to work with Congress, the legislature, in Arkansas, even though you may not have total respect, you've got to work with the system. They were trying to do too many things, not fulfilling any of the goals he set out to do, went in with a real arrogant attitude with the legislature, couldn't work well with them.

"He and I had a lot of words that first term. Things didn't get done. You'd go up there to that office, there'd be a whole bunch of guys running around acting like big shots, not tending to business. I think the thing is, a lot of that went to everybody's head."

Many put the blame on what everyone called the triplets who served as top aides that first term—Steve Smith, Rudy Moore, and John Danner. All were bearded, intense, and liberal; for many, they served as useful lightening rods for any general frustration with Clinton's office, which was common. The "Boy Wonder," as he was called—along with other less savory sobriquets such as "Baby," the "Kid," and a throwaway line picked up from a letter to the editor and made popular by John Robert Starr, "Slick Willie"—could often appear to be all over the map those first years.

Part of it was that the campaign never ended, where he was concerned—the urge to connect, one on one, with everyone he met, to shore up their love, to hear them out, was as strong as ever. He truly was the perpetual candidate, whether he was running a campaign at the moment or not. "He governs as a campaign," John Brummet said. "He's always got a drama, always got a big issue, big vote, big election. His career's been on the line so many times, it's a cliché."

Unfortunately, there were only so many hours in the day. Bill tended to tell everyone to come up and see him sometime if they had a problem, and most of them did, clogging the offices, screwing up any possibility of a schedule, driving his staff up the wall. Told that security was holding a guy who said he was sent to kill the governor, Rudy Moore passed the information on to the scheduling officer with a scribbled note: "See if you can work him in."

Bill's habit of wanting to please everyone, find common ground with all, also came to haunt him. Rose Crane, a childhood friend who worked in his first governor administration, felt this sprang from what she thought of as the "umm hmm" problem.

"His natural inclination is always to talk, that's how he synthesizes his decision," she said. "But that also creates the problem of people thinking he has agreed with them. He talks to everybody, a broad sample of people, and he says 'umm hmm.' It's not 'umm hmm, I agree with what you're saying,' it's 'umm hmm, I hear you and understand you.'

"But these people—when he'd say 'umm hmm,' they thought he had agreed with them. Then when he'd make a decision, they'd say, 'Well, that's not what he said to me.'"

It also became known rather quickly that Bill tended to lavish a great deal of energy trying to convert enemies into friends—much more, often, than he lavished on the friends themselves. The tale is told of how one pro-Clinton legislator, fed up with his inability to get an audience with the governor, finally took the floor at the capitol to bitterly oppose one of Clinton's pet projects. Within a short time, he was summoned to the inner office. "How could you do this to me?" Bill raged. "You're supposed to be on my side."

"Governor, I've been trying to see you for three weeks—this was the only way I could think of to get your attention," the man replied.

Bill also began a practice that would last throughout his entire stint as governor—keeping a running dialogue (monologue, mostly) going with various Arkansas journalists. For years, many would get used to seeing articles they'd written come back from the governor's mansion covered with comments, corrections, asides, suggestions of various readings, penned in his usual hasty scrawl. Bill was incapable of giving up the idea that one on one, man to man, he could convince anyone of his point of view.

They got used to his temper, too. One morning Ernie Dumas, who wrote editorials for the *Gazette*, picked up a ringing phone and was greeted by a burst of gubernatorial vitriol. It took him a few minutes to figure out exactly what the problem was.

"All I hear is this stream of epithets—'You goddamn son of a bitch, this is the worst piece of lying shit'—just went on and on. I said, 'Wait a minute. What are you talking about?'

"Then he kind of calms down—'This is Bill Clinton.' I said, 'I know who it is, what are you talking about?' He says, 'This goddamn editorial this morning, this is the biggest bullshit I've ever heard of'—just goes on and on.

"I was trying to grab a paper with my other hand, saying 'What are you talking about?' I couldn't remember which editorials were in that morning. I said, 'Well, which one?' That first one, on higher education. Criticizing something. I said, 'Well, Governor, I didn't write that editorial. You didn't? 'No, it's Jim Powell. Hold on a second, let me get Jim.'"

Clinton paused for a second, then sighed. "Oh, shit, don't bother, I got it out of my system,'" he said.

He then launched into a friendly twenty-minute conversation.

"Even if I had written the editorial, he would have wound up the conversation wanting me to feel good about him," said Dumas. "He would not have allowed that conversation to end on a harsh note. Never did. Even when he'd sound off he'd find a way to come back, smooth it over, try to make me feel good about him. He does not want *anybody* to go to bed feeling bad about him."

At the end, Dumas told him, mischievously, that he would be sure to pass on his feelings about the editorial to Powell. "Oh, hell no, don't do that," said Clinton. "It'll just get Jim upset. Forget about it, no big deal. I just picked it up and it pissed me off."

Most observers are in agreement in general about what doomed Bill's first term in office, causing him to be resoundingly defeated in his 1980 reelection bid by savings and loan executive Frank White.

"It's what I used to call the five C's," said David Matthews. "Cubans, car tags [Clinton had raised the fees, slightly, infuriating people], coat-tails—the people who were voting for Reagan—Carter, and Clinton. The people who voted against him were mad about Cubans, mad about car tags, wanted to see a Republican sweep, they were mad at Carter and associated Bill Clinton with him—or they were just mad about Bill Clinton. Because he was kind of arrogant, that first term, he'd tried to change too much, embraced so many projects, and people would call and try to talk to him and Steve and Rudy wouldn't let them through."

The Cubans were boatlift refugees, several thousand strong, who were being held at a resettlement camp in Fort Chaffee; in June 1980 a hard-core contingent rioted, burning the camp, wreaking havoc. Addington, who was on the scene as public affairs commander for the Arkansas National Guard, was impressed with Clinton's handling of the situation. He called out the National Guard, "stood up to Jimmy Carter." In all, he felt, Clinton acquitted himself well. But the image of wildly rioting Cubans stayed in the electorate mind—mainly because the Republican candidate for governor, Frank White, kept replaying the footage.

The year 1980 had started well for Bill and Hillary; on February 27, Hillary gave birth by Caesarian section to their first and only child, Chelsea Victoria. There were rumors galore surrounding Hillary's pregnancy; some were calling it an immaculate conception (everyone had heard tales of Bill's adulterous activities); some believed the Clintons had planned to visit a fertility clinic before the pregnancy; others were sure the conception had been sheer accident. Gennifer Flowers, who maintained Bill had initially told her he was sterile because of a bout with the mumps as a child, was infuriated—though she had already discovered the tale itself was a myth, she said, since she herself had gotten pregnant by Bill in 1977 (he had paid for the abortion), according to her tell-all memoir.

Whatever and however, the Clintons were thrilled beyond measure by their beautiful little girl—and this would be one thrill that would not dim with time. Even the most rabid Clinton haters give them points for being deeply involved, caring parents.

Paul Fray, seeing Chelsea for the first time, was fulsome in his praise. "I told him, 'Billy boy, you did a good job, you brought a little girl into the world who looks a whole hell of a lot like your mama.' He just smiled, like man, I've done the right thing." He told Virginia the same thing. "I said, 'Well, you never had a daughter but Billy's got a daughter now that looks a whole lot like you.' And it was like I had just turned on this big old huge light." Virginia thus joined the ranks of millions of mothers-in-law who discover to their shock that somehow even the least congenial daughters-in-law can manage to turn out the greatest grandchildren in the world. She and Chelsea—who called her Ginger—would have an especially close relationship.

Telegrams and presents poured in from everywhere. Carolyn Staley, Bill's longtime friend and neighbor back in high school, had decided to go with simple and tasteful—when her daughter had been born, her husband had brought her a bud vase with three roses, two red, one pink, and she thought it would be nice to repeat the gesture. She drove over to the governor's mansion, letting herself in at the kitchen door. In the dining room were hundreds of mammoth bouquets, sent from people around the country, covering every surface in the room, spilling out into the hall. The smell was overpowering. Staley set her bud vase down and walked away.

A trained musician, Staley then decided to write a song about Chelsea. She made an appointment to come over and sing it to them. Bill later told her it was one of the best presents they'd gotten. Hillary's response was somewhat different. Staley's song included the words, "We may not be worthy, but we'll try to be wise," and Hillary, miffed, took strong exception. "Nice song, but who's not worthy, Carolyn, you and your tape recorder?" she demanded. The very hint of a suggestion that she might not be totally capable of the task—of any task—galled her. Humility was not part of Hillary's makeup.

Still, one of the few self-deprecating tales Hillary has ever told publically involved her first few days as a parent—nursing Chelsea in the hospital, she was terrified to see milk pouring out of her nose. A nurse calmed her down, telling her to hold her up a little more. Later, Hillary said, she had a firm talk with her infant, telling her they were both new at this mother-daughter business, but would improve with time.

It was much more natural for Hillary to be deprecating about others, not herself. In the *Man from Hope* video—at least, the longer version shown at the Hope, Arkansas, railroad depot museum—Hillary told a tale about Bill, who was watching their three-month-old roll over on the bed, mesmerized. It was meant, clearly, to illustrate Bill's great delight in parenthood.

"He yells, telling me to come in quick and I thought he was going to tell me she was rolling over which of course I *knew* . . . but no. He said, look at this, she rolls over to the edge of the bed and then rolls back, she must understand gravity! And I said, 'Oh, right,' and about twenty minutes later I hear this plunk, as my daughter unlearns gravity, right?"

It has the sound of reality, also of a tale told often, but perhaps not always to illustrate Bill's endearing ways as a father. As any parent of a newborn knows full well, such a story is only amusing long after the cries have died down, the recriminations have ceased—and the doctor, quite possibly, has been called in.

Hillary's book, *It Takes a Village*, is laced with anecdotes about Chelsea, every one of them underlining a moral truth, or wise point of some kind. This is natural, given the book's subject matter—the raising of children in America. But it is revealing as well, particularly of the author's rigidity, at least as a public figure. Life is real, life is earnest, and simply getting a kick out of your kids is not its goal. Undoubtedly, Hillary, like any parent, has occasionally laughed herself silly over something Chelsea has said or done—but such a thing is not for public consumption.

The contrast with her mother-in-law is noteworthy—Virginia Kelley in her book tells about Chelsea getting furious because she wouldn't let her help wash the car in her new shoes. Later, she saw her sulking in a back room, muttering to herself, "That is the meanest woman." There is no point to such a tale. It's funny and cute and has no moral purpose whatsoever. Hillary, as always conscious of an agenda, would not have used it in a million years.

BILL'S LULLABY

PART OF THE REASON Bill's loss to Frank White in 1980 hit him so hard was the fact that it came as a total surprise. There were problems, sure—but neither Bill, Hillary, nor any of their entourage had any suspicion they would result in loss of office.

Richard Atkinson, their friend from Fayetteville, remembered Hillary flying up to vote the evening of the election. "She was happy to have 'the diversion of the campaign' over, ready to get back to work," he said. "There was no thought at all that victory would not be theirs. It was a shock."

David Matthews, though, had an uneasy feeling. As campaign manager for Benton County, he'd become increasingly worried in recent months. At the state convention's Third Congressional District caucus, held in Hot Springs in August, he'd watched as the campaign chairman went around the room, asking each county coordinator how things were going in their area.

Everyone was upbeat, totally confident. "They're all saying, 'Frank who? Why, he's nowhere. We're gonna beat him, no problem, we'll get 55–60 percent of the vote.'" Matthews was beginning to feel like an alien—he knew the story in Benton County was very different. Should he say anything?

He decided he had to. "I said, 'Look, the truth is, if he comes—this is August 15—and he stays in Benton County every day, all day, from now until the election, he might get 48 percent of the vote. We're gonna get killed there.'"

There was a shocked silence. Then Nancy Heinreicher, coordinator for Sebastian County, spoke up. It was the same with her county, she announced. He was going to get killed there, too.

"Six weeks later, the election is held and Clinton did not carry a single county in the Third Congressional District," said Matthews. "Not one. The place where he ran for Congress and had almost beaten Hammerschmidt six years before—he did not carry a single county."

White hailed it as a victory for the Lord. The Clinton people were crushed. Overall the loss had not been huge. Still, it was a heavy blow; the scene at headquarters was grim. "Oh, God. Like a wake. Like a funeral," said Meredith Oakley, a *Gazette* reporter, who was there. "People there were grieving. Not just unhappy or sad, grieving. He made his goodbye to the troops. And little old husky Roger Clinton was pounding the air with his fist—'We'll be back, we'll show them.'" Hillary alone seemed to be handling the situation with aplomb, she noticed; she was calm, noticeably dry-eyed.

Bill, reeling, went into free fall for several months. According to some reports, he haunted supermarket aisles, apologizing to everyone he met. Others have taken issue with this—Bill never actually apologized, they say, not for anything he'd done. Bill wasn't big on doing that. What he was sorry about was that he had lost (just as, years later, he'd be extremely sorry about being caught).

"I think he was really numbed by that defeat," said Oakley. "It didn't mean he believed *he* had done wrong, though. If you look at his apologies, they're basically that he didn't do enough to explain to people what he was trying to do. But the wind was sincerely knocked out of him. He didn't expect to be defeated, that didn't happen."

John Brummet felt he was not so much depressed as obsessed. Endlessly, he analyzed the returns, trying to figure out how the unthinkable had happened. Being Bill, none of this went on privately, of course.

"If you'd go to jog at the junior high track he might be there, run along with you awhile, just to analyze. Not to say he was sorry, but to analyze. You'd see him on the sidewalk."

Once, Brummet pulled over and asked if he needed a lift. Bill, on the way to pick up his car, said sure, and hopped in. "In the three blocks it took us to get to the car dealership, he did a soliloquoy on political analysis, what went wrong, why he got beat, how he might come back. Just obsessed. I was just somebody to be there while he did more analysis, out loud."

Bill's closest friends and supporters were as stunned—and as miserable—as he. "It was a pretty hard year, for me," said Rose Crane. "My mother died, and he lost the race. A dreadful year." Only the deepest loyalty could lead a person to equate the two events, but Bill's friends were the most loyal in the world.

Two of those friends, however, were now summarily ejected from the Clinton circle, if not for all time, at least for many years to come: his aides, Steve Smith and Rudy Moore (John Danner had been cut loose some time before). They had been convenient whipping boys throughout the past two years; it was only natural they receive the direct brunt of the loss.

It was Hillary, not Bill, who delivered the blow, and with her usual lack of restraint. "She blamed them for losing, for causing him to lose. She was not diplomatic in how she told them that and there were some hard feelings," said one close observer.

"Steve Smith and Clinton didn't speak again for about a dozen years," said Ernie Dumas, a good friend of Smith's. The night before Bill's first inauguration as president, he held a party in Washington for members of his first gubernatorial administration, most of whom had been estranged from him for years.

"Steve told me a couple of days later, he'd decided he wasn't going to go, then figured, what the hell, he'd go on, and he goes to this thing at the Mayflower or someplace, and Clinton comes up and gives him a bear hug.

"He said, 'You know for eight or nine years in the 70s, he was my closest friend in the world. We were just inseparable companions. All of a sudden I never saw him for ten years. He never had anything to do with me, shunned me. I see him, the night before he's sworn in—he's teary-eyed, gave me a bear hug, we talked about forty-five minutes. It was like nothing ever happened. Nothing was ever said about that long silence.'"

Bill's relationship with Hillary—always so closely intertwined with his political career—floundered badly after the loss. Hillary had little patience with weakness, and no interest in being paired with a loser. Some observers have thought her choice to step in at this point, take the reins, hire tough consultants like Betsey Wright and Dick Morris to help him regain his seat, were all fueled by a desire to save her marriage. But the marriage had never been a separate entity; without Bill's career, without the cause, the race to the top, the marriage itself was empty, a drained vessel.

Besides hanging around jogging courts and supermarkets, Bill filled his time with his usual extracurricular activities, probably stepping up the pace even more. The atmosphere at home was distinctly chilly. Hillary was no shelter-from-the-storm helpmate. In the years to come, it would be noted frequently, she reserved her true anger for the times he had strayed from the path of political viability. That was to her the truest infidelity. A friend recalled visiting him at home during these months, to find him sitting on the floor with baby Chelsea, crooning softly over and over, "I wanna divor-orce."

By the end of the year, the game plan had been reenacted. Bill and Hillary were coconspirators once again. There was no more talk of divorce.

With the advice of their consultants, they made a number of flight corrections. For one thing, they realized Paul Fray and Virginia Kelley's instincts had been right all along: Hillary would have to change her name. The good people of Arkansas had been puzzled and confused that the wife of the governor refused to take his name; even savvy pro-Clinton types agreed. "Why give them that to hit you with?" asked journalist Gene Lyons.

And it wouldn't hurt to get a little fashion advice and do something about that hairdo as well. Hillary's looks may not have been the crucial deciding point in Bill's loss, but there was no question they hadn't helped either.

It was not just her looks, of course—it had never been. Hillary and Arkansas had not managed to warm up to each other in the past six years, and never would. She would earn respect, but outside of her academic friends in Fayetteville, her law firm friends in Little Rock, and a few others, little true affection. While Bill seemed to want to gain everyone's love, she almost appeared at times to purposely repel it—acting cool and abrupt with his oldest friends, giving them the impression they weren't worth her time.

"I remember talking to her on the phone once," said Carolyn Staley. "She'd called wanting information, and suddenly—I thought we were in the middle of a conversation—'gotta go.' And she was gone. We had accomplished what we needed. My sense was, I've got a lot to do, I'm on the clock."

Most of them struggled to accept her. She was Bill's wife, after all. ("It wasn't rude, it wasn't intended personally," Staley rushed to explain.) But it wasn't easy.

"We Southerners," said one, simply, "don't know how to understand Hillary." Many chalked her behavior up to her native origins. "She's a damn Yankee—there's Yankees and there's *damn* Yankees and you know the difference," said one Hot Springs loyalist—of Bill's, not Hillary's.

"There's a Southern mentality and then there's a non-Southern mentality," longtime friend Carrie Owen explained, somewhat more tactfully. "The Southern mentality often can be received as warmer and more inviting. That doesn't mean the Northern can't be the same way, but . . ." she trailed off.

Actually, though, even some Northern family members such as Helen Dowdy had noted Hillary's off-putting ways, long before she left home.

It was her style, her manner—aimless socializing held no appeal for her. There was always a book to read, work to be done, a goal to achieve. When relatives came to the house, Hillary would be cordial enough—but like as not, disappear into her room. It was not meant as an insult; it was just the way she was. Still, it was hard not to get the impression you had been deemed unworthy of her time.

But as the campaign for 1982 got underway, Hillary seemed to make more of an attempt to be consciously pleasant, at least in public. Not that everyone was taken in. "When she makes the effort to be nice, courteous, generous—to me it always seems like a facade, there's an agenda, she'd just as soon slit your throat," said Brummet. Still, she was trying, for the first time, to be an asset as a political wife, not just behind the scenes.

Bill—both Morris and Wright were agreed—would also have to

apologize to the voters. He balked, but finally came up with a wording he could live with. His daddy had never whipped him twice for the same thing, he said in a thirty-second political commercial; reelected, he would not make the same mistakes again. It was vague enough, but his handlers were happy with it, until the returns came in—voters hated it. The ad reminded them of all the reasons they'd voted against him in the first place. It was a lesson Bill took to heart. Even years later, when the entire country wanted nothing so much as a sincere, heartfelt apology, he would be stonily reluctant to oblige. The apologies, when they finally came, would be diffuse, repetitive, canned—and too late, as well.

As the 1982 election neared, it was time for some fine-tuning. Bill, Hillary, and their consultants had spent weeks analyzing every barrier to success, and come up with a big one: the conservative managing editor at the *Arkansas Democrat*, John Robert Starr.

Starr had been on Bill from the beginning, like white on rice. Dumas remembered getting a call from Betsey Wright, early in the 1982 campaign. Bill, she said, was worried about Starr—how could he run, how could he serve, if the conservative *Arkansas Democrat*, a statewide newspaper, was going to continue to harass him nonstop?

"It was true, too," said Dumas. "Everybody had been savaged, all his aides, there'd been cartoons drawn about them, editorials, the whole resources of the paper were turned against him. Bill said, 'How can I ask anybody to serve in my administration if we're going to be hammered like that?' Was it possible to neutralize the *Democrat*? And they'd figured out it was Starr, he dominated the paper, everybody imitated Starr, all the headline writers and commentators took their cue from Starr."

So the obvious answer had to be—fix Starr.

Dumas thinks Hillary was probably the one who figured out how to do it. Starr was a man of obvious and gargantuan ego. His column was published seven days a week, 365 days a year. "The world could not go on without him," said Dumas. Hillary set out on a mission to turn him around. She forged a friendship, meeting him for lunch, calling him for advice. And bit by bit, her efforts began to bear fruit.

"You could see it," said Dumas. "You'd see something in his column saying, Clinton's learned a lot from his defeat. He's a different kind of person, he's developed humility. He'd write about how Clinton had called him up, asked him what he thought about something, would call him to remark on a column. And he'd mention Hillary, how Hillary had talked about how much her daddy loved Starr's column." When Starr had a heart attack a few years later, he reported in his column that Bill and Hillary had come to the hospital to see him.

The Clintons, Dumas thought, had played the man like a saxophone. "He came totally around, and the paper really was neutralized. There was no more harassment." Not infrequently Dumas and Brantley, both from the far more liberal *Arkansas Gazette*, would run into Hillary having lunch with Starr in downtown Little Rock. They always made it a point to go up and say hello. Hillary's smile on those occasions was steely.

The gambit had worked—so well that a year after Bill had been reelected, Dumas had what he counts as his most surreal experience in his career as a journalist. Bill had convinced the *Gazette* he was determined to do something about public education; in the end, his only substantive act that term was to add a penny sales tax. Disappointed, Dumas took him to task editorially, calling it a "vast missed opportunity for a great leap forward."

He expected a call—but not the one he got. The call that came was from John Robert Starr, managing editor of the *Democrat*. "Who hated us! And attacked us every day!"

"Look," said Starr. "I know how you feel and you're right. But Bill is going to come back and get the second bite. This is just the first."

Dumas, stunned, felt he had been dropped into an alternative universe. The Republican newspaper was calling the Democratic newspaper to run interference for the Democratic governor. "Absolutely the most bizarre thing that ever happened to me, in all my years of journalism."

Starr himself, a political columnist at the *Gazette* (which consumed the *Democrat* in 1991, becoming the *Arkansas Democrat Gazette*), admitted in interviews before his death in April 2000 that he rode Bill pretty hard in 1980. "A lot of people believed if I had not opposed him, he would have won, and Clinton was one of them," he said. "I was the first discordant voice, his first critic, the only one really hammering at him, right on up to election."

The first time Starr recalled meeting Hillary was after the election, when Bill spoke at a roast given for him. "He was pretty nasty," he remembered. Hillary, though, made a "tremendous" impression. "I decided, believe it or not, that any man that woman would marry couldn't be all bad," he said. They began to have regular lunch dates.

"Hillary and I talked about her husband all the time," said Starr. "She would say, 'I know you don't agree with me on this,' and I would say, 'Now, Hillary, the only thing you and I don't agree on is whether your husband is worth a damn.'" Hillary, he said, assured him frequently she knew he was acting out of principle, that it was nothing personal.

Clearly, Hillary had learned enough about charm to impress Starr, who found her a woman of fine intelligence and high principles. Bill, too, began to keep in touch. "He would call with a problem, I'd say, 'What do you want to do with it?' He kind of considered me a father figure," Starr claimed.

Starr did not support Bill in 1982—but he did refrain from trashing him. Bill was pleased. The morning after his reelection, Starr got a call. "He said, 'We won, what do you want?' I was just flabbergasted— are you aware I didn't vote for you? 'Yes, I am, but you didn't write anything bad about me, so we won, what do you want?'

"I said I don't want anything except for you to be a good governor. Which kind of took him aback. I guess he was accustomed to dealing with people who wanted something."

The friendly connection lasted a number of years. In 1987, when Bill aborted his presidential run, he and Starr had a private conversation.

"I said, 'You don't have a Gary Hart problem, do you?' And he said, 'Well, yes, I do. Do you want to hear about it?'" He obviously wanted to talk about it, but Starr stopped him. "If he was going to tell me about betraying Hillary then I could not have ever supported him again, I liked her so much. Anyway, I didn't get told. That may have been a bad mistake."

By the time Bill announced for the presidency in 1991, Starr had once again grown extremely disillusioned with him; later he expanded this view to include Hillary. Being first lady had gone to her head, he believed. He'd never seen that in her before. The phone calls and lunch dates had long ceased; Starr has had no contact with the Clintons for years.

Once, when they were still lunch partners, he asked Hillary what she wanted to do herself. "I want to run something," she told him. Her appointment as head of the health care task force, made just five days after Bill's inauguration, had been her "payoff," he thought.

HILLARY'S HEALTH CARE SECRET

HEALTH CARE HAD BEEN an ongoing interest of Hillary's, along with children's issues. But an incident that occurred in her own family during Bill's reelection campaign, in the summer of 1982, had undoubtedly brought it more sharply to her attention.

Hillary, accompanied by two-year-old Chelsea, her mother, Dorothy, and her brother Hughie, had gone to Florida to attend the wedding of Oscar and Helen Dowdy's oldest child, Kim.

Along with Hughie and Tony, Kim Dowdy had been attending the University of Arkansas. Tony dropped out, but Hughie had stayed, receiving a master's and a law degree. The brothers, always close, had taken over Bill and Hillary's old house after they'd left Fayetteville. The house quickly became a typical student disaster area, the housekeeping utterly neglected.

Hillary had not had much time available for family get-togethers, or vacations of any kind. The wedding offered a chance for both, and she took it eagerly. But her relaxation was short-lived. A day after the July 5 ceremony, she called the Dowdys—Dorothy had been taken to the emergency ward of a local hospital, suffering from what looked like an attack of kidney stones.

Oscar Dowdy quickly arranged to have his aunt transferred to a better hospital in the area, then went down to visit her. Dorothy Rodham, lying in her bed, was spitting mad—and not at the accommodations. Dowdy asked what the problem was.

"I can't afford this! I don't have any health insurance," Dorothy cried.

"What do you mean?" said Dowdy, shocked.

"Hugh is covered by the Veterans Administration, but he's too cheap to buy medical insurance for me!"

Dowdy was flabbergasted. "I couldn't believe it," he said. "I thought, 'Jesus Christ, this is insane! He's supposed to be a shrewd businessman, a fairly intelligent guy. Anybody who has the means and doesn't have health insurance for his wife'—that really threw me for a loop."

"You're kidding, right?" he said to her.

"No—that cheap old grump won't pay for it," said Dorothy.

Dowdy knew Dorothy had told Hillary. "If she complained to me, I'm sure she complained to Hillary and everyone else—'I don't have health care, I don't have medical insurance.' It had to have been discussed." Dorothy had certainly never been the type to suffer in silence.

She stayed in the hospital for two days; luckily no surgery was necessary. Dowdy was never sure who handled the bill. "I would assume that maybe Hillary paid it just to get her out of there, then Hugh paid her back."

In retrospect, it seemed to him Hillary's interest in universal health coverage might well have taken a giant leap right then—with the realization that her own mother didn't have it.

"I'm sure she remembered that—how could she forget?" Dowdy certainly never did. "It just seemed totally absurd that somebody who could afford health insurance wouldn't provide it for his wife." And if not, how likely was it that he would have provided it for his kids, either? Everyone in the family knew how cheap Hugh was—Dorothy had complained about it often enough when Dowdy was growing up in Chicago, rarely making any inroads that he could see. "She wants this, she wants that, let her want," Hugh used to say, shrugging it off. Still, this struck him as beyond the pale.

Yet a few months later, both Oscar and Helen Dowdy were witness to one of the few loving moments they had ever seen between Hugh and Dorothy Rodham.

The occasion was Bill's exuberant second gubernatorial inauguration at the mansion in January 1983; the cause was not their son-in-law's success, but a new mink coat, given by Hugh to Dorothy. The Dowdys had never seen either of them so happy.

"They were almost giddy with each other," said Helen Dowdy. "She was really, really happy with it, and it seemed like he was happy she was happy." Hugh, genially expansive for one of the few times in his life, urged Helen to try it on. "That's her new coat, you have to try it," he said.

Helen demurred, but agreed to try on the coat when Hugh insisted. "It was obviously a big thing between the two of them," she said. "That was the first time I saw some peace between them. Real peace, no bickering for once.

"It was the mink coat that did it."

Back in the big house, the Clintons resumed their hectic lives, glad to be on track once again. During the interim, Bill had practiced law in a desultory fashion at Little Rock's most prestigious firm, Wright, Lindsey & Jennings, given a few lectures here and there, but funneled the greatest part of his energies towards the task of coming back. There was no question that getting back in the game—the only game that counted for him—was all he wanted.

The loss had been deeply traumatic, though. From here on in, his primary motivation, above all else, would be his determination never to have it happen again. This would change him in ways both subtle and direct—he would become less the risk taker, more the compromiser; he would lean heavily on the use of polling; and he would depend far more strongly on the advice of political experts—Wright, Morris, and others. His career would thus become a far more well oiled machine—and whatever was discarded in the way of beliefs, spontaneity, innocence, moral fiber, there was no question that the new course would succeed overwhelmingly in at least one respect: Bill Clinton would *never* lose an election again.

*   *   *

It was no real secret, long before it exploded publicly, that Bill had a little brother problem. Roger, his adoring half brother, six years younger, was a wild man, reckless, immature, a three-time college dropout rock musician with a full-fledged cocaine habit. The Clintons would later put the expected spin on the story—Bill hadn't known for sure, he had had suspicions, but that was all, he maintained. "Suspecting is not mutually exclusive from being taken by surprise. You hope against hope," Betsey Wright parsed, later.

Still, it is unlikely Patty Roddenberry was the only one to have encountered Roger's problem directly, before his arrest.

Roddenberry and her husband ran a popular Italian restaurant, Rod's Pizza Cellar, in Hot Springs, one of Bill's favorite stopping-off places when he was in town. A fellow graduate of Hot Springs High who had double-dated with Bill in her younger days, Roddenberry was close to Virginia, and intensely loyal to the family.

It did not make her blind, however. Roger had taken to dropping by her restaurant frequently, invariably ordering a $2.35 sandwich. "He was a spoiled brat," she said. "One day he stood up, whistled, snapped his fingers, and yelled at the waitress, 'Hey, bitch, come here!'

"You don't do any of those things in my restaurant and certainly not in succession. I was out of the kitchen in a flash." Roddenberry, a solid-sized woman, grabbed him by the arm. "I told him, 'I don't need your business or your damn $2.35. Get the hell out of here and I don't want to ever see you again.'

"You can't talk to me that way! My brother's the governor!" Roger howled, trying to shake her off.

"Oh, yeah? Good," said Roddenberry. Holding him in a firm grip, she marched over to the phone, called the operator, and asked to be connected to Bill at once in the governor's mansion. "I said, I want him found now. I have his brother and I want to talk to him."

Roger managed to jerk away and get out the door before Bill picked up the phone. Roddenberry was characteristically blunt. "I said, 'It's none of my business, but your brother's on drugs of some sort. I strongly suggest you come down on him big time, or your butt's gonna be in big-time trouble. And you might save his life.'"

"Did you call Mother?" Bill asked immediately.

"No, that wouldn't do a damn bit of good," said Roddenberry, who knew, as did everyone, how Virginia felt about her sons—criticize either of them to her face and you became an enemy for life. "I'm calling you."

To Roddenberry, at least, the arrest when it occurred came as no surprise. Sometime after her run-in, in spring 1984, the Arkansas police narcotics division, acting on a tip from an informant, set up a sting operation to nail Roger as a cocaine dealer. Bill was told of the investigation shortly after it began; he kept quiet and let the process proceed without interference. Most felt he had taken the only correct and honorable route, though it is impossible to believe Virginia and Roger felt no stray pangs of betrayal, once the story became public.

After holding a press conference to announce the arrest, Bill had an emotional meeting with his mother and brother. According to Virginia's book, Roger raved about suicide. "I caused it, I'm going to end it," he howled hysterically. Bill grabbed him by the shoulders, shaking him furiously. "How dare you be so selfish!" he screamed.

After that, they calmed down, and talked for hours. "We were crying, but we were calm," said Virginia. In the months before the trial they had a number of counseling sessions with a therapist, Karen Ballard. For the first time, the three of them discussed Virginia's habit of denial—which Bill admitted he himself was prey to—as well as stepfather Roger Clinton's alcoholism, and how it had affected the family. Bill was fascinated with the concept of the child-of-alcoholic syndrome, which appealed to him greatly; he would refer to it many times in the future. In some ways, he was almost a textbook example of one type—the savior, the achiever, whose deeds are meant to validate the entire family. There was something else about this theory that appealed to him—as with all the other popular syndromes now in common parlance throughout the country (battered wife, abused child, etc), the main message was that none of this was your fault; these were the cards you had been dealt. Wasn't your responsibility to change it, then, comparatively weakened? Syndromes could be a way to label, to define a person; they didn't necessarily, all on their own, provide a way out, a cure.

The sessions also dealt with addiction. Roger's drug problem, of course, was central, but addictions could come in many forms. "I think we're all addicted to something," Bill told his friend Carolyn Staley, mat-ter of factly. In years to come, everyone in the country would know what he was referring to; many would agree. Yet labeling someone a sex addict was also a simplistic way of approaching the problem. It was neat, it lent itself beautifully to talk shows and bestsellers, it was certainly very all-American pop shrink, and undoubtedly allowed some people to come to terms with their problem. But wouldn't some, again, faced with such a label, simply find it a good excuse?

Addicts have fought their way back, of course (Roger Clinton him-self appears to have managed it); syndrome victims have taken charge of their lives. Defining a problem can be helpful, when it leads to treat-ment, particularly a twelve-step approach. There is no suggestion, how-ever, that Bill's participation in therapy in 1984, where he learned about these terms, changed his own behavior one iota. He filed the new information away, and proceeded to continue living his life in exactly the same manner as before, chasing women.

In January 1985 Roger was sentenced to two years; he served one. Vir-ginia, agonized, realized she had spent a lifetime babying her youngest son, and resolved to finally "stop mothering" him. Whether she was truly able to change such an ingrained habit is not known, but on the day of her funeral, eight years later, Roger Clinton moved many in the audience with his speech. "Today," he said quietly, "my mother made me become a man."

Though not widely known, Hillary herself had something of a little brother problem in the early 80s too, though nothing as notable as Bill's. Tony dropped out of the University of Arkansas in 1982, and took a series of low-level jobs—one of them, in Chicago, as a repo man, repossessing cable boxes.

Tony and Hughie, "the Boys" as they were always called, had oper-ated under a double whammy—there was the shadow cast by their tremendously high achieving older sister, plus the demands of their blustering father, who had no problem letting them know they were failing to measure up to his expectations the way his daughter had. Hughie, who as oldest had received the brunt of his father's criticism, earned a law degree; Tony, a freer type, dropped out. Yet both yearned for nothing more than their father's respect.

"They both always wanted to be like their old man—a wheeler-dealer," said Oscar Dowdy. "They always seemed to be looking for the big score."

In September 1999, this desire, still strong, would land them in hot water, when they attempted to set up a $118 million deal to import hazelnuts from Russia—a deal that had been arranged through the good offices of a Russian political boss who had been accused of having close ties to the Russian mob. The White House, learning the truth, was livid. Under pressure, the boys backed out of the deal. "It would be nice . . . if [Clinton] kept a tighter leash on his own brothers-in-law," commented *Washington Post* writer David Ignatius. Three months later, it turned out they had not completely cut off the hazelnut connection after all—Tony admitted he was still involved in the distribution end of the project. "We do not approve," said the White House, icily.

In the early 1980s, Tony's repo job took him into rough Chicago neighborhoods—and as is not uncommon in the trade, involved him in a number of brawls as well. "It wasn't like he did jail time, but I know he was in trouble a couple of times," said Dowdy. "Probably for bopping somebody."

Hillary, aware of the situation, angrily cut off all contact—she did not speak to her youngest brother for a number of months. When the Clintons arranged to take a vacation in Sanibel, Florida, Dowdy seized the chance to orchestrate a truce; he came down to visit, bringing both boys. "I just told Hillary, I'm bringing Tony with me and you guys have got to quit this bullshit," he said. "You're brother and sister—you have to bury the hatchet." The visit went well, and the Rodham siblings were reconciled.

Bill may have learned something about the uses of prudence and caution in his political life, but his private life in the governor's mansion was as chaotic and out of bounds as ever. The state troopers who blew the whistle on his activities later on painted a Rabelaisian portrait of the lusty young governor—constantly hopping into cars for a swift bout of sex, frequently dropping off for quickies during his morning jogs, entertaining various women in the mansion the minute Hillary left town. The fact that conservative powers were funding the troopers cast doubt on their credibility; even David Brock, author of the original

American Spectator article in which they appeared, later came to question their veracity to some extent.

But of the primary fact—that Bill Clinton was an inveterate, unreconstructed womanizer—there could be no doubt. The rumors were constant, throughout his tenure as governor. Loyal friends fought to deny them valiantly.

Diane Lyons explained the thinking common to many at the time. "There were rumors from the beginning. And you did sort of think, well, maybe there's something to them. He obviously was a good-looking, very charismatic, engaging person. I worked for David Pryor, and there were never *any* rumors about David Pryor. So I thought maybe there is something.

"But then I became pretty well convinced there was a definite movement to discredit him, people making up stuff." The attacks by his enemies seemed so unfair, so vicious and off the wall—drugs (there was a well-publicized allegation that Bill had snorted cocaine with Roger and "had a nose like a vacuum cleaner"), murder, illegitimate babies—she found herself defending him, with more and more fervor, finally to the point of discounting the rumors about his constant affairs, too. It all seemed part of the package, just one more nasty unproven mud sling.

In this way, Bill's enemies may have actually helped him—just as later, Kenneth Starr's tactics would finally repulse people to the point of turning the tide in favor of the president.

For he did have enemies. For some reason, there was something about Bill Clinton that stuck in the craw of a great number of people. He was naturally no favorite of the right, but the enmity was more than a simple matter of political preference. A number of observers struggled to find the reason. Was it simply cultural, a leftover effect of the great 60s rift that had torn the country into opposing sides? Was it gender-based? Bill had a softness to him that appeared almost womanly to some; he was no tough football playing, deer-hunting, beer-slugging good old boy. Was it inverted snobbery—the Ivy League degrees, the Rhodes scholarship, the ties to national politics? Arkansans put a great value on not getting too big for your britches. Or was it, as some believed, a matter of racism? Did it still matter in the South that Bill was, and always had been, a staunch civil rights advocate, a man, as one put it, "without a trace of prejudice in his body."

Or was it something even simpler? "I think some of it was he was such a consummate politician, he was kind of beating everybody at their own game," said Lyons. In other words, sheer jealousy.

Newspaper editor Melinda Gassaway thought so, too.

"There's so much animosity towards him in this state. He was always the lightning rod for controversy. I've tried to analyze why — I think a lot of it's jealousy. Jealousy because he's attractive to women. Some of his worst critics are men. I think, too, like with Carter, the Southern thing — people see him, he wasn't a hunter, the culture down here can be very cruel to people who don't fit the mold. I think they see him as weak."

Rose Crane, his childhood friend, has always seen the anti-Clinton movement as "an emotional-based thing. Between 30 to 35 percent of the people are his core support, ready to fall on their sword for him no matter what he does. Then on the other side you have these people who vehemently despise him, are never ever going to vote for him no matter what he does. There's a balancing that goes on. People respond to him strongly in both directions."

Shirley Abbott, who wrote a memoir about growing up in Hot Springs, thinks the race issue cannot be dismissed. "Any time you're dealing with any subject having to do with Southern politics, if you look long enough you will find that race is at the bottom of it. It certainly has got to be an element in this, in why the Southern right wing hates Clinton so much. Really more than religion. I don't know if we're ever going to get away from that. You dig long enough and there it is."

The two groups — enemies and devotees — eyed each other coldly across a wide abyss, as far removed, as unable to grant an inch, as the prochoice and pro-life allegants. Given such an atmosphere, it was no surprise that many in the Clinton camp were deeply loath to recognize his womanizing — a hard core holding on to their belief in his innocence right up to the point when the DNA report on Monica Lewinsky's blue denim Gap dress became public knowledge. And a few even beyond that, reflecting the age-old human ability to wall off disturbing truths.

Clinton hatred was matched in strength only by the power of Clinton devotion, both passions boundless, intemperate, marked with more than a tinge of religious fervor. In this, as in so many ways, he reminded more than one of the feelings stirred up by another Southern original, one of his personal heroes — Elvis Presley.

HILLARY'S AFFAIR

Denial about the womanizing rumors may have been rampant in the Clinton camp, but such a thing was not as easy to pull off in the Clinton family. The fact that Hillary remained his wife has led many to believe she herself engaged in massive, or at least, serial, denial. Undoubtedly she overlooked what she could. But that she was aware—extremely aware—there can be no question.

Even his flirting was a thorn in her side, and Bill was an unmitigated flirt. John Brummet remembers once accompanying both of them to a hot air balloon show during one of the early governor campaigns. Immediately, getting out of the car, Bill was engulfed in a gaggle of fawning young women.

One of his aides leaned over to Brummet. "You watch, this is going to make Hillary mad," he said, snickering. Sure enough, within minutes, Hillary had stomped back to sit in the car alone, furious.

Even warm encounters with longtime women friends could get under her skin. Patty Roddenberry, a stolid woman, recalled once going to his headquarters to bring him a big mug of Diet Coke from her restaurant, when he was visiting Hot Springs—he had sent a staffer over to ask for one. In her usual casual way, she handed it to him by throwing an arm around him, "bumping him on his butt." Bill returned the hug, kissing her on the top of her head. "No big deal. Nothing more than we've ever done," she said.

But this time, from the back of the room she heard a loud, imperious throat clearing, that went through her like a blast of cold air. It was Hillary. "Real bitchy," said Roddenberry. She froze. "I took my elbow and jabbed him and went, 'Thanks for telling me Hillary was here so I didn't bring her anything, thank you very damn much.' He was grabbing his ribs because I jabbed him pretty good." Bill introduced them, but "she was really frosty." Rodenberry tried to make amends, offering to bring her something to drink, too, but Hillary said icily she would just share Bill's. Later on, when both of them came over to the restaurant for the pizza Roddenberry had promised, it was clear Hillary was still miffed. Years later, hoping to smooth out the relationship, Roddenberry spent hours scouring Hot Springs for a bagel—Hillary, she had heard, liked bagels, not exactly a native Arkansas product. She managed to find one, and presented it. "It was the best I could find," she apologized. Hillary accepted it without a word.

If this was how Hillary reacted in public, how did she respond in family settings?

One event gives a clue. In July 1986, the Clintons again went to Florida, to celebrate Hughie Rodham's marriage to Maria Victoria Arias, a vivacious twenty-eight-year-old attorney whom many have described as possessing Hillary's drive. Hughie, by now a public defender, was thirty-six and had lived in Coral Gables for a number of years, sharing an apartment with brother Tony. The Rodham boys were still very close; only his wife-to-be's adamant insistence prompted Hughie to find a new apartment, a few blocks away—and that not until the day before the wedding. He was, he later said, still hoping to convince her to move in with *both* of them.

The rehearsal dinner, given by Bill and Hillary, and Dorothy and Hugh, was held the night before the nuptials, on July 11. Shortly after the party started, though, Hillary surprised everyone when she stalked off to her room. It seemed odd to the Dowdys—the entire family was sitting in the lounge, relaxed, enjoying the evening, getting to know Maria's family and now Hillary was gone. But it was not as curious as what happened next.

214 STATE OF A UNION

Suddenly, Bill too had disappeared. Dorothy seemed particularly disturbed, Helen Dowdy noticed. "She kept saying, 'Where's Bill? I haven't seen him for a long time.' She was concerned. Really concerned."

And it quickly became apparent that yet another person was missing—one of the wedding guests couldn't find his gorgeous wife. "People were looking for Bill, and suddenly someone else was looking for his own wife," said Helen Dowdy. "Bill's gone and then this woman's gone. It was strange."

Soon "the search was on." Tony was looking, Oscar Dowdy was looking. "It was a literal search."

Bill and Hillary had come to the wedding without bodyguards, and there had been a certain amount of wink-wink, nod-nod earlier, sitting around the hotel pool with Tony and Hughie—"You know, Bill's on his own—let the fun begin." The boys, the Dowdys felt, were well aware of Bill's proclivities. Oscar Dowdy thought it great that Bill had some free time without his shadows. "Yeah, I'm pretty much on my own," Bill had said. "Well, that's cool," Dowdy offered. Bill had laughed.

Now he was gone. Dowdy, concerned, left the lounge to search in earnest. "I started down a long hall, and Bill just kind of appeared, head on. I said, we were kind of worried about you."

"No problem," said Bill. "I just had to go somewhere to get a drink of water." But the bathroom was right in the lounge, which was also where the drinks were. Dowdy eyed him a bit quizzically. "I thought, 'hmmm,'" he said.

Bill rejoined the party, looking quite cheerful. "He had that smuggy Bill thing going on," Helen Dowdy recalled. Dorothy seemed immensely relieved to see him.

The next day Oscar Dowdy felt he ought to say something. "I told him, 'I wasn't trying to stick my nose into your business, I was just concerned. I know you're the governor, but you're family—I was worried. If I stuck my nose where it didn't belong, I'm sorry.'" Bill just nodded complacently.

No one ever discovered what had actually transpired that night, but suspicions lingered for years.

The next night, at the wedding reception, Helen Dowdy, a tall, buff, attractive blonde, had even more direct contact with Bill. The band was playing a slow dance, and Bill suddenly pulled her onto the floor. The dance quickly disintegrated into a grope, with Bill squeezing her much too close for comfort. "It was a very uncomfortable feeling," she distinctly remembered. "He was holding me very close, pulling me into him. It was almost like a teenager would do. It was *so* inappropriate." She attempted to pull back, but "he's a big man."

Unsure what to do, extremely embarrassed, she was suddenly aware of yet another body pressed close to hers on the dance floor—Hillary's. "It was so weird. All of a sudden Hillary came up from behind me and put her arms around me and Bill. She blindsided me. She came up from behind, her arm went around my neck and his neck and there we were. We all just kind of finished the dance as a threesome."

Odd as it was, Helen was glad for the rescue. She had no doubt whatsoever that was what it was.

Off the dance floor, she complained to her husband. "I was irritated," Oscar admitted. "She said he got a little squeezy with his hand up there where it shouldn't have been. I said, 'If it bothers you, I'll do something,' but she said she wasn't going to make a big deal of it. It did seem like there was a little Hillary intervention—'Hey, Bill, cool it.'"

Helen was sure, especially after that experience, and the scandals that would follow, that "Bill and Hillary had to have an agreement. I absolutely, positively feel like that, one hundred percent. An agreement where the wife would say, do what you need to do as long as you don't bother me and don't get caught. I just think that's the kind of marriage they have."

Oscar Dowdy agreed. "Helen and I were not surprised by what happened. We saw over the years that Bill and Hillary—they'd be affectionate, but not overly so. Bill was a big lovable teddy bear and Hillary just kind of had that standoffish attitude with him. It just seemed like a marriage of convenience because they were both headed in the same direction politically, that was the goal, that was the deal."

It was natural for people to wonder whether Hillary also had her innings, and there, too, rumors flew. Unlike with Bill, though, specific Hillary rumors concentrated on one person, Vince Foster, her colleague at the Rose law firm, who along with Webb Hubbell seemed to be her closest friend and associate in Little Rock. The trio ate lunch together nearly every day, often sharing an after-work drink as well. They were "inseparable," said lawyer David Matthews.

Foster was tall and slim with a courtly demeanor and striking patrician good looks. He too had been born in Hope, his family's house a bare stone's throw from Bill's first home; the two had attended kindergarten together. In a less dramatic way than Bill, Foster too had been an Arkansas golden boy—top of his class, now a highly respected lawyer.

"I think women were drawn to Vince not just because he was smart and handsome but because he seemed to keep secrets," wrote Webb Hubbell in his 1997 memoir, *Friends in High Places.* Hillary, he felt, "had no male in her immediate life like us—males around whom she could be the person she wanted to be. With Vince and me, she was a warm friend and a brilliant colleague, with no strings attached. We enjoyed her, respected her, loved her, accepted her."

Once the three went on a business trip to New York together, where Foster bought Hillary a hat, putting it on his credit card. Later he asked Hubbell to reimburse him, so he could tell his wife the hat was for Hubbell's wife. Lisa Foster, who married a judge after her husband's sudden death, was apparently not pleased about the close friendship between her husband and the governor's wife.

Some dismissed the rumor of an affair as highly improbable, given the personalities involved. "All I can tell you about that is if they did, two people never enjoyed it less," said journalist Gene Lyons. "He was an extremely conscientious person, very discreet, with an old-fashioned sense of duty. If he were screwing his friend's wife he'd be so consumed with guilt he couldn't possibly enjoy it."

Others are not so sure. One former Rose law firm colleague had heard the rumors but discounted them. Then, during Bill's first presidential run, "a number of researchers for the television news shows came to town to investigate the tales about Bill's infidelities—and all they kept coming up with were the rumors about Vince and Hillary." Intrigued, he began to ask around, and finally talked with a young woman who had served as a courier for the firm during the 80s and was now living in Dallas. She, he had heard from other law firm colleagues, knew the real story.

"I said, was that a rumor or was that the truth?"

The truth, she said—she had once seen them in a passionate embrace in the building stairwell.

"It's hearsay—but I do believe the person saw it, they don't have any reason to lie."

Paul Fray—who also believed the two had had an affair—got into a discussion with another man on the subject. "He said, 'You know that woman about as well as anybody, are you aware of her and Vince's relationship?' I said, 'I don't give a damn, what difference does it make? If you were to try and make all that public, you realize what would happen?' He looked at me and said, 'Why, by God, it'll ruin her!' I said, 'No, it'll make her. Next question.'"

It was a common reaction. If even a handful of the Bill stories were true, who could blame Hillary for finding a little comfort outside the home?

"I felt like she put up with a lot," said the former law firm colleague, who had no use for Bill. "I admired her for that. I felt this was a lady sincerely committed to marriage, who had a genuine concept about what marriage was supposed to be, for better or worse. She stuck, and I admired her for it. My response to it is touché. She pales in the face of his reputation."

He had also been acquainted with Lisa Foster, Vince's wife. "I never remember being impressed with the warmth between Vince and Lisa. Vince was a little aloof, too. He wasn't the warmest guy in the world. And Lisa was sort of a perky little Arkansas girl." In fact, the personality contrast was not unlike that between Bill and Hillary, with the sexes reversed—though of course, in this case, no one was pointing to a regional cause for the difference.

There were also other, more generalized rumors about Hillary that circulated around Arkansas, and later, Washington, as well—that Hillary was a lesbian, or at least bisexual, and this was what explained their odd marriage. Such talk was perhaps not surprising in Arkansas, where Hillary stood out so dramatically against the fold as a strong personality, a feminist, a tough negotiator, someone who never shrank from adversarial action, and who seemed to have, for years, no interest in dress or makeup or appearance—not the kind of woman Southerners were used to. But the rumors persisted later, too. Mandy Merck, Bill's radical feminist (and lesbian) friend from Oxford, heard them when she visited America in the spring of 1999.

"When I was in New York and Washington, tons of people said

Hillary was gay. I heard 'lover' in New York, I heard 'lover' in Los Angeles."

But Merck asserted, "I never received a single intimation of that the two or three times I encountered her."

Two past associates of Bill's, both avid publicity seekers, also weighed in on the subject. Gennifer Flowers contributed a naughty one-liner in her book, saying Bill had told her Hillary had "eaten more pussy" than he had. One-time Clinton adviser Dick Morris made a series of vaguer comments on a Los Angeles radio talk show in early 1998. "Let's assume some of the allegations that Hillary [is] sometimes not into regular sex with men might be true," he said, offering this as a possible reason for Bill's defections. He later backed down, in the face of White House fury. (He has ruptured his relationship with the Clintons for all time, swore then–Clinton spokesman Mike McCurry.) He had, Morris insisted, just been "floating a scenario." "I do not believe Hillary is gay and I have no evidence she is gay," he declared stiffly a day later.

One particularly peculiar tale circulated among the Washington cognescenti around the time of Clinton's impeachment trial—that a well-known Washington veterinarian, visiting the White House to treat Socks the cat, had opened the wrong door and discovered Hillary locked in a passionate embrace with another woman. The oddest thing about this tale was who was telling it: it had been passed on by a stalwart Clinton loyalist, a man who had repeatedly demonstrated his willingness to fall on his sword in defense of the president.

Then again, perhaps not so odd after all. There was a huge divide between Bill people and Hillary people, which had widened ever more in the wake of the Lewinsky scandal. The two groups, at least in private, never shrank from exchanging sniper fire. To imply, or at least hint, that Bill's wife had alternative interests—what was it but a giant justification for all Bill's foibles?

But in truth, there was never a shred of hard evidence. The lesbian rumors came from publicity-seeking spinmeisters, from disgruntled ex-bimbos, from fanatic Bill-loyalists, Internet gossip columnists, and from those for whom the mere sight of a strong, successful woman was enough to set off prurient gongs. Unlike the Vince Foster rumors, these had no grounding in reality. According to one source, when informed about the gay rumors, early on, Hillary responded only with a terse three-word growl: "Fuck this shit." She refused to dignify them by rebuttal.

The Vince Foster situation, though, was different. "I had a good friend who was an attorney in Little Rock, who said part of the reason for that rumor was because of Vince's actions and reactions," said a well-placed Arkansas source. "He was different around her, there was this softness. He'd say, 'You just have to undertand her, she's never been loved.' This attorney said they all felt like there probably was a special relationship.

"She had to have somebody to talk to, somebody she trusted. She doesn't trust too many people. Whatever transpired, Vince is the one she felt she could go to, share things with."

Their law firm colleague explained it simply. "You take two people, who probably found each other to be intellectual equals, working close together on things—it would have been natural for something to happen."

There was, at the very least, a special connection between them, which makes Vince Foster's fate—he committed suicide in July 1993, only seven months after Bill took office as president—all the more tragic and complex.

"A decent, honest guy," said Ernie Dumas. "Never had anything to do with politics. Why in the world he went to Washington, a young man who was always perfect, top of his class, president, best-liked kid, goes to Davidson, then University of Arkansas law school, finishes top of his class, a top litigator, never lost a case, just a paragon of virtue, president of the bar. No one has uttered a word of criticism to him in his life, the apple of his daddy's eye, always honest.

"He goes to Washington, and first thing you knew, he was attacked in the *Wall Street Journal*. He just went crazy. People who saw him said he was totally distracted. Someone saw him a few weeks before, he was on an airplane, and didn't even know where he was going.

"If you're a lawyer in Little Rock and get a chance to go to the White House, you don't turn that down. Though I guess he should have."

Whatever the relationship between Hillary and Vince Foster was or had been, there was no question it underwent a radical shift when he came to work at the White House. Hillary was no longer a peer, she was now his superior—and one he felt he had failed, particularly in the matter of the early botched Justice Department nominations. If, as many believe, he was still in love with her, the failure would have been all the more unbearable.

In his book, Hubbell portrayed Foster as deeply upset about the change in their relationship. "It's just not the same," Foster told Hubbell. "She's so busy that we don't ever have any time to talk." His sense of grievance was acute, the feelings expressed were "more in the nature of a lament," Hubbell said.

Conspiracy buffs, especially those in the anti-Clinton camp, theorized endlessly about Vince Foster's death—had it truly been a suicide? Yet the picture of a careful, prudent man unable to deal with the overwhelming pressures and criticism that came with being thrust suddenly into the national spotlight rang true. "Here, ruining people is considered sport," he wrote in a final note, found torn to pieces in the bottom of his briefcase and pieced together much later. From all reports his behavior in his last weeks clearly bespoke growing depression. Conspiracy seekers laid a great deal of weight on discrepancies in the reports of the U.S. Park Police—a slim reed, for those familiar with the Byzantine workings of that particular bureaucracy.

Terry Guzman, who had been at law school with Vince Foster, visited the White House with her family not long after his death. Hillary did not mention his name. "The subject was clearly not to be touched," she said. "It was too close." Bill shared his pain—and everyone else's—with the world; Hillary kept hers inside, locked away. Anger she had no difficulty unleashing, jealousy, rancor, resentment, spite. Hurt, though, was private.

CHELSEA AND THE GARY HART PROBLEM

So RARE WAS IT FOR HILLARY to show anguish of any kind in public that the sight of a single tear, running down her cheek, riveted every eye. The time was July 1987; the occasion was Bill's announcement that he could not, he had decided, run for the presidency in 1988 after all. Hillary, who had encouraged the idea, appeared devastated, observers said.

The most important reason for this decision, Bill said, was "the certain impact this campaign would have on our daughter." His voice throbbed with emotion—no one doubted the utter sincerity of his desire to protect his beloved daughter, to do nothing to disrupt their relationship.

Nor did anyone doubt that the main reason a presidential campaign might prove so disruptive and disturbing to a young girl had a great deal to do with the travails of another Democrat, Gary Hart. Hart's potential candidacy—his entire political career, in fact—had been smashed to smithereens two months earlier, in May 1987, when it was revealed he was having an affair with Donna Rice. In what struck many as a spasm of pure self-destruction, Hart had actually pulled the roof down on himself, taunting the press with a challenge to "follow me—I promise, you'll be bored." They did; they weren't; and the ensuing scandal not only buried Hart forever as a national figure, it marked a watershed in relations between press and politicians in America.

From here on in, adultery or other sexual improprieties on the part of a candidate would be deemed viable campaign issues, worthy of investigation by the news media. The tacit understanding that had stood for so many generations, that such matters were not fodder for legitimate journalist inquiry—an understanding that had served so many so well, no one better than Bill's teenage hero, John Kennedy—was now officially moot.

In some ways this was the worst possible thing that could have happened for Bill. The rules had changed on him midstream—Bill who had reveled so in tales of JFK and LBJ White House dalliances. The ancient, old boy, turn-a-blind-eye collusion between politicians and press had now been ruptured for good, and the ramifications for the rest of his career would be far-reaching and dire. Because despite his famous intuitive skills, his ability to endlessly remake himself, his amazing grasp on the zeitgeist, this would be one sea change he would never be able to deal with, or even fully understand.

Even while the impeachment trial was raging, he managed at one point, speaking to a reporter, to bring up the old Lincoln anecdote—told General Grant was a drunk, Lincoln announced his intention to find out what liquor he liked, so he could send a bottle to all his other generals. The comparison with his own situation was bizarrely inappropriate, the implication unavoidable—despite everything, the president still just didn't get it.

The immediate effect though, back in 1987, was to douse his interest in a 1988 run. The atmosphere, in the wake of Gary Hart, was charged, making the current national political scene, as Dick Morris put it, "a terribly inhospitable environment upon which to tread." He chewed over the problem—was there, he asked one friend, a statute of limitations on infidelity? Would there ever be dispensation for someone who was perceived to have come through a bad time, and gotten his house in order? Perceived, of course, being the operative word.

Chelsea, though, was the reason Bill gave the world for not running in 1988. She was only seven, she needed a father, the campaign would take him away. He repeated this mantra so many times over the next year it became rote. Appearing on the Johnny Carson show in the summer of 1988, in a quick-fix attempt to rebuild his image after his disastrous nominating speech at the Democratic convention, he said it yet again. Chelsea was only seven, she needed a full-time father. The next morning he received a stony call from his daughter. "I am eight now," she informed him coldly. Bill presumably noted the correction for future use.

No one doubted the sincerity of his concern, though. The Clintons doted on their bright, active daughter, never missing a softball game, dance recital, or school program. "I can't think of a thing they could have done for Chelsea they didn't do," said Max Brantley, whose daughter Martha was a good friend. "All the things we did, they were there, too. Special math programs that required a carpool, soccer, softball, music, ballet, trips together."

They also did something else, a little less common—according to Hillary's book, *It Takes a Village*, they began quite early to coach Chelsea, using a form of role-playing, to build up her defenses against political attacks.

They started when she was six, and Bill was about to run for reelection as governor once again. Daddy is going to run again, Hillary told her one night at the dinner table, and other people may try to beat him by saying terrible things about him. They would be lies, of course, but she should be ready for them.

Chelsea didn't understand why people would lie—didn't they know it was wrong? Why would they do that?

"I didn't have a good answer for that one. (I still don't.)" said Hillary.

With Chelsea playing the part of Bill, both parents began to attack her, causing the little girl to begin to cry. After several more bouts over the next weeks, though, "she gradually gained mastery over her emotions," Hillary reported proudly. As an added device, they also had her take the part of former governor Orville Faubus, a possible opponent. The role-playing, in one form or another, continued over the years. In the end Hillary felt they had done the best they could do to protect her. She hoped the immunization would work, that they had prepared her well enough to withstand whatever came her way, never suspecting, of course, that in the end it would be not lies but the truth that would deal the most devastating blow of all.

The fact that Chelsea was an extremely aware, resourceful child comes through clearly in Hillary's book. At one point, in first grade, her parents noticed she seemed oddly unwilling to demonstrate her new reading abilities at home. Her teacher, too, when asked, said Chelsea seemed less than enthusiastic about reading in class. Eventually, Bill and Hillary figured out the problem—Chelsea was afraid if her parents knew she could read, they would stop reading aloud to her every night. Recounting the tale, Hillary seemed unaware of both its oddness and its obvious implication: that this was a young child fighting to hold onto whatever portion of her parents' attention she could, against tremendous odds.

But of the fact that both Bill and Hillary were utterly smitten, devoted parents there could be no doubt. Even their most scathing critics admitted it. "The apple of their eye, absolutely," said journalist Meredith Oakley, no particular friend.

"I was always touched by what caring, devoted, loving parents they were," said Carolyn Staley, whose two girls often babysat for Chelsea. "There was a real sense of let's get home, every minute we're away from Chelsea is too long."

On the other hand, as Chelsea herself was clearly aware, these were busy people, who lived separate lives to a great degree.

"My recollection is Bill and Hillary were apart more than they were together," said Max Brantley. "I think they covered more ground that way. If they'd gone together as a couple, they couldn't have covered as much ground. They doubled the territory. There were always dual tracks going on."

One glimpse of how their lives operated stayed with him. Early one morning, in summer 1991, before Bill had formally announced his candidacy, Brantley met him at the Little Rock airport—both fathers were putting their daughters on the plane for the German language camp in Minnesota they attended together every year. Waiting in the lounge, Bill told him Hillary had just gotten back from an education conference in Scandanavia a few hours before and was flying back out to Washington later that day.

But what struck Brantley most was that in the short time between Hillary arriving and Bill taking Chelsea to the airport—it couldn't have been more than an hour—they had managed to totally debrief each other. "He knew all about the conference she'd attended, he was regurgitating what she said." He had obviously filled her in on the status of his exploratory committee. In some supercharged cyber-speed manner, they'd been able to connect, download, reboot, and move on without dropping a line. Not unlike two sportscar racers pulling into the pit for thirty-second tune-ups, then roaring back onto the track.

It wasn't marriage, or family life, as others knew it—but when had Bill and Hillary ever had a marriage like anyone else's? After Bill's decision not to run in 1988—the decision that publicly upset Hillary and brought a tear to her eye—there were signs, once again, that things were fraying badly. His behavior had thrown a whammy into the works, deflecting his bid for at least four years, making it a true sin, in Hillary's eyes. She herself had become a much more prominent figure in the last few years, heading up the educational reform movement, traveling the state, lecturing, impressing many with her cool analytical intelligence.

"Gentlemen," announced one legislator famously, after she had appeared on the floor, "I think we've elected the wrong Clinton." There is some indication Hillary herself may have been thinking along the same lines—one persistent rumor was that she was thinking of running for governor of Arkansas next.

According to several reports, Bill had also become deeply involved with another woman around this time—though whether this meant he had cut back on his other womanizing activities is unclear. At any rate, there is at least some evidence that both Clintons did some private muttering to friends about the possibility of divorce around this time. The dream of getting to the White House had not died, after all—it had only been postponed. And while Reagan may have broken one taboo, by becoming the first divorced man to ever be elected president, his divorce had been far in the past, long before the start of his political career.

It would be entirely different were a candidate to get divorced on the very eve of a presidential run; that could hardly fail to present a problem.

In the end, Bill and Hillary ended up in pastoral marriage counseling. They would hang tough, salvage what they could, patch over the rest—and adhere to the master plan. As long as the plan was alive, divorce was, and would continue to be, unthinkable. Bill and Hillary were yoked together forever—or at least, till the end of Bill's presidency.

CLINTON VS. BUSH

WELL INTO 1991, with the success of the Gulf war still reverberating, George Bush was riding so high he seemed untouchable—there was even some jocular talk about skipping the 1992 election completely. What was the point? Bush seemed a shoo-in for reelection. No political observer could have predicted the sudden precipitous slide that would leave him so vulnerable only a few short months later.

Bill was no different. According to friends and observers, he had no expectations at all about his chances of winning a presidential run in 1992; he was as convinced as everyone else that the popular wisdom was right—Bush had it sewed up. If he ran, it would be for name recognition only, a chance to present himself as a strong potential Democratic candidate, hopefully the obvious choice for 1996.

In typical fashion, he discussed his thoughts on the subject compulsively, asking for input from nearly everyone, nearly everywhere. No setting was off limits. Warren Maus, his high school classmate, who ran into him at a governor's conference in Hot Springs in 1991, was asked for his opinion in the men's room, while the two men stood at adjoining urinals.

226

"We went to the john together, were chatting a little bit, you know, like guys do. I said, 'You gonna give it a run this time?' He said, 'I dunno, what do you think?' I said, 'What do you got to lose? You got the name recognition, with that hour and a half speech [at the 1988 Democratic convention].'

"I think at the time he had no idea he was going to really try for it," said Maus. "It was just an opportunity to get his name in the national spotlight and then run in '96. Because Bush was unbeatable."

Garrick Feldman, publisher of three small Jewish newspapers in Arkansas, heard about it while sitting with Bill on the steps of an auditorium where their daughters were about to perform in a dance recital. "It was May 1991. He told me, 'I'm going for name recognition. I'm not going to win, but I'm going to get ready for 1996.'" Feldman was sure he was one of the first to be told. Perhaps he was, at least that day. Bill had the unique ability to make nearly everyone feel like a special confidant.

Max Brantley got the news in the airport, while the two men waited to put their daughters on a plane for summer camp. "This was about four months before he announced. By that time Hillary was really pushing for it, thought it was the right decision, he told me. That seemed pretty significant to me, because I felt she was a pretty strong influence." Brantley, at least, had no illusions that he was being singled out for special treatment. Bill was just being Bill. "He lays out scenarios for all sorts of people, and listens to what they say," he said. Brantley later wrote about the incident in the *Gazette*. The two had long had an understanding that nothing Bill said to him would be off the record; it was the only way to handle it.

And Gene Lyons discussed it with him in October 1991, the day of the last Arkansas-Texas football game—ironically, also the day the liberal *Arkansas Gazette* closed its doors forever.

"We ran into them outside the stadium. He had just announced he was going to run for president, and was going around basically asking for permission," Lyons said.

Diane Lyons gave Bill a warm hug and told him she agreed, he ought to go for it. Lyons, though, "just to be perverse, just to see if I could shake something loose from the tree," reacted differently.

"I said, 'I think you all are crazy. Why would you want to do this?

It's the end of your private life forever, do you know what they're going to do to you?'"

At the time, of course, he had no way of knowing just how bad it was going to get, Lyons acknowledged ruefully.

Bill simply shrugged, undisturbed, but Hillary exploded—it was obvious Lyons had hit a nerve. "Her fear and contempt for the press all just came flying out. We had a very lively discusion for about 10 minutes—about local newspaper people and how much she hated the press, what weasels they were and how they were all working off childish grudges. You couldn't make them happy, the best thing you could do was ignore them, there was no way of satisfying them.

"She just talked about her fear of and contempt for the press and characterized them as a bunch of emotionally damaged malcontents, basically—people who make their living hurting other people."

At the time, of course, the press Hillary was referring to, the only press the Clintons had come into contact with on a regular basis, was the homegrown variety—mainly the *Arkansas Gazette* and the *Arkansas Democrat*. The *Gazette*, generally pro-Clinton, had endorsed him for every election, while the conservative *Democrat* had been under the sway of John Robert Starr, the editor they had managed to neutralize so successfully. For all her distaste, Hillary was close to being a media virgin, someone to whom the age-old charge, *"You ain't seen nothing yet,"* definitely applied. She hadn't. But that was going to change.

"I think they were stunned to find the Washington press just as dishonest and almost as mean. Meaner. Meaner because smarter. If an idiot insults you it doesn't hurt as much," said Lyons.

"I don't think they expected that."

Oddly enough, shortly after her antipress diatribe to Lyons, possibly within hours, in fact, Hillary took the time to make a private sympathy call to a member of the very group she had just been deriding so scathingly—journalist Max Brantley, who had just returned home after learning about the death of his paper, the *Gazette*.

"The paper closed, they sent everybody home with their boxes, their pitiful little belongings. Nobody knew what the next day or year was going to hold. I drove home after packing my stuff up, drove to the house, walked in, and the phone was ringing."

It was Hillary. "She'd heard about it and wanted me to know how sorry she was. At that point I was just an unemployed newspaper guy. Couldn't do a thing for her, wouldn't have known if she hadn't called, didn't expect it." To Brantley, this sort of private kindness reflected a side of Hillary he had seen before, which always impressed him, but which he felt few were aware of. She was unfailingly attentive and responsive when it came to the personal problems of others. Years later, he would see another example, when she spent an entire day on the phone attempting to track down his wife, Ellen Brantley, to let her know a mutual friend of theirs had been diagnosed with terminal cancer—at the very moment when her husband's fate was being decided in Congress.

"It was in the middle of everything, they were going to impeach her husband and bombing a foreign country, and she was calling people she knew because she knew they wanted to know. She didn't need to do it, she could have had a maid do it. She just did it, because she knew how much [our friend] meant to us," Brantley said.

He was also convinced that Hillary, in addition to making the sympathy call the day the newspaper closed, had done a little work behind the scenes to help the failing *Gazette*, toward the end. "She was on the Wal-Mart board, and I'm reasonably sure she was responsible for efforts made to see if we could get some Wal-Mart advertising."

If intelligence is, as some believe, the ability to hold two opposing views simultaneously, and act on them, Hillary, as much as Bill, clearly topped the charts. She was perfectly capable of despising the press, yet going out of her way to comfort an individual newsman.

On the other hand, her intelligence was no help to her when it came to seeing down the road. Kwan Kwan Wang, Hillary's friend from law school, who saw her in the early months of the campaign, also got the distinct impression neither Clinton had any expectation of actually winning—in fact, that they viewed it all as a sort of lark.

"My sense was that they thought they'd make a try, that they just thought they'd run, see what happens. Everyone thought Bush was not defeatable." Wang wished her good luck.

"Well," said Hillary airily, in what had to be one of the least astute judgments she would ever render, "Whatever happens, it's going to be fun, anyway."

Perhaps it was, at least at first. This was, after all, what they'd been aiming for from the beginning. Bill, as ever, was at his best on the cam-

paign trail, meeting hoards of people, impressing them with his enthusiasm, knowledge, intelligence, and charm. Reporters across the country found themselves reacting in a rare way to this candidate—they
were disarmed, intrigued, excited. So much has been made over the
last few years about the Clinton haters, it is easy to forget that many
journalists, meeting him for the first time during that first campaign,
had quite another reaction—they fell in love.

An editorial page editor at a big eastern metropolitan daily remembered interviewing Bill along with several colleagues, at a lengthy get-
acquainted session early on during the campaign. "Amazing," he said
years later. "This guy—he had read the books, he had done the research,
he *knew* what he was talking about." Impossible not to leave the room just
a bit dazed, just a bit infatuated.

The magical Bill-effect, so noted by Arkansas journalists over the
years, was still strongly in play, of course. Eric Rozenman, the editor of
a small newspaper in Florida, met with Bill early on, for a private interview. He came out dizzy, enthralled. "This man seemed to say all the
right things, to believe exactly what I believed." He rushed back to his
desk to transcribe his notes. Puzzled, increasingly upset, he searched
through his notebook for all the quotes he remembered, flipping the
pages again and again.

"There was nothing there," he said, still stunned. "He had said
nothing. Not a single thing I could use."

Bill's formal announcement that he was a candidate for the presidency on October 3 was expected by most, hailed by many, and
sharply criticized by a few—notably *Arkansas Democrat* columnist
John Robert Starr.

"Clinton ran for president without telling Starr first," said Ernie
Dumas. "He hated him for it. Bill had indicated he wasn't going to run
in 1991, Starr wrote that in his column, then he embarrassed him by
running, so he's a lying no good . . ." Of course by then, the Clintons
no longer needed his approval.

Even before the announcement, Bill and Hillary had taken it upon
themselves to defuse—they hoped—what they considered the primary
obstacle they would have to face in the campaign: the persistent
rumors about Bill's womanizing. They appeared together before representatives of the national political press at an off-the-record event held

in Washington, the Sperling Breakfast (named for Godfrey Sperling Jr. of the *Christian Science Monitor*). Reporters had been urged to ask about the rumors, but proved curiously reluctant. Finally, right at the end, one managed to pop the question.

Bill, clearly prepared, launched smoothly into his defense. He thought, of course, the subject had little to do with his ability to serve. But yes, since he had been asked, like anyone else, he and Hillary had had some difficulties over the past twenty years; but they were together now, committed to each other, and intended to stay that way.

He hoped that would be the final word on the subject; as it turned out, of course, it was only a dress rehearsal.

The womanizing issue did indeed raise its ugly head, and most dramatically, in January, courtesy of Gennifer Flowers's tell-all appearance in the tabloid *Star*. But even before that, two other problems would come up—marijuana and the draft. All three issues gave the country a good chance to see Bill in defensive mode for the first time. It was not an appealing sight.

Faced with an accusation, Bill seemed to rely on certain typical techniques—denial, obfuscation, self-pity, redefinition, wordplay, spin. As the country's first viable baby boomer presidential candidate, it was not surprising to find him being questioned about drugs and the draft. But those hoping for a direct, honest response would be disappointed.

Age-old political wisdom, of course, has it that a candidate must lie, or at least waffle, on certain subjects—to speak the truth is too dangerous. But recent years have featured a number of admissions, however tepid, from various political hopefuls, about using soft drugs in their youth, for instance—and these statements have done them no notable harm. The knotty issue of draft dodging was a more difficult matter to confront, of course—but again, Vietnam had been a situation on which honorable men had disagreed; surely there was no harm in reminding the country of this. Bill, hardly a violent war resister, had nonetheless opposed the war; like thousands of young men he had worked diligently to find a way out of the draft, using his vast talents for manipulation, not always savory, then after receiving a high lottery number, had defaulted on his promise to join ROTC. He had done nothing genuinely illegal—and nothing particularly admirable, either.

Unfortunately, that was the point. Since there seemed to be nothing gained by admitting the truth, Bill, enthusiastically backed by his advisors, continued to spin, to deny, to confuse the issue, just as he would with the Gennifer Flowers story, with one handler finally coming up with the plaintive line that he was being constantly harassed about "a draft I never dodged, a woman I never slept with" (an adroit combination of a questionable truth and a full lie, as it turned out). It worked, in that he ended up elected to the presidency. It did not work, in that he ended up being the Bill Clinton we inherited.

It is at least possible without too much trouble to imagine an alternate universe. "Yes, I did smoke pot a few times when I was in college." "Yes, I strongly opposed the war, and was willing to do what I could within legal boundaries to stay out of it." Yes, even, "I did stray earlier in my marriage." Not simply "caused pain . . . I think the American people know what I mean"—but "strayed." It could, of course, have lost him the election. It might also have ushered in a breath of fresh air, a new day.

Because the truth was, the vast majority of Americans, whether they were friends or foes, believed these things anyway. At one point during the Academy Awards in March 1992, emcee Billy Crystal muttered under his breath, sarcastically, "I didn't inhale," Bill's famous claim. The entire hall exploded.

Gennifer Flowers went public in the *Star* in January; on Super Bowl Sunday, January 26, Bill and Hillary appeared on *60 Minutes*, poised and coifed, a united front. They were for the most part unflappable. Theirs was a genuine love match, no arrangement, they insisted. Bill admitted causing pain. Asked whether or not he denied the Flowers story, Bill gave the national audience its first chance to see his special semantic talents in action: "I've said that before," he said. And so he had.

Later, in a scene shown in the *Man from Hope* video played at the Democratic convention, Bill told of how he and Hillary had viewed the taped interview with Chelsea. It was a brief, but remarkable tour de force.

"Once early in the campaign when I'd been beat up a lot by the press, Hillary and I went on national television and basically acknowledged we'd had some problems in our marriage and were proud of the fact we'd managed to keep it together. When the show aired, the three of us went upstairs to watch it together. It was pretty painful to have your child watch that. After it was over I looked at her and said, 'What do you think?' And she said, 'I think I'm glad you're my parents.' After that I knew whatever happened it'd be all right."

This supposedly homey anecdote was in fact as slick, or as sleazy, an appeal as he would ever make, carefully orchestrated for maximum effect—especially since the Clintons had always pledged *not* to use Chelsea, to keep her private at all costs. It combined, in a tight 102-word spiel, flat-out bids for pity, stout claims of virtue, and finally, the direct, calculated use of his eleven-year-old.

He was certain after that exchange that everything would be all right.

With all the bullets flying around his head in the early months of 1992, the word went out—Bill needs help. His friends responded at once. Vast numbers of devoted Arkansans turned up in New Hampshire, in the closing days before the primary, to lend their support. They hit the streets, knocked on doors, pressed the flesh, did what they could to help.

David Matthews, the lawyer Bill had first met at the University of Arkansas, was typical. "He didn't ask me to go, didn't know I was there," he said. "He was getting the thunder beat out of him. I thought he was being treated unfairly, so I went up there to do what I could do. I ended up going around, trying to rally the troops, speaking at various headquarters, going up to people on the street, just kind of doing a kamikaze."

Matthews was on hand to hear Bill give what he still considers the best speech of his life, the famous "last dog dies" speech, in Dover.

"It was one of the most electrifying moments you'd ever want to see," he observed, "He was on the ropes and everybody knew it. On the ropes and the press expected him to fold and he wasn't folding, he was fighting. He talked about the work of his life, how the election was about the people of New Hampshire. It's not about me, he said. I'm gonna be fine if I win or lose. This is about you. "It was an incredible speech. [Cartoonist] Gary Trudeau was in the crowd that night, other writers—many said it was the greatest political speech they'd ever heard. It was a huge crowd. packed to the gills. An unreal experience. He was just giving an old-time speech from his heart. Not note one. And it was unbelievable."

If the country had earlier gotten a glimpse of Bill at his waffling, side-shuffling worst, this was a chance for them to see him at his best.

Back against the wall, counted out, he had come back blazing, a phoenix soaring up from the ashes. It was an amazing performance, an incredible rebirth that put him solidly back on the path to the presidency.

Shortly after the speech, Matthews got a glimpse of how Hillary was holding up. The campaign was barely four months old, but it was clear she had already revamped her earlier opinion, the one expressed to Kwan Kwan Wang. Whatever this was, "fun" was not the word for it.

"Sometime after the Dover speech he had to give a speech to the New Hampshire general assembly," Matthews said. "And when we made the walk from the state capitol back down to where we were staying, there was this throng of people. Hillary told me later it was the most scary moment of the campaign—physically scary. There was this throng of reporters with boom mikes and they just engulfed us. Hillary was walking between Bill and me, we were trying to hold her up and push our way through this group. People were getting knocked down, one man got stepped on and actually was hurt, had to go to the hospital. It was scary, a mob thing."

Back in the hotel, Bill having left to talk to yet another group, Matthews and Hillary sat breathing quietly, trying to recover. Hillary looked at him, shaking her head.

"You know," she said quietly, "if I didn't think we could change the world, it really wouldn't be worth this."

Bill did not actually win in New Hampshire; he came in second. But this mattered not at all. He had turned it around, he was still a viable candidate. He knew it, his staff knew it, his friends and family knew it, and their reaction was ecstatic.

Mauria Aspell, his longtime pal, had also come up to New Hampshire to lend support. She was in the crowd the night the results came in, surrounded by shrieking fans. Everyone was elated, wildly enthusiastic, drunk with victory. Standing in the midst of all the joy, she realized she alone was on the outside, not sharing it. She wasn't even sure why.

"I felt such a powerful sadness all of a sudden," she recalled vividly. "My husband said, 'What's going on?' I said, 'I just feel something negative. I don't know whether I feel like I'm going to lose him as a friend to the world for a long period of time, maybe forever, because he'll get bigger and more indifferent . . . and I always counted on the closeness . . . or whether some part of me is concerned something will happen to him.'

"As it turned out, neither happened completely, both happened somewhat. But I remember tears coming in my eyes. I was so happy for him. But there was just that feeling of, he belongs to too many people. And fear. And fear. I didn't want to turn around. Everybody was watching the results and I had these tears in my eyes."

As the campaign progressed, with the annoying women/draft/pot issues continuing to circle around Bill's head like so many gnats, other friends were called in to help. One, Saul Benjamin, who had been at Oxford and later served in the first administration, tracked down Bill's old Oxford pal Mandy Merck, who was teaching at Cornell for the year. It was a call she would never forget, and it underscored how the Clinton operatives operated.

"He called me to check on whether I was going to say anything indiscreet in the press about Bill," she said. "He said, 'Hi Mandy, what's happening, is the press hassling you?' I said, 'A little bit, the English press in particular.' And he said, 'And of course we're going to be impeccable and say the right things, aren't we?' I said, 'What do you mean, Saul?' He said, 'Well, of course Bill and Hillary have always been deeply happy together, haven't they?'"

Merck was taken aback. The English journalists who had contacted her had only asked about pot and the draft, not Bill's sex life. "And I honestly couldn't remember Bill smoking dope. Though [a student] later reminded me Bill liked dope in cookies." She didn't know the marriage itself had become a central issue. She had met Hillary only twice, briefly, and had no idea what shape the relationship was in. Still, she was quick to calm Benjamin.

"I said, 'You know, Saul, no way am I going to talk about dope or the draft or any bad thing, because I want the fucker to win. Of course you can trust me.'" Benjamin, reassured, asked her if she wanted to attend the election night party in Little Rock.

"I said sure, send me an invitation. He didn't—the asshole, especially considering he was doing all this arm twisting, which he didn't need to do."

In the end, of course, Bill made it—the draft, the pot, the womanizing, the waffling nonwithstanding. Straight through to the nomination, then to the election itself. There were those in his native state who gnashed their teeth, who vowed dark revenge, but they were not the ones in the spotlight at that first inauguration. To the casual observer, it looked as though a majority of the Arkansas population had turned out to rejoice and share in the miraculous moment. An impressive number of good men out of Arkansas had achieved political power over the years — William Fulbright, Dale Bumpers, David Pryor, even Wilbur Mills, who despite his personal problems and sorry end with a stripper named Fanne Foxe had been well respected as a legislator. But never before had the state produced a president.

Melinda Gassaway, editor of the *Hot Springs Sentinel*, echoed the feeling of many. "We thought, an Arkansan being elected president — this really is affirmation. We are not all barefoot and pregnant."

Over a thousand people showed up at the Arkansas Ball, the night of the inauguration. They milled around, forming small groups, sharing anecdotes and memories, waiting for the moment when Bill would finally appear. The man who had always told them he would be president someday, and who had made good his word.

Nearly everyone in the large room felt they had a personal connection to the new commander-in-chief. Including one woman who stood a bit off to the side. A slim, attractive woman, olive skinned, with shoulder-length brown hair and unusual green eyes: the "college girl" — Marla Crider.

"We were waiting for them to show up," she said later. "I had a great vantage point, he would have seen me right away." The minutes ticked by; at any moment, the doors would open, the band would burst into "Hail to the Chief," and the new president would walk in, arms outstretched, radiating joy, to greet his folks, the people who knew him best, who had watched him, tended to him, believed in him over the long haul.

And suddenly, she knew she couldn't do it. She couldn't be there. She hadn't been able to resist coming to Washington for the inauguration, it was the kind of moment that would never happen again. But she realized that was enough. She didn't need to face him directly.

"I looked at my husband and said, 'I don't want to do this. I don't need to see him. I know him very well, I'm happy for him, but I don't want to do this. I don't have to see him now he's president.'"

They left, minutes before Bill arrived. Later in the evening they found themselves at a smaller party, filled with Arkansans, most of whom had been in the hall earlier. Rudy Moore, Bill's onetime aide, during his first term as governor, was one. He and Bill had had their problems in the past, of course—he and Steve Smith had been cut off completely after that first term, with Hillary brandishing the ax and Bill allowing it to happen. And yet he was here. How could you not be? It was still Bill, someone who had been an important figure in his life, someone he still cared for. He spotted Marla across the room and came over, greeting her warmly. He had seen her leave earlier, and wondered about it.

"Marla, you didn't stay to see him?" he said. "Why not? What happened?"

Marla just smiled. "I didn't need to do that," she said.

POLITICAL GAFFES, PERSONAL TRAUMA

FIVE DAYS AFTER THE INAUGURATION Bill appointed Hillary to head up the Health Care Task Force. This was clearly not a casual decision; no first lady in history had ever been named to a political position of any kind, much less such an important one. First ladies were expected to spend their time in soft, noncontroversial pursuits. But Bill and Hillary had known from the start, long, long ago, that if—when—they reached the White House, there would be a hefty reward in it for Hillary.

Bill had certainly hinted as much during the campaign. "You get two for one," he'd announced several times, until his handlers shut him up; the concept was not going down well with the public, who had the odd idea they wanted to vote for the person who would lead the country, and were wary about Hillary anyway. Some of her ill-advised spontaneous comments on the trail ("I could have just stayed home and baked cookies"; "I'm not just standing by my man like some little Tammy Wynette") had managed to alienate a significant number of people.

There were some reports Bill had initially considered elevating

Hillary to a cabinet post; luckily he was persuaded such an appointment would have caused an even harsher reaction than John Kennedy's decision to install his brother Bobby as attorney general.

Appointing Hillary to head up health care, which many Americans felt was one of the most crucial issues of the day, would prove unfortunate enough. She would reveal herself, to Congress and the country, as extremely intelligent, knowledgeable, articulate—and utterly unbending, with very little understanding of the art of compromise. Part of the problem had to do with her personality, her unswerving belief in the correctness of her approach; even more had to do with the fact that when it came to Washington, she was a total neophyte.

Hillary had had no previous experience working with Congress, no real understanding of what it took to push through a program. Other than her time on the Watergate committee and her work in Arkansas for the Clinton education reforms, she had had no dealings with any legislative body at all—and never, of course, as an elected official. As most politicians and lobbyists know—or discover, shortly on their arrival in Washington—working with Congress is an art, a craft, a complicated skill it can take years to master. Only someone with a sizable ego, well laced with hubris, riddled with blind spots, would ever believe they could pick it up on the fly within a few short weeks. Among other things, it requires a true aptitude for people-skills, knowing just who to push, who to coddle, and how and when. Hillary had never been good at that sort of thing—that was Bill's department.

However Hillary, utterly confident, was sure she would be up to the task. She wasn't. While in fact presenting a program to Congress is only the beginning of the process, Hillary, at the point she handed over the thirteen-thousand-page proposal she and former Yale Law School classmate Ira Magaziner had developed, thought she had reached the end of the road. And of course she had, as had any real chance for new health care legislation under the Clinton administration. The failure cannot be laid solely at her doorstep, of course; there were too many complicated factors involved. But there is no question she shared responsibility for the final result. By all rights it should have been a humbling experience for her. There is no indication that it was.

Later, looking back on the trials of that first year, Hillary said she was reminded of a favorite poem—one that she felt "summed up the absolute unpredictability and frequent unfairness of life: 'As I was standing in the street/As quiet as could be/A great big ugly man came up/And tied his horse to me.'"

It was a revealing comment. The rhyme perfectly summed up Hillary's reaction to almost anything bad that happened to her, from personal tragedy to political criticism—she considered all of it equally undeserved, unwarranted, unfairly dumped at her feet. Introspection was not Hillary's forte; self-criticism had never been a part of her makeup.

The health care debacle was not the only low point of 1993 for the Clintons; it was a bad year in other respects as well, reminding many back in Arkansas of Bill's first term as governor, when he had tried to do too much too soon and ended up infuriating almost everyone. Just like that earlier time, there again appeared to be a preponderance of brash young staffers around. Bill himself seemed to be all over the map those first months, mishandling any number of issues, from Haitian refugees to gays in the military to a series of ill-planned Justice Department appointments, followed by clumsy withdrawals, of a number of women, including his old Yale friend Lani Guinier.

At the same time, Bill and Hillary experienced a series of difficult personal losses. Hugh Rodham, Hillary's father, was the first.

He had not been well, and by the time the Rodhams moved from Park Ridge to Little Rock in 1987, his health was failing badly. He was taking medication for his heart, and had a severe limp caused by a bad knee and hip that forced him to wear a built-up shoe and later use a cane. Doctors had suggested hip replacement surgery but Rodham refused; he felt the procedure was too new.

The heart condition surfaced suddenly while he was in Little Rock for Bill's second gubernatorial inauguration in January 1983—he experienced severe chest pain and was taken to the University of Arkansas Medical Science Hospital, where Dr. Stephen Van Devanter performed a three-hour bypass operation. Van Devanter was impressed with Hillary's cool demeanor. "It was amazing because with the inauguration and all the other stuff going on, Hillary handled it very well, no tears," he said.

A decade later, on March 19, 1993, as Hillary's first public hearing on health care loomed, her father suffered a massive stroke. Hugh had been in high spirits, having just made a cameo appearance on the TV sitcom *Hearts Afire,* one of several high-rated shows produced by Bill and Hillary's pals and advisors, Harry Thomason and Linda Blood-worth-Thomason, key players in the Clintons' Hollywood crowd.

Her father comatose and on life support, Hillary, along with Chelsea, flew immediately to Little Rock, while Hughie and Tony jetted in from Florida, beginning a long emotional vigil at St. Vincent Infirmary Medical Center. At night the family stayed in the Rodhams' small red brick condo. Hillary kept in close telephone contact with her White House health task force, and spent time briefing Vice President Al Gore, who was chairing the hearing in her absence. Bill arrived in Little Rock a week later, to join the family.

With doctors offering little hope for Rodham's survival, the family began to plan for the funeral. Scranton historian Nick Petula received a tip from a friend in the Secret Service. "You're going to have some excitement up there," he was told. "Hillary's father's dying and he's made a wish to be buried in Scranton."

After a couple of days, Bill flew back to Washington; he needed to make final preparations for his upcoming first summit with Russian president Boris Yeltsin, the White House announced. There was another reason for his return, however—he was expecting a special overnight guest.

"I was going over to see Hugh at the hospital, and thought I might see Hillary just to speak to her, see how she's doing, and boom—she's gone," said Paul Fray. "When I got there, I said, 'What happened, where is she?' And this guy said, 'You don't want to know.' I said, 'What the hell are you talking about?' He said, 'This is off the record—but it looks like Bill's got tied up with Barbra Streisand up at the White House.' I said, 'Man, you're talking a bunch of crap.' And he said, 'Well, why else did Hillary go home while her daddy's laying here getting ready to die?'"

Hillary had, in fact, rushed back to the White House after getting the news that Streisand—who performed at the inauguration—had spent a night in the plush and historic Lincoln bedroom while Hillary was grieving over her comatose father in a depressing and sterile hospital room. (The White House spin was that Hillary had returned to handle urgent business regarding her health care program.) She had also heard that during her absence Bill, spiffy in a black-sequined tuxedo, had escorted Streisand and his mother, who had become very friendly with the singer, to the Gridiron Dinner, an annual media-politico event. There, in a party-hardy mood, the president wailed on his sax to the Coasters' golden oldie, "Yakety Yak."

Hillary was livid. Soon after her return, reporters noticed a vicious-looking scratch on the president's face. Queried, White House spokeswoman Dee Dee Myers dismissed it as a shaving cut. Later, after leaving the White House, she hedged. "I'm the idiot who said he cut himself shaving before I'd seen him. Then I saw him—it was a big scratch, clearly not a shaving cut. Barbra Streisand was clearly around at the time," she said.

Tales of a bloody confrontation between the Clintons prompted by Streisand's visit circulated wildly. Paul Fray put it succinctly: "Hillary left Little Rock like a rocket, went back, and caught the son of a bitch. You know who got hit in the chops, who got smacked around."

There were tabloid reports at the time, denied of course, that Bill and Barbra had had an affair, and that the First Lady had banned the singer from the White House permanently. "She, more than any other film figure," commented London's *Daily Mail*, which took a sharp interest in such matters, "has swift and easy access to Bill Clinton's White House. She has stayed overnight at the mansion. The President drops everything to take her calls. Around the dinner tables of Washington, there is light gossip about a romantic liaison between the President and the formidable Streisand."

As it turned out, Barbra Streisand was one subject about whom both Hillary and Monica Lewinsky seemed to see eye to eye, according to one of Linda Tripp's secret tapes. Like Hillary, Lewinsky reportedly suspected Streisand had been one of the president's women.

"Ugh. I hate her," whined Monica. "She's soooo annoying." Tripp responded: "She gets prettier as she gets older." But a catty Monica replied: "Where do you think that's from? Plastic surgery probably. She's probably had everything done but her nose."

(If there had been a falling out between Hillary and Streisand, the diva attempted to smooth things over with money—she was listed as an early contributor to Hillary's senate campaign.)

Hillary was still in Washington on the evening of April 7, when her father died, at age eighty-two. The Clintons immediately returned to Little Rock to be with the grieving widow. Two days later a private memorial service was held at the First United Methodist Church in Little Rock, where Bill gave the euology. It was a full military service with U.S. Navy pallbearers and a flag-draped casket; Hugh, after all, had been a World War II veteran, albeit a safely landlocked one.

Then the family accompanied Rodham back to his boyhood home for the final service and burial. Hundreds of Scrantonites hoping to catch a glimpse of the first couple stood in a teeming rain as the presidential motorcade and the hearse pulled up in front of the Court Street Methodist Church, a block and a half from Rodham's boyhood home, and two blocks from Scranton Lace. "It was such a bizarre scene," recalled Petula, who lived directly across from the church. "The local politicians acted like it was a circus. The city administration must have had the street sweeper and the cleaner go by twenty times; they were patching every little hole in the street. If they had the time I think they would have repaved the street. The cemetery was a mess and at the last minute they were putting flowers around all the graves, sprucing up the areas around where the grave site was."

To get in the church, everyone had to pass through metal detectors; men were frisked; women's purses were thoroughly searched; sharpshooters were posted on nearby roofs. The first mourner invited inside was Manny Gelb, a veteran Democratic ward leader in Scranton, who had known Hugh for decades. "My father used to tell the story about how after the war he went out to Chicago to look for a job and stayed with Hugh and Dorothy," Gelb's daughter, Natalie Solfanelli, said. "My father used to take Dorothy dancing because Hugh had to work."

Once again Bill gave the euology. "He talked about having a tough time winning Hugh's graces for Hillary's hand, but having an even a tougher time because he was a Democrat," said Oscar Dowdy, one of the family mourners.

Few noticed the one odd touch in the open casket. "They had a very brief viewing and when I looked inside I saw a cigar in Hugh's hand," Dowdy said, chuckling. "I'm guessing Hughie or Tony was responsible for it. In life a cigar in Hugh's hand was pretty predominate. He gave up smoking them, but he used to buy pretty good cigars to chew on, not smoke, but just roll around in his mouth."

Stogie in hand, Hugh Rodham was laid to rest in the family plot at the Washburn Street Cemetery. By January 2000, his name had still not been placed on the monument. "I think it's very weird," commented Scranton genealogist and Rodham-Clinton family watcher Cecille Champagne. "After all, he's Hillary Clinton's father. Someone should have put his name on it by now." On the other hand, such a discrepancy was not unique at the cemetery, where one of Hillary's great uncles, Reese Jones, buried in 1913, still has no marker attesting to his presence. "They buried him, then they buried [Hillary's grandmother] on top of him," Champagne said. "They call it a double-death interment."

After the burial, the first family and guests retired to Cooper's Restaurant for a wake of sorts. "The president drove the Secret Service crazy," Scranton journalist Joe Flannery recalled. "He broke loose and was walking through the crowds shaking hands, talking to people like a campaigner. Cooper's carries hundreds of kinds of beer and Clinton left on the plane with a bag of sandwiches and a six-pack of weird beers put out by tiny breweries—'Pig's Head Beer,' whatever."

Hugh Rodham had been old and failing. Three months later, the Clintons were hit with a much harsher, utterly unexpected tragedy— the suicide of Vince Foster.

The death itself was so bizarre and shocking, it inevitably gave rise to rumors of conspiracy, which would continue to swirl around the Clintons for the rest of the administration. Not surprisingly, it also breathed new life into the stories that Hillary and Foster had had an affair. It would not be until the next millennium however—seven years later— that anyone would have the temerity to actually pose the question directly and publicly (though the Office of Independent Counsel Kenneth Starr had sniffed around the relationship, as did right-wing anti-Clinton groups.)

"You're going to hate me," said Buffalo, New York, radio host Tom Bauerle, interviewing Hillary during her still-not-quite-announced senate campaign on January 19, 2000. Then he hit her with it—had she ever been sexually unfaithful to the president? Specifically, had she had an affair with Vince Foster?

"You know, I do hate you for that," Hillary replied. Those kinds of questions were "out of bounds."

Bauerle persisted. "Is the answer no?"

"Well, of course, it's no," Hillary said. "It's an inappropriate question." Questions like that, speculations of that nature, "all of that diverts attention from really talking about and working on what we can do together to help people."

It was not quite a last-dog-dies New Hampshire moment. But for those with a fine ear for political resonance, the echo was there.

At the tail end of the first year in the White House, Bill and Hillary experienced their third personal loss—the death of Bill's mother, Virginia Kelley.

Virginia had been diagnosed with breast cancer in 1990; she had a mastectomy and a course of chemotherapy, and as always, faced it in her usual upbeat, optimistic manner. Her sons' troubles could derail her, but not her own. "Cancer was my problem and I could handle it," she said.

But in June 1991, she was informed that the cancer had spread to the nodes of her arm; as a nurse, she knew exactly what that meant. She made her decision at once: "If they ask, you tell my boys I'm fine," she told the doctor. She threw herself into Bill's presidential campaign. A year later, learning the cancer had spread to her bones, necessitating radiation, she remained adamant—the boys could not be told. It wasn't until months after the election, and then only when Bill himself became suspicious, that she allowed her doctor to tell him the truth. It wasn't just because she wanted to keep her boys unaware—she couldn't stand the idea of people crying over her. With less than a year left, Virginia wasn't about to stop living life on her terms.

She managed, even with the ongoing chemotherapy, to rejoice in Bill's inauguration. She and her current husband, Dick Kelley, a food broker, visited the White House several times. ("People would ask her how many times she was going to get married. And she was so quick, she would say, 'As many times as it takes,'" said her friend Rachel Heffernan, fondly. By all reports her marriage to Kelley, a tall, courtly man with an easygoing manner, who shared her love of the racetrack and travel, was extremely successful.) Their last Washington visit was over Christmas 1993; Virginia returned home, then flew out to Las Vegas to see her friend Barbra Streisand perform over New Year's. She died in her sleep on January 6.

"My mother," Bill told James Morgan, who worked with Virginia on her book, *Leading with My Heart*, published after her death, "had a big sprawling life." He had never ceased to respect her tremendously, for her indomitable spirit, her refusal to let herself be broken, her determination to make her own choices.

"I think the reason Bill's been able to survive is that he has a lot of his mother in him," said Melinda Gassaway, who got to know Virginia well, as editor of Hot Springs's newspaper. "She just refused to give in to many things."

Virginia's funeral was as big and sprawling as her life had been, with thousands of friends, family, and celebrities—Streisand of course being one of the most visible—showing up to celebrate her life. Patty Rodden-berry had been put in charge of bringing in food to the president's party, a mammoth task, particularly since the Secret Service insisted on check-ing each item. Finally, when one particularly officious type began to carefully go over a shipment from McClard's Barbecue, she broke—seiz-ing his hand, she plunged it deep into the vat of baked beans. "I said, we want to make sure I don't bring in anything to harm the president, don't we? Of course the guy hated me from then on but I didn't care," she said. Later, Bill teased her—"I hear you're giving the Secret Service a hard time," he said. "He deserved it," said Roddenberry calmly.

A few of Bill's oldest friends—Mauria Aspell, David Leopoulos among them—gathered at Virginia's house in Hot Springs to be with Bill the first night he came back to Arkansas after his mother died. "We stayed real late the first night he got home. When we were leaving, two in the morning, I went over and hugged him, and he looked up and just said, I miss my mama. I said, I know you do," said Aspell.

Earlier in the evening, she had glimpsed a rare moment between Bill and Hillary. "I looked up and they were standing behind some people, arm in arm, and he rested his head on her head and she was resting hers up against his shoulder. There was no one to impress. It was just a very sweet tender moment between them that was genuine."

The next night she, Bill, Leopoulos, and Jim French rode around Hot Springs together—trailed, of course, by the Secret Service. "We went down memory lane, drove all over Hot Springs, looked at different places. Bill was real nostalgic. We went into the high school and he wrote on the blackboard, 'I remember Miss Mackey'—the assistant principal who was such a powerful woman—and then he put 'Bill Clinton, class of '64,' and made us all sign it."

The next day the high school officials discovered the message and were thrilled. "They were gonna keep it forever, but the guy in charge put some solution on it to preserve it and it just dissolved," Aspell laughed. "Ahh, Arkansas."

After the funeral, which had to be held in the Hot Springs Convention Center to accommodate the huge crowd, Virginia was taken back to Hope for burial, near the house where she had grown up.

It had been a hard first year. Yet despite the problems, the Clintons' optimism, particularly Bill's, was not seriously affected. Dark times were ahead—scandals, investigations, congressional revolts, finally the horror of a full-scale impeachment—yet never would he doubt this was where he wanted to be. At a reunion of his Hot Springs High School class held at the White House late in 1999, he would repeatedly avow his deep belief that this, the job he had been striving for all his life, was the best one in the world. "He said several times that if he could run again he would," said class president Marty Elam Walker. "He's going to miss it."

Certainly the first year had done nothing to dampen his spirits. Melinda Barran, mayor of Hot Springs, was on hand to greet the Clinton family when they flew back to Arkansas after Christmas 1993—and found their general mood buoyant.

"Bill and Hillary and Chelsea and Roger and his then fiancée [now wife] Molly, they all flew into Hot Springs, between Christmas and New Years. A lot of people were there to welcome them, and I was included in the crowd because I was mayor."

Afterwards, walking back to airport parking lot, she bumped into an ebullient Roger Clinton. "Roger had had an awful lot to drink, he was in his cups. We were just chitchatting. I said, how's it looking?"

Roger, grinning hugely, had a ready answer. "Well, the plan is—Bill for eight and Hillary for eight after that. We'll have the White House for sixteen years!" he whooped. Barran, shocked, just stared at him.

"It could have been just his opinion, of course, but I've never felt he was an independent thinker," she said later. Troubles or not, it was clear the family's confidence was riding high.

There would be times in the coming months, however, when even Bill would feel momentarily beaten down by events. Late in 1994, after the dramatic upheaval in Congress, which left him the first Democratic president to be faced with both a Republican House and Senate, was a definite nadir.

"It was a really low point. It just looked like he was dead," said Arkansas journalist Ernie Dumas. "The Republicans had taken both houses, all these scandals [Paula Jones had filed her sexual harassment suit in the spring of 1994] were mounting, investigations right and left."

Dumas was at home in bed recovering from heart surgery when he got a call from Bill, who quickly launched into a lengthy recitation of his own troubles. "He spends another thirty minutes talking about himself, his problems with Congress. Mainly he wants to know what to do about the press, they all hate him, all the national press hate his guts, nobody's giving him a fair shake."

Dumas, weakly holding the phone to his ear, felt trapped. There seemed to be no end to the monologue. With anyone else, you could hang up, but how do you hang up on the president of the United States?

At last he was able to mutter a reply. "I said, 'Well, I think you're gonna bounce back from this.'" Finally, thankfully, the call ended.

Bill did bounce back—and continued to bounce back from one blow after another; his ability to absorb, recover, and reemerge seemingly unscathed struck many as close to superhuman.

"It's like that clown in our youth with the round bottom, you knock it over, it comes back up," said Mauria Aspell. "No matter what you do to him, he comes back up."

David Matthews was more thoughtful. "I guess if you grow up the way he did, with your father dead before you're born, your mother struggling to get an education so she can provide for you, the abusive stepfather situation, bouncing back, dealing with difficult things, realizing you can make it becomes second nature. He's always looking forward—like the theme song of '92, 'Don't Stop Thinking about Tomorrow.' I think that's what he does."

Hillary did not fare as well; she had always been a grudge holder, and once in the White House, the opportunity for grudges multiplied wildly. Travelgate, Whitewater, Troopergate, Paula Jones, the constant press criticism; Hillary took all of it very personally.

"Ultimately some of her flaws really hurt them," observed Max

Brantley. "Hillary's fundamental distrust of the media—and you'd have to say in a way, of the public, the process. She's always been secretive.

"Some of it does have to do with principle—the privacy thing—but it's unrealistic principle. Now more than ever, if you offer yourself for public service, you give up some of the rights to privacy. You know the story various aides have written in which they said they counseled her to just dump every Whitewater document they had. And she just fought that notion tooth and nail, and only to her detriment. Everything was stripped bare anyway and left her looking like she had something to hide. Very sad."

One popular theory, which emerged as more and more Americans wracked their brains trying to define the Clinton marriage, was that Hillary tended to redirect her anger, turning it away from Bill and towards other targets—the press, political enemies, "the vast right-wing conspiracy." If so, it was nothing new.

"She really manifests this bunker mentality, this beleaguered attitude that 'everybody is against us, jealous of us because we're so successful and so smart,'" noted John Brummet. "That's the way she sees the world. She's always seen it that way. It's like the Clinton's are Jesus—you're either for us or against us."

For all her much-touted intelligence, Hillary suffered from a kind of tunnel vision—an inability to see the complete picture, even when it involved things going on under her nose. Perhaps years of compartmentalization, of purposefully ignoring certain distasteful realities in her marriage, had heightened this tendency. Or perhaps it was simply her own form of denial.

She was a global thinker, a purposeful planner; intuitive leaps eluded her. Certain details held no interest for her—especially those from the past.

After Virginia's burial in Hope in 1994, Barbra Streisand took a few moments to visit the house where Virginia had grown up, the one where Bill had spent his first years. The house, which would open to the public a few years later, was being carefully redone so as to resemble the original as closely as possible in decor and furnishings. The final re-creation was successful enough that Bill, when he visited a few years later, was actually reduced to tears.

Hillary did not visit the house that day; this is not the sort of thing that held much interest for her. Yet it is filled with clues to Bill's char-acter—the highchair where he sat, every morning, while his grand-mother taught him his letters and numbers; the table in the front room, site of perennial card games.

Had she visited that day, she would have seen something else, as well: a portrait prominently displayed in the living room of a glowing young Virginia who, with her dark hair, round cheeks, bright eyes, and curving mouth, bears a startling resemblance, noted by nearly every-one who walks through, to someone who was about to enter Bill's life and change it forever.

THE INTERN

SHE WAS BORN ON JULY 23, 1973, in the midst of a long hot summer when talk of presidential resignation and impeachment, secretly recorded tapes, and grand jury perjury exploded on the national scene. Hillary was at the center of the drama, working with the Senate Watergate Committee, while Bill was in Arkansas, laying the groundwork for his first-ever political run. At San Francisco Children's Hospital, the baby's mother had had a long painful labor and delivery, but her seven-and-a-half-pound girl was startlingly beautiful, with dreamy hazel eyes and the longest lashes.

From the beginning, Monica Samille Lewinsky was precocious, strongwilled. By twenty-four months she was talking incessantly, walking everywhere, knowing her own mind. Three-year-old Monica's determination and obstinacy was underscored on the day of a relative's wedding when the child adamantly refused to wear a blue flower-girl dress until her self-described "nonconfrontational" mother, Marcia, cut off the sleeves to avoid a tantrum.

In 1976, Monica's father, Dr. Bernard Lewinsky, an oncologist, decided to go into private practice in the city of Los Angeles. Wanting the best for Monica, the Lewinskys bought a pricey Spanish-style three-bedroom home with a pool in Beverly Hills, and later enrolled her in the exclusive Thomas Dye School, a private academy whose high-powered alumni included, ironically, the son of the owner of the *Washington Post*, the newspaper instrumental in bringing down Richard Nixon. However well-intentioned, the Lewinskys' decisions to raise Monica in one of America's most ostentatious communities and to send her to a snooty private school proved to be disaster.

She complained that she was teased, locked out of cliques, patronized and put down because of her looks and her weight—the latter an albatross throughout her life. When she wasn't on the guest list for one of classmate Tori Spelling's A-list birthday parties, Monica felt as if she'd been hit by a truck, and when a boy she liked nicknamed her "Big Mac" she was crushed.

"Monica never fit in," observed her aunt, Debra Finerman, a close confidante. "If she had been very thin and in with the [Beverly Hills] fast crowd she would have been OK. But it wasn't really her."

Monica also was dispirited at home and found life "unpleasant" in the house with a live-in maid on North Hillcrest Drive. The description of that world, as offered to Monica's biographer, Andrew Morton, rings of the Rodhams of Wisner Street in Park Ridge, without the glamour. Like Hugh Rodham, Bernie Lewinsky was "very autocratic, very stern," a father with a violent temper who belittled his children, asserted Marcia Lewinsky. Like Hillary's father, Monica's dad "worked a lot," " and family dinners "were often unpleasant," Monica declared. As with Hugh and Dorothy Rodham, Bernie and Marcia Lewinsky "fought . . . They weren't very affectionate or loving towards each other . . ."

While she dreamed of being "daddy's little girl," Monica was closest to her mother who, like her daughter, also felt ill-starred—so much so that in September 1987, when Monica was fourteen, Marcia Lewinsky suddenly filed for divorce after learning that her husband was having an affair with a nurse at his office.

The breakup could not have come at a worse time. Monica was an emotional wreck when she entered socially competitive Beverly Hills High—an overweight, clumsy girl struggling with intense anger, confusion, and disappointment, while surrounded by scores of beautiful classmates who scorned her. "Everybody looked great . . . being overweight was not acceptable. The pressure was horrid." Depressed and angry she cut classes and watched her grades plummet as her heft soared.

At sixteen, Monica saw a therapist and entered an eating disorder program for the first, but not the last, time. Moreover, she found a place where she felt accepted. In the drama department at school she won a prize for designing an Elizabethan costume, and was cast in a small role in *The Music Man*. But she also began a friendship that quickly turned into an obsessive, emotionally damaging five-year affair with a soon-to-be married twenty-five-year-old instructor named Andy Bleiler.

From 1991 to 1993, Monica attended a run-of-the-mill two-year community college, where she was unhappier than she had ever been in high school. It was during this period that she suffered a virtual nervous breakdown and began seeing another psychotherapist, billed as a shrink to the stars. All the while she had liaisons with Bleiler, giving up her virginity to him when she was nineteen, seeing him regularly even when his wife was pregnant, having quickie sex in edgy places like the auditorium light booth at Beverly Hills High. Though he tried to break off their affair a number of times, he kept returning—as Bill Clinton would later. After the Clinton affair, Monica observed: "I came to learn with married men that they feel guilty, say they want to stop it and then succumb to temptation anyway. So they always come back."

In the fall of 1993 Monica moved away from home for the first time to attend Lewis and Clark College in Portland, where she majored in psychology. At the same time, her affair with Bleiler became even more twisted when she befriended his wife, Kate, and the couple's children. And when she discovered that Bleiler was seeing another girl she took revenge by having a fling with his younger brother.

In May 1995, a very mixed-up Monica graduated with a Bachelor of Science degree in psychology. Still deeply in love with Bleiler, but desperate to break off their obsessive bond, she decided she should leave Portland.

But to where? To do what?

It was her mother, now living at the Watergate in Washington, who suggested that she take a coveted White House internship that was arranged by an influential family friend, millionaire businessman Walter Kaye, a Democratic fundraiser with ties to the first lady. (Despite the scandal to come, Kaye remained a supporter of Hillary's, contributing at least twenty-one thousand dollars to her New York senate campaign war chest.)

The emotionally troubled and needy twenty-one-year-old, who cared little about politics and knew nothing about national affairs, was assigned that July to work on correspondence in the office of the White House chief of staff. The six-week unpaid internship, Monica thought, would be exciting and look good on her résumé, nothing more.

But that changed after she saw Bill Clinton in the flesh from a distance for the first time on the White House lawn. Instantly, she developed an obsessive crush—attending White House events in order to catch his eye, which she did at a ceremony just a few weeks after starting her job. As she recalled the moment, the president had given her "the full Bill Clinton," as she put it. "It was this look, it's the way he flirts with women . . . we shared an intense but brief sexual exchange. He undressed me with his eyes."

At some point early in what would become the world's most infamous office romance, Bill had in fact become infatuated with Monica, there is little doubt of that. He hungered for love, and she had an unlimited supply to offer. Hillary had long ago washed her hands of him, not because of his womanizing, but because of his getting caught womanizing. For years the word has been that the two sleep in separate beds, putting on a united front for the public and the media, but disappearing into their own separate worlds in private.

As a close friend of Bill's observed in early 2000: "Other than their mutual love of Chelsea—and their shared political goals—Bill and Hill's marriage was dead and buried a long, long time ago. Had it not been for public office, they undoubtedly would have gotten divorced. There was lots of talk of it, going as far back as their early Arkansas days. Monica came along at a time when Bill felt lonelier than I had ever known him to be. His mother's death had devastated him. He was a wreck, terribly vulnerable. However off-the-wall Monica was, she was a breath of fresh air for him at a time when he desperately needed resuscitation.

"I know how he is with women. But she was different. He was literally hooked on her, and pursued her with the same level of adolescent obsession that she pursued him. He desperately needed to be loved — I'm not talking just about sex, but a caring kind of love, and Monica probably more than any other woman — except his mother — filled that need. Certainly Hillary never did. From things he has said since, I truly believe that Bill would have run off with that girl if he had the chance, if things had been different."

Monica closely resembled a young Virginia: vivacious, energetic, enthusiastic, soft and feminine. Bill had noticed it immediately. At one point during their affair he told her she was "full of piss and vinegar" like his mother, and on another occasion he declared adoringly, "She would have liked you. You are very much alike."

On November 15, 1995 — just four months after coming to the White House (her internship was extended for a second six weeks, and she was then hired full-time) — Bill and Monica had their first sexual encounter, sparked by her now-famous panty thong flash as the two stood in the chief of staff's office. Later that day after some necking and groping, the intern performed oral sex on her boss — while he talked on the phone to a member of Congress. "I told him that I wanted to complete that," she stated later. "And he said that he needed to wait until he trusted me more. And then I think he made a joke that he hadn't had that in a long time."

After their initial meeting, and up until March 29, 1997, Bill and Monica had at least ten sexual encounters, usually lasting fifteen to twenty minutes each, frequently in his private study near the Oval Office, as documented by Ken Starr's investigators. When they weren't together, they had long phone calls filled with sex — ten to fifteen such chats — one of which concluded suddenly when the commander in chief began snoring.

During their clandestine meetings, Monica usually performed fellatio, but Bill always avoided climaxing; however, the first time he did ejaculate, at her insistence, he left an indelible mark on her navy blue Gap dress — and in the history books; the dried presidential semen proved conclusively that they had had a sexual liaison. In another particularly bizarre and now legendary incident, the commander in chief inserted a cigar in his playmate's vagina, then put the stogie in his mouth and remarked, "It tastes good."

During one of their more introspective liaisons — they were never fully unclothed, and always were on the alert for trespassers—Bill revealed that he had had literally hundreds of affairs before he was forty, but was making a concerted, desperate (but seemingly not very successful) effort to be faithful to Hillary. In fact, he held out hope to Monica that a post-presidency divorce wasn't entirely out of the question. Overjoyed, the ever-optimistic Monica boasted to a friend that one day she might become the second Mrs. Clinton.

On April 5, 1996, five months after her first presidential tryst, Monica was fired from her job at the White House—considered a stalker and a troublemaker by her immediate supervisors. Her transfer to the Pentagon press office left her brokenhearted, and Bill extremely distressed. "Why did they have to take you away from me?" he asked at an emotional meeting in the wake of her dismissal, and vowed that if he won reelection that November he would bring her back "just like that. You can do anything you want. You can be anything you want." Monica jauntily asked whether she could be "assistant to the president for blow jobs," and Bill responded, "I'd like that."

Despite his promise, Monica was blacklisted permanently from White House employment by members of the palace guard. Irate, she demanded presidential help to get a job in the private sector—feigning exposure of their relationship if he did not. Her declaration, made in a fit of anger, infuriated Bill who warned her that a threat against the president was illegal. Bill, however, suspected that Monica had blabbed, and in fact she had—revealing their affair to at least eleven people: her psychologist, her mother, her aunt, and a number of friends. "This wasn't bragging," Monica explained later. "It was more like just treating him like a normal boy . . . I know all about my girlfriends' boyfriends . . . the President was no different."

There were a number of emotional conversations between Bill and Monica during the period of what would become an ill-fated job search, which was spearheaded by Washington power broker Vernon Jordan, a close friend of the president's. One extraordinary telephone exchange took place at two-thirty in the morning of October 11, 1997—Hillary and Bill's twenty-second anniversary. "All I think about is you and your job," Bill told Monica. "I'm obsessed with you and finding you a job. I wake up in the morning and it makes me sick thinking about it. My life is empty except for you and this job search. All I have is my work and this obsession. I'm on your team."

At the Pentagon, meanwhile, Monica once again in her young life bonded with the wrong people.

One, an older man, with whom she had a three-month affair, got her pregnant, and she was forced to have an abortion, borrowing the money for the procedure from her aunt because her ex-lover refused to help.

The other was an older woman, a seemingly sympathetic and warm career civil servant who seemed to have Monica's best interests at heart.

LIES, DENIALS, AND REBUKE

A DRAB, DOUR DIVORCEE in her late forties with two children, Linda Tripp had worked at the White House, first for Bush, then briefly for the Clintons—assigned to Vince Foster's office where she claimed to have served him his last hamburger. In the controversial aftermath of his mysterious suicide she also helped stir the conspiracy kettle with talk of suspicious White House activities surrounding his demise. While fond of the Bushes, Tripp came to hold the Clintons and their liberal staffers in contempt, and had visions of cashing in with a tell-all book—"Behind Closed Doors: What I Saw at the Clinton White House"—focusing on presidential womanizing that she and a circle of conservative cohorts hoped would eventually destroy the President.

Spurring her on beginning in 1996 was a member of that circle— Lucianne Goldberg, a New York literary agent. In her sixties, Goldberg had a curious background. She had arrived in the nation's capital years earlier after dropping out of high school. During the Johnson years she held a White House job one step above that of intern. In his book *A Vast Conspiracy*, Jeffery Toobin mentioned that Goldberg had bragged to friends that she had had an affair with LBJ. After publication,

Goldberg vehemently denied this story. During the 1972 presidential race, Goldberg had worked as a paid Mata Hari for the Nixon camp, posing as a journalist to gain information about liberal Democrat George McGovern.

Like Tripp, Goldberg despised Clinton; she thought of him as virtual "trailer park trash."

Bill, Monica, and Tripp, along with other key figures in the drama—players such as Kathleen Willey, the attractive widow who claimed she was groped by the president in the Oval Office when she went to speak to him about a job in November 1993—all merged in a classic "she said, he said" legal battle. Had it not been for the unprecedented sexual harassment lawsuit filed on May 6, 1994, by Paula Corbin Jones, a secretarial school dropout who was working as a $6.35-an-hour documents examiner for the state of Arkansas—and the subsequent nuclear fallout—Bill Clinton might have left the White House in January 2001 with his legacy virtually intact.

Jones, who favored lots of makeup, tight miniskirts, high heels, and hair bows—an ex-boyfriend sold nude photos of her to *Penthouse* after she got her fifteen minutes—claimed that on May 8, 1991, when she was twenty-three, and working for the Arkansas Industrial Development Commission, she was invited to a suite at the Excelsior Hotel in Little Rock, where the then-governor was waiting for her. She alleged that during their introduction he "lowered his trousers and underwear exposing his erect penis" and asked her to "kiss it."

To buttress her allegations, Jones asserted that there were "distinguishing characteristics" in the governor's genital area that she could identify. In an affidavit that is considered one of the strangest legal documents ever, she stated that Bill's penis was "five to five and one-half inches, or less, in length . . . a circumference of the approximate size of a quarter, or perhaps very slightly larger" and "was bent or crooked from Mr. Clinton's right to left, or from an observer's left to right if the observer is facing Mr. Clinton. . . ."

Though Jones's suit was eventually thrown out on April Fools' Day 1998 by a federal judge on the grounds that Bill's conduct did not constitute sexual assault, he subsequently agreed to pay her $850,000 in January 1999—but with no acknowledgement of any wrongdoing. Curiously, the settlement—which came out of his insurance policy and a trust fund—was $150,000 more than the damages Jones had originally sought.

But all of that was still to come.

Back at the Pentagon, when Monica finally faced the cold reality that her chances of returning to a White House job and to her man were zero to none she confided her affair to her new best friend, the seemingly kind-hearted and concerned Linda Tripp, who gloatingly and expeditiously informed Lucianne Goldberg. At the agent's suggestion, Tripp began tap-ing her telephone conversations with Monica, apparently unaware that she was violating the laws of the state of Maryland where she lived. Later, Tripp would be prosecuted for her one-sided electronic eavesdropping.

By late 1997 Paula Jones's attorneys, who had been seeking to estab-lish a "pattern and practice" in Bill's relationships with women other than Hillary, had learned of Monica from Tripp and served her with a subpoena. On January 7, 1998, Monica gave an affidavit denying any form of association with Bill. Referred to in *Jones v. Clinton* as Jane Doe No. 6 to hide her identity, Monica swore under the penalty of per-jury that, "I have never had a sexual relationship with the President, he did not propose that we have a sexual relationship, he did not offer me employment or other benefits in exchange for a sexual relationship. He did not deny me employment or other benefits for rejecting a sex-ual relationship. I do not know of any person who had a sexual rela-tionship with the President. . . ."

Later, Monica explained why she had lied. "When I saw that the document said that I did not have sexual relations I thought that I could buy that, as we had never had sexual intercourse."

Events moved swiftly after Monica's false statement was filed: Tripp tipped off Starr to Monica, handing over her secretly recorded tapes; Starr received permission from Attorney General Janet Reno to probe Bill and Monica's relationship; in a sting operation, Starr wired Tripp to trap Monica as prosecutors listened in; Monica was effectively taken into custody and given two options—cooperate, or face more than a quarter of a century in jail for perjury, obstruction of justice, subornation of perjury, witness tampering, and conspiracy.

On Saturday January 17, 1998, the day after Monica was questioned by Starr's people, Bill became the first sitting president to be deposed under oath in a lawsuit, and on videotape, as part of the Jones case. A number of times in the past he had stated unequivocally that he didn't remember ever meeting Jones, let alone exposing himself to her. As for Monica, Bill felt secure; he had read her false affidavit and believed they were on the same page: they both would agree there was no intimate relationship. The last word he had received from one of his lawyers, Bob Bennett, before testifying was not to lie. "They will try to impeach you if you lie."

At first Bill was relaxed, confident. Yes, he said, he knew Monica. She was, he stated, a friend of his secretary, Betty Currie. That was one of the few half-truths told in the entire deposition. Most of his responses were lies and denials. "I have no specific recollection," he said, when asked whether he had ever been alone with Monica in any room in the White House. As the deposition proceeded, Bill became visibly nervous and difficult to hear. Worse, his lawyers were having conniptions because it was clear the Jones team knew devastating details of the relationship that they were unaware of—information garnered from Tripp and her illegal tapes, for the most part. Asked whether he had had "an extramarital sexual affair" with Monica, he answered, "No." Would it be a lie if Monica had told someone that she did have a sexual affair with him beginning in November 1995? "It's certainly not the truth . . . I have never had sexual relations with Monica Lewinsky. I've never had an affair with her."

Even as Bill was testifying, rumors were furiously flying in the media—but not yet published—of the affair. *Newsweek* reporter Michael Isikoff, allied with sources such as Linda Tripp, Lucianne Goldberg, and others who were bent on nailing Bill, was about to break the story. But an intrepid Internet gossip named Matt Drudge—with the help of Goldberg—became the first to publish a story. While not naming Monica in his cyberspace posting in the *Drudge Report*, he predicted that the exploding scandal was "destined to shake official Washington to its foundation."

At five o'clock in the morning of Wednesday January 21, a sleepless Monica opened the door of her mother's Watergate apartment, where she had been holed up, picked up the *Washington Post*, saw the headline about her affair with the president—reported in the mainstream press for the first time—and began to sob. Shortly after seven o'clock, just blocks away in the family quarters at the White House, an anguished Bill awakened a groggy Hillary with the words, "You're not going to believe this . . ."

Now that the scandal was public, their lives would never be the same.

That night Bill and Hillary's overnight guests were a high-powered divorce lawyer—their close friend David Matthews—and his wife, Mary Beth. "Of course, Bill spent the entire evening denying any involvement with Monica," stated a mutual friend who was privy to the grim proceedings. "David, who believed Bill, kept saying, 'Go out and tell the public. Tell them. You gotta talk to the people. You didn't do this, Bill. Get straight with all of this.' But Hillary, who I believe in retrospect knew Bill was lying, was saying, 'No. No. No. You do not understand how it is here [in Washington]. It doesn't matter what you say to the press—they're not going to believe us. It's just not worth it.'"

Later, Matthews said, "It was a tough, obviously disconcerting time for them. We tried to be as supportive as we could. I was with them that night and I just know that she believed him. She did not think that he was fooling around on her with Monica. She knew he'd strayed at some point in their marriage, but they'd worked on that. I've counseled hundreds of women in twenty-five years of practicing law. Hillary's pretty tough, but I've been a divorce lawyer long enough to know it ain't ever going to be the same for them. Hillary's been embarrassed and humiliated. She may forgive him, but they've had a substantial part of themselves stolen from them."

In the next week, both of the Clintons denied to the nation: Bill looked into the eye of a TV camera from the Roosevelt Room of the White House and lied: "I did not have sexual relations with *that woman*—Miss Lewinsky. I never told anyone to lie, not a single time— never. These allegations are false." And the next morning a defiant Hillary made her now famous "right-wing conspiracy" allegation on the *Today* show.

Behind closed doors, though, the Clintons' union—the pact they had made years earlier—was all but shattered by the scandal. Hillary yelled and cursed and threw things, and on at least one occasion smacked Bill in the face. When she wasn't venting her fury, she flatly refused to even acknowledge his presence. "It was hell," a family friend noted sadly. "None of us could do anything, none of us could help." In the family quarters, Bill often sat alone, his eyes red from crying, or he stared blankly into space. Long past midnight, he'd sit up making sad, lonely calls to a few close friends, rationalizing what had happened, seeking support and guidance. He spent hours alone with his dog, Buddy, talking to him, as if to a confidante. "Bill," said a close friend, "was an emotional wreck. Like in a film, he was watching his whole life pass before his eyes—and he saw himself and his legacy going down in flames. We all feared for the worst. If he had been in jail, there would have been a suicide watch. There's no doubt the Secret Service guys were ordered to keep a tight guard on him, to watch for any acute signs. Suicide was not out of the question, at least in the minds of those who knew his emotional state during that hellish period."

Hillary, meanwhile, turned to her mother for some solace.

"Aunt Dorothy had input and advice," acknowledged Oscar Dowdy. "They talked in probably some depth. Hillary expressed what her thoughts were and knowing Dorothy she'd say, 'If you did this, then this or that might happen.' Dorothy is a smart lady and she's been around, if you will. She may have been a little naive in the beginning, probably disbelieving or thinking that the media was being unfair as far as Bill goes. But a blind-deaf person would have known what was going on. Bill and Hillary pretty much lived separate lives from almost day one.

"As talented and as smart as she knows Bill is, Dorothy can't overlook what he's done to Hillary. I'm sure Dorothy's disgusted with him, but understands that Hillary's making the choice to stay with him for whatever is going to help them politically. Whatever goals they have, they will do what's necessary to achieve those goals—and I'm sure Dorothy's supporting her for that reason. She certainly respects Hillary's decisions and decision-making processes.

"But if Dorothy had her way, she would have Hillary kick Bill to the curb."

The spring and summer of 1998 became even more unreal: glamour cover photos were taken of Hillary for *Vogue*, and of Monica for *Vanity Fair*; Ken Starr issued an unprecedented subpoena to Bill to testify before the grand jury; in exchange for full immunity, Monica agreed to tell the panel the full and complete story about her relationship with the president.

Testifying for some four hours before the grand jury from the White House via a video hookup on August 17, Bill, testy and angry, admitted his relationship with Monica for the first time, but showed little remorse. That night, in a four-minute broadcast to the nation, he declared, "I know that my public comments and my silence about this matter gave a false impression. I misled people, including even my wife. I deeply regret that."

The public and the press felt his words weren't enough. Was there no real remorse? Was he sad only because he had gotten caught?

After months of White House and prosecutorial leaks, career-making TV punditry, huge book deals, blaring tabloid tales, and sophomoric Letterman Top 10 Lists, all of Bill and Monica's encounters as documented ad nauseam by Ken Starr and his team were finally made public by Congress on September 11, 1998.

Appropriately, the unprecedented 445-page report was wrapped in an ordinary plain brown cover with an equally innocuous and bland title:

REFERRAL
TO THE
UNITED STATES HOUSE OF REPRESENTITIVES
PURSUANT TO
TITLE 28, UNITED STATES CODE, § 595(C)

SUBMITTED BY
THE OFFICE OF INDEPENDENT COUNSEL
SEPTEMBER 9, 1998

Some newspapers, like the *New York Daily News*, which published a special section detailing all of the naughty bits, felt compelled because of the steamy content to warn of "sexually explicit details that some readers may find offensive."

Like most members of Congress, Tom Davis, a Republican from Vermont, was shocked by the pornographic details of the president's sexual adventures. "It is gross," he gasped. "It's not the way normal people act."

Starr's seven-month probe—an investigation that would eventually cost taxpayers more than $50 million—uncovered "substantial and credible information that President William Jefferson Clinton committed acts that may constitute grounds for an impeachment."

Starr listed eleven impeachable acts—ranging from lying in the Paula Jones deposition, to witness tampering, to engaging "in a pattern of conduct that was inconsistent with his constitutional duty to faithfully execute the laws."

Bill's eyes were downcast, filled with tears, and his voice cracked. "I have sinned," he told a hundred ministers, priests, rabbis, and imams at a White House prayer breakfast the day the Starr Report became public. Almost a month earlier he had given a confident, combative TV address to the nation about his "inappropriate" relationship with Monica. Now, he appeared distraught, devastated, on the verge of collapse. Seemingly.

"It is important to me," he said, reading words he had written the night before, "that everybody who has been hurt know that the sorrow I feel is genuine: first and most important, my family; also, my friends, my staff, my cabinet, Monica Lewinsky and her family, and the American people. I have asked for their forgiveness." He also read a passage from the Gates of Repentance, a Yom Kippur liturgy, that he noted had been given to him a few days earlier by "a Jewish friend of mine."

While showing contrition, he emphasized that he had no intention of resigning, that he fully intended to fight impeachment. "I will instruct my lawyers to mount a vigorous defense, using all available appropriate argument," he declared. And sounding like Bill the campaigner, he noted: "I will intensify my efforts to lead our country and the world toward peace and freedom, prosperity and harmony, in the hope that with a broken spirit and a still strong heart, I can be used for greater good, for we have many blessings and many challenges and so much work to do."

At the end, a Texas minister offered a prayer and emphasized that "the only difference between a sinner and a saint is that one's found forgiveness, the other ain't."

A month after the Starr Report was issued, the House of Representatives voted along party lines to begin an inquiry into possible grounds for the president's impeachment. "It is not in my hands," Bill stated that day. "It is in the hands of Congress and the people of this country—ultimately in the hands of God. There is nothing I can do."

And there wasn't.

On December 11, the House Judiciary Committee voted to impeach him and remove him from office for perjury and obstruction of justice. Three Articles were approved and a fourth count was passed the next day. Appearing anguished, Bill spoke for several minutes in the Rose Garden. "Mere words cannot fully express the profound remorse I feel . . . These past months have been a torturous process of coming to terms with what I did . . . the pain I have caused my family. There is no greater agony."

Five days later House Republicans were forced to postpone the impeachment vote when Bill suddenly and suspiciously ordered air strikes against Iraq, claiming that the country had refused to abide by a promise to allow the United Nations to conduct on-site inspections for weapons of mass destruction. The general feeling about the timing of the attack ranged from skepticism to disbelief. As one pundit noted, ". . . the President came face to face with the stinging reality that his credibility was crumbling. . . . Some sober, experienced leaders no longer take him at his word. . . ."

Meanwhile, Bill and Hillary's disintegrating relationship began to manifest itself in public. It became known that she had canceled the family's annual holiday vacation in the Virgin Islands where, a year earlier—when he was still involved with Monica—the first couple were photographed snuggling and dancing in bathing suits. In Israel as impeachment neared at home, Hillary publicly gave Bill the cold shoulder—turning and pulling away from him as he tried to hold her arm at the grave of slain Israeli prime minister Yitzhak Rabin. On the flight over on Air Force One, Hillary had stayed in a separate compartment, and she never once mentioned Bill as she mostly traveled on her own during the trip.

Back at home, breaking weeks of a steely silence, she made a weak effort to stave off the impeachment of her husband, stating, "I think the vast majority of Americans share my approval and pride in the job that the President's been doing . . . that view is shared . . . by people all over the world, as I saw recently on the trip to the Middle East . . ."

But her remarks fell flat. Bill's aides were hoping for a firm statement forgiving his philandering, and a plea to the country to move on; his strategists had been pushing Hillary for weeks to take such a dramatic stand—but she had adamantly refused.

On December 19, Bill Clinton became only the second president in history to be impeached, charged with perjury and obstruction of justice by a divided House of Representitives. That afternoon, with a stiff-faced Hillary beside him, he vowed defiant but red-eyed to serve "until the last hour of the last day of my term." That day Hillary had surprisingly described herself in a closed meeting with the House Democrats as "a wife who loves and supports her husband" and accused Republicans of "hounding him out of office" because they opposed his politics. It was her first major defense of him since the *Today* appearance and was reminiscent of her tough "stand by my man" statements on *60 Minutes* years earlier when he denied his affair with Gennifer Flowers. Hearing her words, one Ohio congressman declared, "She's so terrific. It's lucky for America we have a woman with her strength to lead the nation right now. And everybody understands she is one of the leaders of the nation right now, as much as the president."

But the next day Hillary was gone from Bill's side when he attended church with only Chelsea and some friends. The next day, though, they were photographed together cooking Christmas lasagna at a soup kitchen, a scenario certainly set up by White House spin doctors.

Little more than three weeks later, on February 13, 1999, a harrowing year of scandal came to an end when the Senate acquitted Bill Clinton—not because of a lack of evidence, but because the lawmakers of the land, some believed, did not want to defile the office of the presidency itself.

But as Dale Bumpers, the former Democratic senator from Arkansas and close family friend, declared in a wrenching personal appeal to the Senate not to remove Bill from office, "[The Clinton family] has already been about as decimated as a family can get. The relationship between husband and wife, father and child, has been incredibly strained, if not destroyed."

Like a giant brush fire, the Monica Lewinsky scandal had roared across the land, scorching every community in its wake. Fascination, repulsion, delight, disgust, whatever the reaction, there was not a solitary person in the country—man, woman, or child—who was not in some way affected.

But no group of people were hit harder, or affected more deeply, than those from Bill's beloved home state, Arkansas.

These were the people who had known him, grown up with him, believed in him, fought for him, given him, in newspaper editor Melinda Gassaway's words, "their time, their hearts, their money."

Their reactions ran the gamut. They were heartsick, defensive, furious, shell-shocked. The closest friends wracked their brains to come up with mitigating pleas—it was Monica's fault, it was Hillary's fault, it was Starr's fault, it was the media's fault, the right wing's fault.

Yet all but a very few diehard loyalists recognized, too, that Bill himself, their brilliant, talented golden boy, had some deeply imbedded kink in his psyche—and that he was in fact the most responsible.

"He embarrassed Hillary, embarrassed us, embarrassed the public—and he did it to himself," Marge Mitchell, Bill's mother's oldest friend, put it flatly. Through the years Bill had always wanted to hear her opinion, knowing she would give it to him straight. Had she said anything to him during the Monica scandal? Mitchell threw back her head and laughed heartily. "You betcha," she said, but would reveal no more.

"Arrogance, arrogance, arrogance. The arrogance of power," Melinda Gassaway pronounced, sadly. "I am angry at him, I'd like to throttle him. We know he lied. He behaved abysmally. I know he's angry—no one's personal life has been that exposed—but he brought it on himself. That's what I think has angered so many people in Arkansas. They feel humiliated."

In the wake of the scandal, Beckie Moore, the executive director of the Clinton birthplace foundation, was forced to play the reluctant host to hundreds of angry visitors who dropped by the restored Clinton home in Hope—only to vent their spleen. "Where's Monica?" some asked. "Do you have a gallery with pictures of all the women?" Occasionally, she was unable to keep from snapping back—"Oh, Monica's only here on Tuesdays." One lady stormed in, furious. "How in the world can you stand to work for this sinner?"

Carolyn Staley, Bill's close high school friend and neighbor, could not resist attempting to trace possible precipitating factors for what had happened. Before getting involved with Monica, she noted, Bill had experienced a number of personal losses—the deaths of Foster, his mother, Commerce Secretary Ron Brown, Israeli Premier Ytzhak Rabin, all important figures in his life. He also was nearing the point when his beloved Chelsea would be leaving the nest. All these events were heavy psychological blows, Staley felt—believing that if you sustain enough of them, something cracks.

And then, too, the Monica business had sprung to life in a strange, otherworldly atmosphere—during the government shutdown. "Everyone else was gone, it was like a snow day, a kind of fantasy land in the White House," she said. "And there's Monica—in all her thonged glory."

Bill, Staley knew, was a man who thrived on emotional relationships. Being isolated in the White House could not have been good for his health. Shouldn't his need for friendship, for people he could simply relax with, have been recognized more? Wouldn't it have been better for all of us if it had?

Theories, explanations, attempts to understand—all were ways people who knew and admired Bill attempted to deal with the situation. But there was another reaction that lay deeper, just beneath the skin— sorrow, pain, a wistful longing for what might have been.

Perhaps Marla Crider, who had known him and loved him so long ago, back at the beginning, expressed it best.

"There is a part of me, after twenty-five years, who would love to sit down one more time, one on one, with unlimited time, to talk to Bill Clinton about everything," she said. "To satisfy myself whether the Bill Clinton I know is still in there somewhere.

"Because externally he's not there. The things he says, actions he takes, it's just not the guy I believed in in 1974. It's all got spin to it, it's all for the cameras . . . and it's sad. I guess, bottom line, it's sad.

"In my eyes back then, I really felt like he had all the makings of greatness. And I'm one of those people who's been very, very disappointed along the way. I still like him as a human being, still look forward to maybe sometime conversing with him again, joking, laughing, talking about the good old days. But I'm sad because he never did get, was never allowed to be, the Bill Clinton he started out being."

Hillary, meanwhile, did not walk away. She chose to stay, horrifying many, while winning the admiration of many more: as the number one betrayed wife in America, her approval ratings shot straight for the stratosphere. Many applauded her grace and dignity; others, shaking their heads, wondered if she was about to apply for sainthood. How could she stay with him? Yet, as first lady, how could she leave? Hillary had no option.

Yet in fact, as always, she had her own agenda, and knew she would need Bill's help, and her position as first lady, to bring it off.

Hillary had decided it was time to set up her own franchise.

HILLARY ON HER OWN

Thirty-five years earlier, a thirty-eight-year-old political icon named Bobby Kennedy had decided that his road to the White House involved a temporary detour through New York as a U.S. senator. Now, Hillary had decided to take that same route—and members of her circle were certain that if she won the New York senatorial election in 2000, her next goal would be the presidency.

Like Kennedy, Hillary's decision to seek elective office garnered enormous support in part because of the sympathy factor; both had decided to seek the U.S. Senate seat on the heels of tragedy: Bobby had lost his brother in Dallas, and his popularity ratings had rocketed; Hillary had lost Bill in the arms of Monica—or at least that was the public perception, making her the most admired and sympathetic woman in the country, if not the world.

Despite the intense positive public feelings for Kennedy, he ran headlong into the carpetbagger issue: How could he represent the people of New York State, the media and his adversaries asked, if his image was emblazoned on the state of Massachusetts, his professional life

271

stamped and sealed in Washington, and his personal world centered in the rolling country landscape of Hickory Hill in northern Virginia?

At campaign stops after he announced his candidacy on August 25, 1964, Bobby faced multitudes of hecklers carrying signs that read, "Get a Roadmap and Go Home"; "Carry Me Back to Old Virginny"; and "Take Your Carpet and Bag it." Bobby scoffed at the accusations, while Ethel, his ruthlessly loyal wife and mother of their enormous brood, defended him against what she termed "a false issue." Bobby, of course, won, and little more than three years later announced his tragically ill-fated presidential candidacy, knocking Eugene McCarthy, whom Hillary had actively campaigned for at Wellesley, out of the box.

But by the millenium the carpetbagger issue wasn't as organized and strident against Hillary, who had been raised in Illinois, educated in Massachusetts and Connecticut, and lived most of her adult life in Arkansas and Washington. Nevertheless, she acknowledged that she was trying to transform herself into a New Yorker—in part by reading Kennedy's speeches from his campaign, and watching videotape footage of him. Though she had absolutely no ties to New York—not even a Manhattan hotel suite such as the one the Kennedys had maintained at the Carlyle for years—the only real question appeared to be whether she would wear a Yankees cap rather than a Cubs.

Credibility was more important. Though Kennedy and Hillary had never run for elective office prior to their respective New York campaigns, Bobby had served as the brilliant chief counsel for the Senate Rackets Committee, battling the likes of Jimmy Hoffa, and as U.S. attorney general under his brother Jack, winning round after round against J. Edgar Hoover, the Kennedys' nemesis. With all of that experience under his belt, Bobby was considered the consummate politician whose every step was made with great deliberateness—and with a brain trust of brilliant advisors. Hillary, meanwhile, sought the Senate seat following a series of personal and public humiliations—the most political of which was the health care debacle.

Unlike Bobby who rarely made a misstep in his race for the Senate, Hillary's campaign would be littered with false moves and errors of judgment.

Midway between Bill's impeachment and his acquittal, two leading members of Congress publicly floated the first media trial balloons of a

Hillary-for-Senate run, and from all appearances she had a clear field. The predictable front-runners—the Bobby Kennedy Jrs., the Andrew Cuomos—had let it be known that they had other fish to fry, allowing Hillary, if she wanted, to make her move. "One can see Mrs. Clinton as a senator," wrote Joe ("Anonymous") Klein, in the *New Yorker.* "She has a senatorial sense of personal inevitability. . . . She is probably more qualified for high office than many of the professional wrestlers and talk-show hosts entering the lists across America these days."

A statewide poll had already disclosed that despite the Monica scandal, Hillary could beat any Empire State contender—except for Republican front-runner, New York mayor Rudy Giuliani.

Hillary's popularity, the survey showed, was high among the elderly—the health care issue being key to winning that bloc, and she had already grabbed the gold ring among women; after all, she was a national heroine who had once again appeared to stand by her man—at least publicly. She was the favorite of two out of five New York State women. "It's a sign of the public's support for her handling of the Lewinsky issue," explained pollster John Zogby.

Hillary immediately showed up in the Big Apple to trade national TV quips with native New Yorker and supporter Rosie O'Donnell, and soon after shuffled off to a hockey arena in Buffalo where she was cheered wildly by thousands who waved flags and carried hand-lettered signs that read "Run Hillary Run!" and "Hillary, Move to New York!"

The momentum was there—as was the Clinton's ever-present complex union.

Noting that fact, a lead editorial in the *New York Times* observed: "Running while her husband is still President would certainly be a dramatic break with tradition, and it also suggests a First Lady who is thinking beyond the tarnished record of Bill Clinton. Her candidacy would represent a remarkable change in the dynamics of a marriage in which his career has come first."

The staid *Times* had no idea.

Back at the White House Hillary had thrown her political plans in Bill's face, letting the dishonored, beleaguered lame duck know in no uncertain terms that she now intended to follow her own agenda, her own passions—and he had better play ball as she had done for a quarter century. "The bottom line of what she told him," revealed a close friend of the Clintons privy to the conversation was, "It's my turn, my day in the sun . . . I'm outta here . . . You better support me, or else . . . And by the way, go fuck yourself."

Not long after, at a Democratic fundraiser in Manhattan's swank Le Cirque 2000, a seemingly repentant and chastened Bill Clinton told the ten-thousand-dollar-a-head crowd: "It's highly likely that I will increasingly be known as the person who comes with Hillary to New York." Days later he commented directly on her possible candidacy, declaring she would be "a great" senator. "She and I both would like to continue to be useful in public affairs when we leave office."

But their battles continued behind closed doors—as his political career waned and hers burgeoned. When he returned wistfully to Hope to dedicate his boyhood home—a deeply sentimental, emotional occasion—Hillary was not at his side, blaming her absence on scheduling conflicts; the two had abruptly ended a Utah ski vacation after spending virtually no time together; she canceled her scheduled plans to go on a trip to Central America with him—claiming a back ailment, which curiously did not keep her from a series of hectic appearances in New York; on a trip with Chelsea—but without Bill—to Egypt, talk of her crumbling marriage continued when respected columnist Anis Mansour of the state-owned newspaper *Al-Ahram* maintained, "Their relationship is completely over. The divorce proceedings will go very smoothly because the judge will not have to summon witnesses. Almost all of the globe's population are witnesses to Clintion's infidelity."

It was clear to many that the Clintons' marriage was in shreds, held together only by their years-long political alliance. From Washington to Cairo an eerie marital deathwatch had set in.

During virtually all of 1999, Hillary waged a shadow campaign, establishing an exploratory committee, and teasing about when she would make her formal announcement, and where she would live. But she stated emphatically, "I do plan to live in New York no matter what I end up doing . . ." Clinton marriage watchers in the media, of course, pounced on her use of the word "I"—and its real meaning.

Meanwhile, her popularity among New Yorkers rose and fell depending on the extent of her latest political gaffe—of which there were many.

Jews were furious after she was acclaimed anew as a champion of

Palestinian nationhood—and sat smiling through an anti-Israeli diatribe by Palestinian leader Yasser Arafat's wife. "The severe damage caused by the intensive daily use of poison gas by the Israeli forces in the past years has led to an increase of cancer cases among Palestinian women and children," Suha Arafat declared. Afterward, Hillary kissed her. Israeli Prime Minister Ehud Barak issued a swift denunciation, as did Washington. Scrambling to recover, her advisors claimed she didn't understand the translation of Arafat's words, and shifting into full damage control mode Hillary quickly rebuked Mrs. Arafat "public inflammatory statements." In an editorial headlined, "Mrs. Clinton Missteps," the *New York Times* observed, "More important to the voters than the tactical clumsiness are her substantive positions on Israel, the Palestinian Liberation Organization and the Mideast peace process. She has sown uncertainty with past comments endorsing a Palestinian state and later supporting the idea of Jerusalem as Israel's capital, a position the White House says can be settled only by the peace negotiations."

Back in New York, a shell-shocked Hillary met privately with Orthodox Jewish leaders hoping to deflect criticism and to exhibit her asserted firm support of Israel—but she received a lukewarm reception. Meanwhile, pundits and Giuliani backers, such as Manhattanite Joan Rivers, gloated. The outspoken one-time standup, who now had a national radio talk program, commented that the reason Hillary had recently shown up as a surprise speaker at a Mount Sinai Medical Center fundraising luncheon was "because she figured—'Jews! I can make up for Arafat, kissing Arafat's wife,' . . . if you don't see what a phony she is . . . She's so anti-Jewish."

The Arafat controversy had erupted only within weeks of the revelation that Hillary, the long-avowed practicing Methodist, had Jewish roots, touching off another furor over whether she was pandering to Jewish voters by leaking the bombshell. A *New York Daily News* reader seemed to sum up the general consensus, writing, "The Clintons can pull any trick out of a hat when it suits them. . . . I may be Jewish, but I'm not stupid. Go, Giuliani."

Months later, as the Yankees and the Mets were beginning Spring training for the 2000 season, and only a few weeks after Hillary formally threw her hat in the ring, she was still desperately trying to win over reluctant Jewish voters, holding secret meetings with Orthodox women and appearing unannounced at Friday night synagogue services on Long Island.

Aside from alienating untold numbers of Jewish voters, Hillary had stirred up passions in the barrios of the city's five boroughs—and across the country—when she became embroiled in Bill's highly controversial decision to free a group of imprisoned Puerto Rican terrorists—a move that infuriated law enforcement officials and ignited Republican accusations that Bill was helping Hillary curry favor with New York's powerful Hispanic vote, another bloc crucial to her election. With that in mind, she announced her support of Bill's decision to offer clemency to sixteen inmates who were part of the Armed Forces on National Liberation, known as FALN, which was dedicated to restoring independence to Puerto Rico. It was one of two groups that waged a terror campaign, carrying out at least 130 bombings in the 1970s and 80s, though those convicted were charged with armed robbery, weapons violations, and sedition.

Instantly, Hillary's support of clemency was viewed by upstaters and suburbanites—an even stronger voting bloc than the Hispanics—as being soft on crime and terrorism. Faced with a firestorm of criticism and the realization that she'd lose non-Hispanic voters, Hillary reversed course once again and declared her opposition to Bill's plan. To make matters worse, before performing her flip-flop she never bothered to confer with New York's sensitive Puerto Rican leaders and elected officials who felt more than a bit slighted—and that miscue again sparked intense debate about her political acumen. In the end, Hillary was forced to concede that the situation had been badly handled.

At the same time, the Clintons denied they had ever conferred about the clemency issue, attempting to shoot down the conspiracy theory that they were in cahoots to help her seduce Hispanic voters, "It is as if Bill Clinton looked us directly in the eye, and wagging his finger, said: I want you to listen to me. I never discussed clemency for terrorists with that woman, Mrs. Clinton. Not a single time. Never," noted conservative *Times* columnist William Safire.

Even the Clintons' purchase of their first privately owned home since the earliest years of their marriage ignited a scandal with the revelation that a close friend and Democratic fundraiser, businessman Terry McAuliffe, agreed to spot them $1.35 million of his own money, in cash, to help them buy a $1.7 million three-story, five-bedroom, four-bath Georgian colonial in the New York City suburb of Chappaqua.

The Clintons desperately needed McAuliffe's help; they were saddled with millions in legal debt from the scandals—McAuliffe was involved in raising money for their legal defense fund, too—and Hillary needed to quickly establish New York residency for her campaign. But critics questioned whether the financial arrangement complied with federal campaign contribution and gifts laws. "For Mrs. Clinton," the *Times* said, "renouncing the McAuliffe loan would be smart politics. It would give voters fatigued by the Clintons' odd propensity for scandal a heartening signal that, on her own, she is ready to break from the ethical sloppiness of the Clinton White House."

The White House had defended the deal and Hillary, on the stump, stonewalled when questioned about it—but in the end Bill and Hillary backed off the McAuliffe deal and were approved for a favorable bank mortgage.

On January 5, 2000, the Clintons spent their first night together in the new house—along with Dorothy Rodham. They claimed they had stayed up well past midnight arranging furniture and unpacking. "This is a lot of excitement and hard work for us," Hillary said, "but we are so pleased that we are finally here and moved in."

The next day they returned to Washington.

Did Bill actually plan to move into the house when he vacated the White House in January 2001. "I love the house," he said. "You know, we picked it out and we like it, and I'm looking forward to living there when I leave here . . . I've got a job to do, and she now has a campaign to run, and so we'll have to be apart more than I wish we were . . . but we'll manage."

With Bill on stage in the background, Hillary finally made it official on February 6, 2000, declaring her candidacy as a "new Democrat"— one who viewed government as neither the cause nor the solution to the problems faced by the nation—and emphasizing the themes of children and education. "I care about the same issues you do . . . I'll fight my heart out for you every single day," she declared in response to any nagging carpetbagger questions. The event was choreographed from start to finish—from the soft biographical video that painted a sympathetic portrait of her and copied the style of Bill's campaign video, *The Man from Hope*, to the jumbo banner behind her that read "Hillary." During the half hour Bill spent on stage in the packed gymnasium at the State University of New York campus in Purchase, he never spoke a single word.

Over the next several months, Hillary and Giuliani waged cutthroat campaigns: She attacked him for "dividing the city" in his defense of policemen involved in the shootings of four unarmed men. The mayor had clearly made a major misstep—and Hillary moved ahead in the polls. While the Clinton administration took heat over its "Nazi-like tactics" in the Elián Gonzalez case, Hillary slammed Giuliani for what she asserted were "divisive attacks" against the federal agents—he called them "storm troopers"—involved in the Easter weekend raid on the home of the boy's Miami relatives. By early May the closely watched race was thrown into total disarray when Giuliani revealed he had prostate cancer. But sympathy turned to disbelief a week later when he acknowledged a relationship with a woman other than his wife, Donna Hanover, whom he had married sixteen years earlier at a church called St. Monica's. The Giulianis soon announced a split, and she angrily alleged Hizzoner had had a previous affair with a staffer. Hillary, who'd been there, done that, remained mum. The embattled Guiliani decided to leave the race.

Meanwhile, ghosts of scandals supposedly past appeared: a federal judge ruled that Bill "committed a criminal violation of the Privacy Act" by releasing personal letters to undermine the credibility of Kathleen Willey in the midst of the Lewinsky drama; the White House claimed it was immune from the federal act. Ken Starr's successor, Robert W. Ray, was reportedly considering indicting Bill after he left office on charges relating to whether he lied under oath to a grand jury, and whether he asked Monica to lie about their relationship. Ray also said he would release several reports through the fall of 2000 related to "Travelgate," and Whitewater, which could turn out to be problematic for Hillary.

"I won't be surprised by anything that happens, but I'm not interested in being pardoned," a clearly irritated Bill declared during an appearance before a gathering of newspaper editors. "I am prepared to stand before any bar of justice I have to stand before."

*   *   *

The state of the union address, delivered at the beginning of each year by the incumbent president, rarely offers much chance for drama; usually it is a rather mundane, predictable political speech. Most Americans tune in to hear the first address given by an incoming head of state, and skip the others, except in times of national crisis. Presidents traditionally use the free air time to congratulate themselves on what they've done well, excoriate the other party in Congress for not letting them do everything they wanted, and to ramble vaguely and at stultifying length about what they'd like to do in the future. Few sound bites emerge; rarely, if ever, is new ground broken. It is generally a civil enough evening, broken by genial applause and polite standing ovations, invariably coming from the expected side of the aisle. No more.

Bill's last three state of the union addresses, however, were in a whole different category; it is probable they attracted some of the largest audiences in history. This was a man on the ropes, scandal exploding all around him. No one in the nation was thinking primarily of policy issues as they sat waiting for him to come through the door in 1998, 1999, and 2000. Their concerns were a lot more basic and visceral. Could the big guy pull it off? Would he slip? Lash out? Break down emotionally? Lose it for all time?

People waited, anxious, thrilled, breathless, deliciously fearful, on the edge of their seats—this was an expert stuntman headed over the Niagara in a barrel, a trapeze artist taking a triple somersault without a net, a fighter pilot trying for a tricky landing with a failed engine. And more. This was the president of the United States caught in the gears of a terrible, messy, unspeakably embarrassing situation, about to address the nation. The man was human—surely something would crack.

Yet the Bill Clinton who ascended to the podium those three consecutive Januaries was as calm, as seemingly nondistraught, as coolly smooth as any head of state in history. Stunned, the country watched as he managed, through some almost unimaginable feat of will, to deliver each address as if nothing in the world had gone wrong—or as if none of it mattered in the slightest. It was at once reassuring and oddly chilling; denial raised to the level of presidential fiat.

In 1998, the state of the union address was delivered on January

27—incredibly, a mere twenty-four hours after Bill's finger-waving declaration on national TV that he had "not had sex with that woman,
Miss Lewinsky" (a statement that many found as telling as Nixon's "I
am not a crook" assertion). In addition, it was also given only hours
after Hillary had appeared on the *Today* show to defend him, lashing
out at a "vast right-wing conspiracy."

The following year the address came on January 19, 1999, smack in
the middle of the congressional impeachment hearings—almost midway between the House vote to impeach, on December 19, and the
Senate's final decision to acquit, on February 12. The president was in
deep trouble; it seemed impossible to think there would be no indication. Yet again, his delivery was flawless—though his face, heavily
bagged, showed evidence of the strain he was under.

The atmosphere around Bill's last state of the union address of his
notorious two terms, on January 27, 2000, was different, of course—there
was no exploding scandal, no congressional investigation going on outside the hall. Yet people were still eager to gauge his emotional barome-
ter—he had been deeply humiliated, he was a lame duck, he had been
reduced to the position of silent partner in his wife's campaign for the
Senate (formally announced a week later). Again, they tuned in primarily to see if he could pull it off, manage to act presidential in the face of
everything everyone knew.

But there was another reason why the world awaited Bill's last three
state of the union speeches with all the bated breath expectation of a
championship prizefight crowd: Hillary.

Interest in Hillary, and the state of their union, had risen over the years
to the height of acute national concern. Photographs of the two were
scrutinized for possible clues; comments, actions, the sudden dropping of
a hand, a clenched arm, a tightened lip—all were analyzed endlessly, in
talk shows, living rooms, office cafeterias, opinion columns: she was leaving, she hadn't spoken to him in months, she refused to be in the same
room, they planned to divorce when he finished his term.

At times, her barely concealed rage was clear to everyone—as in the
famous walk across the White House lawn, separated by their valiant
daughter, en route to Martha's Vineyard in August 1999—only days after
it had been confirmed that the DNA stain on Monica's Gap dress was
unquestionably presidential in origin. "Hillary is really angry at me," Bill

confided to a friend a short time later. "We've been angry before, but she is angrier than I've ever seen her in my life."

Few in the country were unaware of this. People were not tuning in just to watch Bill; they tuned in to watch Hillary, too. The entire country was avidly, deeply fascinated, desperate for any glimpse they could get of this complicated, unique, to many utterly inexplicable, marriage.

They saw, of course, very little—nothing they couldn't have predicted. In each speech, Bill referred to her several times, warmly, lovingly, as if they were not in the midst of navigating the roughest patch any marriage had ever faced, and in full view of the nation. He grinned, beamed, held out his hand towards her for all the world as if the marriage was strong and viable. And of course, for all the world—considering the strange and tortuous history of that marriage—it may have been.

In 1998, when he was under attack, and Hillary had stormed to his defense, his references to her were warmly casual, husbandly— "Hillary and I" had launched a White House millennium program, "Hillary and I" had traveled to Sarajevo, he said. Reminding the world that the two of them stood together, united against enemies foreign and domestic, ready to face the new world. Hillary nodded, pleased, when the camera sought her out. Not a crease, not a tremor revealed any doubt: she was in full battle mode, standing by her man.

In 1999, post-DNA, midimpeachment, her face was stolidly inexpressive. Careful arrangements had clearly been made: Hillary sat flanked by two immensely popular figures, Sammy Sosa, the surprise home run champion whose feats had almost surpassed Mark McGwire's in the recent baseball season—and Rosa Parks, one of the true icons of the civil rights movement. A baseball player, a civil rights heroine, and the number one betrayed wife in the country—a trio of sympathetic figures.

To ensure that the seating arrangement would escape no one's notice—certainly not the camera's—Bill made sure he mentioned Hillary when he referred to Sosa and Parks. Hillary, he said, had visited the Dominican Republic after the hurricane had hit the country, had rededicated a hospital. "With her was someone else who has been very important to relief efforts," he added, launching into his tribute to Sosa. Parks, he said a bit later, was "sitting down with the first lady." Each time, Hillary's face filled the screen.

He made a final reference that night as well, to the fact that Hillary had "traveled all across the country" to spur support for saving American landmarks. Again Hillary allowed herself a small icy head-dip of acknowledgement as the camera stayed with her for a long moment. Her face was unreadable, but the nation read it and knew: there had been no forgiveness, and was likely to be none, ever. Most interpreted it personally, through the lens of their own marital history—who would forgive a bum like that? Only a very few understood the deeper meaning. Bill, to Hillary, had done far more than break a marriage vow; his weakness had severely crippled his presidency—the presidency they had strived for their entire lives. He had broken their pact.

In the last state of the union address Bill would ever give, on January 27, 2000, his references to Hillary were far more direct. "I am forever grateful to the person who's led our efforts from the beginning and who's worked so tirelessly for children and families. . . . my wife . . . and I thank her," he enthused, with a wide, loving smile, flinging his arm out dramatically in her direction.

The applause rose sharply—with no one in or out of the chamber unaware of all the other things he might be forever grateful for. The first lady sat, the familiar Gioconda smile plastered tightly on her face. The camera switched—from his face to hers—as the applause continued. Then Bill, whose presidency had been so full of history-breaking moments, added yet another—with the camera on him, with the whole country watching, he became the first president in history to gaze soulfully at his wife in the middle of a state of the union address and mouth the words "I love you."

Quickly, the camera sought out his wife, eager to pick up the slightest glimmer of reaction. But there was none. Hillary continued to stare straight ahead, through the lens, out toward the nation of viewers, who had never understood her, no matter how they tried. Her face remained utterly impassive.

ACKNOWLEDGMENTS

A BIOGRAPHER DEPENDS—more than perhaps any other writer—on the kindness of strangers. In this case, considering how many people had already been besieged—and often, burned—in the past when talking to journalists about the Clintons, that kindness was nothing short of phenomenal.

A very special debt of gratitude is owed to Marla Crider, Paul and Mary Lee Fray, Oscar and Helen Dowdy, Donald Rodham, and Tony Rodham—all of whom tirelessly answered probing questions. Their candor, honesty, and courage illuminate this book.

A special debt of life gratitude is also owed to the wonderful people in Arkansas, who were so open and candid: to Rosalind Hudson, Patty Roddenberry, and the delightful members of Virginia Kelley's Birthday club: Clover Gibson, Berneice Lyon, Mimi Ryan, Pat Switzer, Edie West—and most especially, Nancy Adkins and Rachel Heffernan. Thanks also to Mauria Jackson Aspell, Wilma Booker, Dick Kelley, Marge Mitchell, Beckie Moore, Marty Elam Walker.

For sharing their early memories of the Clintons at college: James Blumstein, Janis Ennis, Pat Fry, Steve Hadley, Jerry Hafter, Art Kaminsky, Michael Medved, Mandy Merck, Richard Porter, Kwan Kwan Wang, among others.

To the Clinton-watchers, who gave their time and insights so generously: Max Brantley, John Brummett, Ernie Dumas, Garrick Feldman, Barbara Feinman, Seth Gittell, Gene Lyons, Melinda Gassaway, Meredith Oakley, Dr. Stanley Renshon, Eric Rozenman, John Robert Starr, Judith Warner.

To the many sources in Scranton, Pennsylvania, who contributed their memories of the Rodham family, Scranton Lace, and the city itself: Harry Arnovitz, Andy Bates, Henry Belin IV, Robert Clarke, Hillary Collins, Bob Hine, Rosie Nemeth, Mary Padeletti, Hazel Price, Marjorie Rodney, Natalie Solfanelli, Isabelle Starvinsky. A special thanks to genealogist Cecille Champagne and historian Nick Petula, for sharing their research, and candid memories, and to Joe Flannery, for his half-century of journalistic knowledge. Also a debt of gratitude to Marianne Moran, Lackawanna Historical Society.

A special thank-you goes to the former Scranton woman who once was engaged to Hillary Clinton's father, and who decided to speak candidly for the first time.

Thanks as well to the alumni of Penn State University and Jefferson Medical College, in Philadelphia, for their memories of Dr. Russell Rodham and the Rodham brothers, Hugh and Willard: Dr. Stanley Clader, Alex Cowan, Dr. John Deardorff, Dr. Rudy Hecksher, Dr. Daniel Hilferty, William Joachim, Dr. Bernard Miller, Dr. William Potter Rumsey, Robert Seigler, and in particular, Dr. Leonard Davitch. Thomas Jefferson University archivist Beth Bensman did a superb job of finding records and information regarding Russ Rodham, and a thank-you to Dr. Benjamin Bacharach, associate Dean, Alumni Records, at Jefferson.

In Chicago, researcher Richard R. Seidel was unrelenting in piecing together details of the lives of the Rodhams in the Windy City. Praise also goes to others in Chicago who participated in research for this book: Colleen Vander Hye, librarian, *Chicago Tribune*; Shah Tiwana, Municipal Reference Collection, Harold Washington Library; Mary Jo Doyle, Rogers Park Historical Society; Jack Bess,

Rogers Park News; Commander Will Knight, media relations, Chicago Fire Department; among others.

Helpful in securing and expediting federal government records were Clifford Amsler, assistant director of military records, National Personnel Records Center, St. Louis; and William Bassman, chief of the Reference Service Branch, at NPRC.

And kudos to the dozens of others who agreed to be interviewed, offering candid memories, perceptions, guidance, and insights. They include: Shirley Abbott, Ron Addington, Richard Atkinson, Melinda Barran, Mike Binstein, Ken Brown, Dolly Kyle Browning, Steve Clarke, Arlene Crane, Rose Crane, Dave Criner, Jeanne Drewsen, Selig Drezner, Paul Elward, Clay Farrar, Enrico Ferorelli, Tim Fry, Bill Granger, Eleanor Graves, Mort Gittelman, Terry Guzman, Ray Guzman, Don Harrell, Chris Hedgedes, Dr. Jean Houston, Cliff Jackson, Steve Jones, Richard Johnson, Dan Kennett, Phil Kunhardt, John Laibovitz, John Loengard, Ruth Love, Paul Lukes, Diane Lyons, Warren Maus, David Matthews, Neil McDonald, Jim Morgan, Steve Nichols, Carrie Lockwood Owen, D. A. Pennebaker, Roy Reed, Nicole Rodham, Martha Saxton, Dr. Bill Schooley, Steve Smith, Brian Snow, Carolyn Yeldell Staley, Nancy Stuercke, Alan Stone, Dave Thomas, Dr. Stephen Van Devanter, Marjorie Voss, Richard Voss, Jane Wilson. I'm grateful to all of you for opening the door, including those others who sought anonymity for personal and professional reasons.

Of all the books written about the Clintons, a few stand head and shoulders above the rest. David Maraniss's *First in His Class*—as the first, and thus far only, truly substantive biography of Bill Clinton—was an indispensable aide. Shirley Abbott's beautifully written memoir about growing up in Hot Springs, *The Bookmaker's Daughter*, provided rich insights. Virginia Kelley's own book, *Leading with My Heart*, written with James Morgan, was invaluable. The early biographies of Hillary—by Judith Warner, *Hillary Clinton: The Inside Story*, and Donnie Radcliffe's *Hillary Rodham Clinton: A First Lady for Our Time*—were also helpful, as was Stanley E. Renshon's exploration, *High Hopes: The Clinton Presidency and the Politics of Ambition*.

Several of the best minds in publishing saw the value of this project from the beginning. The first was my fine literary agent, Joni Evans, who helped guide this book from the proposal stage onward. With the precision of a television network programmer, Joni placed my idea with one of the most savvy editors in the world of books, Larry Ashmead, whose devotion to the project, and support of the author, was unfailing. The team at HarperCollins is superb. I owe my allegiance to Jane Friedman, Cathy Hemming, Vincent Virga, Allison McCabe, and Elliott Beard.

Finally, there would not be a book called *State of a Union* without the tireless dedication and journalistic expertise of my colleague Judy Oppenheimer, the finest reporter and writer I know. In her own right, Judy has been a journalist and editor all of her adult life, and has authored two highly acclaimed books: *Private Demons: The Life of Shirley Jackson* (Putnam, 1988), and *Dreams of Glory* (Summit Books, 1991). I commend her for her intrepid reporting, insightful writing, invaluable insights, and respect for the truth—throughout the course of this project.

NOTES AND SOURCES

THE LETTER
1–4 Exclusive interviews with Marla Crider.

THE MEETING
6 Seven eventful years: *Washington Post*, 8/22/99.
7 "I asked her one day": Interview, Paul Fray.
7 "I don't think she cared": Interview, Art Kaminsky.
7 "Everyone wanted to date": Interview, Michael Medved.
8 "Universally popular": Ibid.
8 "She had a great laugh": Interview, Steve Hadley.
9 "I never heard her say": Interview, Kwan Kwan Wang.
9 "Everybody believed Yale": Interview, Jerry Hafter.
10 "Eddie Haskell": Medved, op. cit.
10 Kwan Kwan Wang remembers: Wang, op. cit.
11 "You're going to sleep": Interview, Marge Mitchell.
11 "Everybody at Yale": Medved, op. cit.
12 "I specifically remember him": Ibid.
12 She collared Steve Hadley: Hadley, op. cit.

12 "He was sort of larger than life": Ibid.
12 "Over the top": Medved, op. cit.
12 "A suprisingly hot couple": Ibid.
13 "Poor baby, I know": Ibid.
13 "You would not have normally": Kaminsky, op. cit.
13 "I was dating": Hafter, op. cit.
14 "I've seen it said": Ibid.
14 "The basic trick to Yale": Interview, Richard Atkinson.
15 "It's a secret about Yale": Kaminsky, op. cit.
15 "Hillary is smart": Interview, Gene Lyons.
15 Kaminsky remembered: Kaminsky, op. cit.
15 "She was smart but": Hadley, op. cit.
15 "He told me she was": Fray, op. cit.
17 "Bill had never ever": Interview, Mary Lee Fray.

HILLARY'S POLITICAL ROOTS

18 "Ordinary, that's the only way": Interview, informed source.
19 "There were shootings": Interview, Nick Petula.
20 "The crimes were mostly": Ibid.
20 She had "2 on a Monday": Rodham family memorabilia.
21 "After he had a series": Interview, Donald Rodham.
21 "He was the only": Interview, informed source.
21 "Because of my dad's": Rodham, op. cit.
22 "Bernie was a black widow spider": Interview, informed source.
22 "Bernie saw my father": Rodham, op. cit.
22 "The club was a facade": Interview, Joseph X. Flannery.
23 "If Bernie was George's mentor": Ibid.
23 "The slot machines were illegal": Ibid.
24 "Daquino was an Italian society": Ibid.
24 "People would come down": Rodham, op. cit.
25 "When you've got that": Ibid.
25 "They'd tell me": Petula, op. cit.
26 "Hugh used to talk": Interview, informed source.
26 "I lost my virginity": Flannery, op. cit.
26 "The Babe loved": Petula, op. cit.
27 "My dad did what": Rodham, op. cit.
27 "George Rodham tried to": Interview, Tony Rodham.
27 "He boasted that": Petula, op. cit.

SCRANTON LIFE

29 "I started on the lowest job": Interview, Rosie Nemeth.
30 "I can't say enough about them": Interview, Marjorie Rodney.
30 "They were a typical American family": Interview, Bob Clarke.
30 "You had to know them": Rodney, op. cit.
31 "Life was tough": Interview, Tony Rodham.
31 "There weren't that many Jews": Interview, informed source.
31 "Willard was sort of a follower": Interview, Donald Rodham.
32 "was something else": Tony Rodham, op. cit.
33 "sentimental reasons": Rodney, op. cit.
33 "I didn't see him": Interview, Hazel Price.
33 "He died of loneliness": Tony Rodham, op. cit.
33 "Hugh decided to sell it": Price, op. cit.

THE MYSTERIOUS DR. RODHAM

34 "Uncle Russell was the genius": Interview, Tony Rodham.
35 "Russ was always looking": Interview, Dr. William Rumsey.
35 "It happens that I'm Catholic": Ibid.
35 "I felt anti-Semitism": Interview, Dr. Leonard Davitch.
36 "He had a brilliant future": Ibid.
36 "I soon discovered": Interview, Dr. Rudy Hecksher.
37 "ambulance chaser": Interview, informed source.
37 "He was screwing around": Davitch, op. cit.
37 "There was lots of beer": Rumsey, op. cit.
37 "Russ called me": Hecksher, op. cit.
38 "I always thought": Rumsey, op. cit.
38 "Jefferson was kind of a closed little family": Interview, Dr. Bernard Miller.
39 "Elizabeth was a nurse": Interview, Hazel Price.
39 "The Rodhams were": Ibid.
40 "When Uncle Russell went": Tony Rodham, op. cit.
40 "That's so shocking": Interview, Marjorie Rodney.
40 "It was very sad": Tony Rodham, op. cit.
41 "I picked up the evening paper": Price, op. cit.

THE WORLD'S GREATEST SALESMAN

42 "When my wife and I see": Interview, Bob Clarke.
42 "Hugh was the consummate pitchman": Interview, informed source.
43 "At Lehigh University": Interview, Donald Rodham.
43 "I've heard people say": Interview, Dr. William Rumsey.

43 "a bag of wind": Interview, Robert Seigler.
44 "Dad was the world's *greatest* salesman": Interview, Tony Rodham.
45 "Hugh was pretty forward": Interviews with the woman who requested anonymity.
45 "Being it was the Depression": Ibid.
45 "It was after college": Clarke, op. cit.
46 "He didn't tell me": Anonymous woman, op. cit.
46 "That's when he got": Donald Rodham, op. cit.
46 "Hugh was a hotshot": Interview, informed source.
49 "We would do the typical family things": Interview, Oscar Dowdy.
49 "That's a lot of gray area": Ibid.
50 "My grandmother was a pretty hot number": Ibid.
50 "His smile was as wide": Interview, informed source.
50 "Max had come from desperate poverty": Dowdy, op. cit.
50 "He would buy every bad mortgage": Ibid.
51 "Max was like": Interview, Helen Dowdy.
52 "There was a bit of a rift": Oscar Dowdy, op. cit.
52 "I can remember": Ibid.
54 "They always lived well": Oscar Dowdy, op. cit.
54 "Our mother had a tough life," Tony Rodham, op. cit.
54 "Our mother decided": Ibid.

HUGH RODHAM RUNS FOR OFFICE
55 "I think she was afraid": Interview, informed source.
56 "I don't know whether they": Interview, Tony Rodham.
56 "In fact, my mother said": Interview, Oscar Dowdy.
57 "in some little nightclub": Ibid.
57 "Uncle Oscar was not one of the brightest men": Rodham, op. cit.
58 "What I heard was": Dowdy, op. cit.
58 "But you'd think": Interview, informed source.
58 "I heard the story": Dowdy, op. cit.
59 "They were both hustlers": Ibid.
60 "Dad was in the process": Rodham, op. cit.
61 "Dad was working": Ibid.
61 "The reason why Hugh": Interview, informed source.
63 "Keenan was very formidable": Interview, Selig Drezner.
63 "By the time the election": Rodham, op. cit.
64 "He loved to sit": Interview, Marge Mitchell.
64 "Uncle Hugh": Dowdy, op. cit.

AND HILLARY MAKES THREE
66 "Our mother hated": Interview, Tony Rodham.
67 "Hillary had managed to wiggle": Interview, Oscar Dowdy.

PORTRAIT OF A MARRIAGE
69 "In Park Ridge": Interview, Richard Voss.
70 "Our mother was pretty tough": Interview, Tony Rodham.
70 "Our mother was probably": Ibid.
71 "Dad loved *The Honeymooners*": Ibid.
71 "very private": Interview, Marjorie Voss.
71 "was a nasty old bugger": Interview, Oscar Dowdy.
71 "It bothered me": Interview, Helen Dowdy.
72 "Helen and I": Oscar Dowdy, op. cit.
72 "during the Depression": Rodham, op. cit.
72 "I just didn't feel": Helen Dowdy, op. cit.
73 "There was a time": Oscar Dowdy, op. cit.
73 "They eat and sleep": Roger Morris, *Partners in Power: The Clintons and Their America* (New York: Henry Holt, 1996), p. 114.
73 "The house was worn": Interview, Nancy Stuercke.
74 "There was no hugging": Ibid.
75 "it is very true": Rodham, op. cit.

THE BIG I AM
76 Dad sold a lot of material": Interview, Tony Rodham.
76 "Hugh was a wheeler-dealer": Interview, Oscar Dowdy.
77 "Our father was a drapery salesman": Rodham, op. cit.
77 "Uncle Hugh's office": Dowdy, op. cit.
77 "It was always my opinion": Interview, Donald Rodham.
78 "If Hugh had a significant estate": Interview, Paul Lukes.

DADDY'S PRINCESS
79 "Hillary was *always* Dad's princess": Interview, Tony Rodham.
80 "I was a quick learner": *Family Circle*, May 18, 1993.
80 "She was absolutely daddy's girl": Interview, Oscar Dowdy.
81 "Hillary was definitely": Interview, Helen Dowdy.
81 "Especially in the summer," Interview, Marjorie Voss.
81 "Hillary got the love": Oscar Dowdy, op. cit.
82 "Hughie tried real hard": Ibid.
82 "Our father was a tough guy": Rodham, op. cit.

82 "She could multiply": *Chicago Magazine*, September 1994.
82 "cut a very singular figure": Ibid.
83 "an incredible amount of heat": Ibid.
84 "We were messing around": Ibid.
85 "had a crush on the cutest boy": Ibid.
86 "Because we were kind of the same age group": Helen Dowdy, op. cit.
86 "Hillary today is": *Chicago Magazine*, op. cit.
87 "When we'd come to a stoplight": Ibid.
88 "After we dropped her off": *Washington Post*, January 19, 1993.

FROM REPUBLICAN TO DEMOCRAT
89 "As soon as we got to campus": Interview, Patricia Coffin Fry.
90 "Hillary just took to Wellesley": Ibid.
91 "She was off campus": Ibid.
91 "At Wellesley College": Interview, Tony Rodham.
91 "We spent a lot of time": Gail Sheehy, *Hillary's Choice* (New York: Random House, 1999), p. 45.
91 "You can't accomplish": David Maraniss, *First in His Class* (New York: Simon & Schuster, 1995), p. 257.
91 "Hillary was a big woman on campus": Fry, op. cit.
92 "stated a burning desire": Sheehy, *Hillary's Choice*, p. 74.
92 "When her mother asked": Interview, informed source.
92 "Hillary confided in Addie": Interview, Oscar Dowdy.
93 "Addie wasn't what Dorothy": Interview, Helen Dowdy.
93 "We were sitting": Ibid.
94 "Dorothy's lifelong grudge": Oscar Dowdy, op. cit.
94 "I have many memories": Letter, January 7, 1999.

WHO'S TO BLAME FOR BILL
97 "They said, 'Wilma, . . . '": Interview, Wilma Booker.
97 "I said, there wasn't anything": Ibid.
98 "All I knew of his life": Virginia Kelley with James Morgan, *Leading with My Heart* (New York: Simon & Schuster, 1994), p. 45.
100 "I'll tell you this": Interview, informed source.
101 "I want to go on record": Interview, Marge Mitchell.
101 "It's clearly ridiculous": Interview, Dr. Stanley Renshon.
102 "A very, very small": Interview, Dr. Bill Schooley.
102 Marty Elam Walker, who went to high school: Interview, Marty Elam Walker

102 "The dirty little secret was": Interview, Clay Farrar.
103 "You learned in your cradle": Shirley Abbott, *The Bookmaker's Daughter: A Memory Unbound* (New York: Ticknor & Fields, 1991), p. 63.
103 "What you saw on the surface": Interview, Melinda Barran.
103 "Melinda [Barran] has always": Interview, Melinda Gassaway.
104 "There really are two Hot Springs": Interview, Roy Reed.

THE KID WANTS TO BE PRESIDENT
105 "People didn't call people alcoholics": Interview, Rose Crane.
106 "A million games": Ibid.
106 "never . . . ever . . . touch my mother again": Virginia Kelley with James Morgan, *Leading with My Heart* (New York: Simon & Schuster, 1994), p. 134.
107 "I saved it": Interview, Ken Brown.
108 "Our group was known": Interview, Mauria Jackson Aspell.
108 "He asked me what I thought": Crane, op. cit.
108 "Bill was like an adult": Interview, Carolyn Yeldell Staley.
109 "a certain amount of boy-girl stuff": Aspell, op. cit.
109 Marge Mitchell, Virginia's nurse buddy: Interview, Marge Mitchell.
109 "People say, did you": Interview, Warren Maus.
110 "He's one of the most": Aspell, op. cit.
110 "In my mind": Maus, op. cit.

HILLARY RODHAM VS. VIRGINIA KELLEY
113 "Maybe because I was pregnant?": Interview, Mary Lee Fray.
113 "I thought, my God": Ibid.
114 "My husband was looking": Mary Lee Fray, op. cit.
115 "It really was extraordinary": Interview, John Brummet.
115 "She told me, 'My God, . . .'": Paul Fray, op. cit.
116 "Your average Southern girl": Interview, Gene Lyons.
116 "I want you to know": Virginia Kelley with James Morgan, *Leading with My Heart* (New York: Simon & Schuster, 1994), p. 191.
116 "Bill told me later": Mary Lee Fray, op. cit.
117 "Because I'll tell you this": Kelley, *Leading with My Heart*, p. 198.
117 Brooding over this: Ibid., p. 200.
117 "He told me": Interview, Carolyn Yeldell Staley.

HIDDEN AGENDA

118 "I said, 'You need . . .'": Interview, Paul Fray.

118 "The faculty was concerned": Interview, Steve Clark.

119 Representative Barney Frank: Spring 1996 speech, Hillel, George Washington University.

121 "He would write": Interview, Brian Snow.

121 "Finally I said, 'Bill . . .'": Interview, Ron Addington.

122 "We told Bill": Interview, Mary Lee Fray, op. cit.

122 "We had planned": Ibid.

122 "Here, why don't you": Ibid.

123 "Am I confused?" Interview, Michael Medved.

123 In her book: Meredith Oakley, *On the Make: The Rise of Bill Clinton* (Washington, D.C.: Regnery Publishing, 1994), p. 68.

123 "He thought it was": Interview, Meredith Oakley.

123 "He told me about": Interview, Cliff Jackson.

123 "Bill and I were riding": Paul Fray, op. cit.

124 "He told me he thought": Interview, Mandy Merck.

124 "We'd be out": Paul Fray, op. cit.

125 "An extreme exaggeration": Merck, op. cit.

THE COLLEGE GIRL

(All of Marla Crider's quotes and narrative regarding her in this chapter are from a series of exclusive interviews.)

128 "He tore into her ass": Interview, Paul Fray.

131 "She told him she'd gone": Ibid.

133 "Back in those days": Interview, Brian Snow.

133 "I don't remember that": Interview, Steve Clark.

133 "Hughie Rodham went after that girl": Fray, op. cit.

134 "That's totally false": Interview, Tony Rodham.

135 "He would go, sit around": Interview, Ron Addington.

135 "Just a good kid": Ibid.

135 "In Arkansas one of": Rodham, op. cit.

136 Steve Smith, who'd become: Interview, Steve Smith.

136 "He'd be up at six": Addington, op. cit.

136 "There's not a son of a bitch": Fray, op. cit.

137 "I was very honest": Interview, Terry Guzman.

138 "It was kind of a hard choice": Interview, John Laibovitz.

THE HILLARY SURPRISE

140 "Bill handed me the phone": Interview, Ron Addington.

141 "The Hillary surprise," Interview, Marla Crider.

141 "There were few people she tolerated": Ibid.

141 "None of those kids": Interview, Paul Fray.

141 "When Hillary arrived in August": Addington, op. cit.

143 "I used to have a lady": Interview, Steve Clark.

143 "The three of us were in the car": Addington, op. cit.

144 "Call them and tell": Crider, op. cit.

144 "She would ask me a question": Fray, op. cit.

144 "Apparently my wife": Interview, Brian Snow.

145 "The better friend": Clark, op. cit.

145 "She almost caused": Crider, op. cit.

146 "giving away the ranch": Interview, Max Brantley.

146 "I was watching him": Crider, op. cit.

146 Mary Lee Fray has offered: Interview, Mary Lee Fray.

147 "the first time in my life": Interview, informed source.

147 "Bill had been telling me about her": Snow, op. cit.

148 "She would have never told my father": Crider, op. cit.

150 "Oh, Marla, . . . What if": Ibid.

HILLARY USES THE "J" WORD

152 "I said, 'Bill, what in the devil . . .'": Interview, Brian Snow.

152 "He said Faubus had been in touch": Interview, David Matthews.

152 "The night we lost": Interview, Ron Addington.

153 "Hillary said, they're stealing the votes!" Ibid.

153 "You fucking Jew bastard": Interview, Paul Fray.

154 "You don't talk about my forefathers": Ibid.

154 "Yeah, it happened": Interview, Neil McDonald.

154 "I never asked Bill point-blank": Fray, op. cit.

155 "Hillary always knows": Interview, informed source.

155 "He said, 'How could that damn . . .'": Fray, op. cit.

155 State trooper Larry Patterson: *More Than Sex: The Secrets of Bill and Hillary Clinton.* Interview conducted by journalist Christopher Ruddy, NewsMax.com.

155 "I think he was possibly": Fray, op. cit.

155 Hillary's uncle Russell Rodham: Interview, Dr. William Rumsey.

156 "Harry was a bastard": Fray, op. cit.

156 Dr. Jean Houston: Interview, Dr. Jean Houston.

157 At a Christmas party: *Washington Post*, 12/14/99.
157 Dorothy never forgave Max: Interview, Oscar Dowdy.
157 "Aunt Dorothy would say": Ibid.
158 "Watch out, Max": Interview, informed source.
158 "It's sad, but Dorothy's always mad": Interview, Helen Dowdy.
159 "The way I see it": Oscar Dowdy, op. cit.
159 "We knew about Rosenberg": Interview, Tony Rodham.
159 "He said, 'What is wrong . . .'": Fray, op. cit.
160 "I've had a lot of guys": Ibid.
161 "Hey, he has some major flaws": Ibid.

UNIVERSITY LIFE
162 "We were socializing": Interview, Brian Snow.
162 "He would come in from that campaign": Ibid.
163 "There was a total contrast": Interview, Ray Guzman.
163 "Even then, she was" Ibid.
163 "Professor, the notion": Ibid.
164 "Hillary in unguarded moments": Interview, Max Brantley.
164 "She was the kind of person": Interview, Steve Clark.
165 "He walks in—": Interview, Terry Guzman.
166 To him, Bill Clinton was: Snow, op. cit.
166 "She was very engaging": Ibid.

MARRIAGE FROM HELL
167 "People thought I was": Interview, Ron Addington.
168 "Hillary came down": Interview, Mary Lee Fray.
169 "Goodbye, my white flower": Interview, Mauria Jackson Aspell.
169 "Should he get married": Ibid.
169 "I don't think they looked": Interview, Oscar Dowdy.
170 "There had to be around": Addington, op. cit.
170 "Bill called and said": Interview, Marge Mitchell.
170 "All I could focus on": Virginia Kelley with James Morgan, *Leading with My Heart* (New York: Simon & Schuster, 1994), p. 219.
170 "As far as we knew": Mitchell, op. cit.
171 "When he said, you know": Dorothy Rodham, *Rosie O'Donnell* show, 12/23/99.
171 "Well, my daughter's married": Interview, Robert Clarke.
171 "My parents actually liked Bill": Hillary Clinton, *Rosie O'Donnell* show, 12/23/99.

171 "I went, 'Oh, here we go'": Mary Lee Fray, op. cit.

172 "The honeymoon wasn't": Oscar Dowdy, op. cit.

172 "Bill said all he could see": Clarke, op. cit.

173 "Bill would call": Addington, op. cit.

175 "We were talking about a woman": Interview, John Brummet.

THAT OLD CLINTON MAGIC

177 David Matthews remembered: Interview, David Matthews.

178 "Regardless of whether I win": Ibid.

178 "He speaks differently": Interview, John Brummet.

179 "I'm like everybody with Bill": Interview, Max Brantley.

179 "He used to call her Hige": Interview, Paul Fray.

179 "He was just so much fun": Hillary Clinton, *Man from Hope* campaign video, 1992.

180 "He's always deferred": Interview, Ernie Dumas.

BILL, GENNIFER, AND JUANITA

183 "These women have misinterpreted": Interview, Max Brantley.

184 The *Journal* piece: *Wall Street Journal*, 2/19/99.

186 "if that was rape": Interview, informed source.

186 "To put it crudely": Brantley, op. cit.

"SLICK WILLIE," HILLARY, AND CHELSEA

187 "It was to be Hillary and Bill": Interview, Enrico Ferorelli.

188 "You know," she added: Interview, Eleanor Graves.

188 "If they say that's what happened": Interview, Phil Kunhardt.

188 "I don't remember Hillary": Interview, John Loengard.

188 "I've said that in my classes": Interview, Ron Addington.

189 "He governs as a campaign": Interview, John Brummet.

189 Told that security was holding: David Maraniss, *First in His Class* (New York: Simon & Schuster, 1995), p. 364.

189 "His natural inclination" Interview, Rose Crane.

190 "All I hear is this stream": Interview, Ernie Dumas.

191 "It's what I used to call": Interview, David Matthews.

191 "stood up to Jimmy Carter": Addington, op. cit.

192 "I told him, 'Billy boy . . .'": Interview, Paul Fray.

192 Carolyn Staley, Bill's longtime friend: Interview, Carolyn Yeldell Staley.

193 "Nice song": Maraniss, *First in His Class*, p. 375.

BILL'S LULLABY
195 "She was happy to": Interview, Richard Atkinson.
195 David Matthews, though: Interview, David Matthews.
195 "They're all saying:" Ibid.
196 "Oh, God. Like a wake": Interview, Meredith Oakley.
196 "I think he was really numbed by that defeat": Ibid.
196 "If you'd go to jog": Interview, John Brummet.
197 "It was a pretty hard year": Interview, Rose Crane.
197 "She blamed them for losing": Interview, informed source.
197 "Steve Smith and Clinton": Interview, Ernie Dumas.
198 A friend recalled visiting: David Maraniss, *First in His Class* (New York: Simon & Schuster, 1995), p. 394.
198 "Why give them that": Interview, Gene Lyons.
199 "I remember talking": Interview, Carolyn Yeldell Staley.
199 "We Southerners": Interview, informed source.
199 "She's a damn Yankee": Interview, informed source.
199 "There's a Southern mentality": Interview, Carrie Lockwood Owen.
199 It was her style: Interview, Helen Dowdy.
199 "When she makes the effort": Brummet, op. cit.
200 "It was true, too": Dumas, op. cit.
201 "A lot of people believed": Interview, John Robert Starr.
202 "I said, 'You don't have . . .'": Ibid.

HILLARY'S HEALTH CARE SECRET
204 "I can't afford this!": Interview, Oscar Dowdy.
204 "If she complained to me": Ibid.
204 "I'm sure she remembered that": Ibid.
205 "They were almost giddy": Interview, Helen Dowdy.
206 "Suspecting is not mutually exclusive": David Maraniss, *First in His Class* (New York: Simon & Schuster, 1995), p. 420.
206 "He was a spoiled brat": Interview, Pat Roddenberry.
207 "I caused it": Virginia Kelley with James Morgan, *Leading with My Heart* (New York: Simon & Schuster, 1994), p. 251.
207 "I think we're all": Maraniss, *First in His Class*, p. 422.
208 Virginia, agonized: Kelley, *Leading with My Heart*, p. 255.
208 "Today, my mother made me": Interview, Nancy Crawford Adkins.
208 "They both always wanted": Oscar Dowdy, op. cit.
209 "It wasn't like he did jail time": Ibid.
209 "I just told Hillary": Ibid.

210 "There were rumors": Interview, Diane Lyons.
211 "I think some of it was": Ibid.
211 "There's so much animosity": Interview, Melinda Gassaway.
211 "an emotional-based thing": Interview, Rose Crane.
211 "Any time you're dealing": Interview, Shirley Abbott.

HILLARY'S AFFAIR
212 John Brummet remembers. Interview, John Brummet.
212 "You watch": Ibid.
212 Patty Roddenberry: Interview, Pat Roddenberry.
214 "She kept saying": Interview, Helen Dowdy.
214 "I started down a long hall": Interview, Oscar Dowdy.
214 "He had that smuggy": Helen Dowdy, op. cit.
214 "I told him": Oscar Dowdy, op. cit.
215 "It was a very uncomfortable feeling": Helen Dowdy, op. cit.
215 "I was irritated": Oscar Dowdy, op. cit.
216 They were "inseparable": Interview, David Matthews.
216 "All I can tell you": Interview, Gene Lyons.
216 "a number of researchers": Interview, informed source.
217 "He said, 'You know . . .'": Interview, Paul Fray.
217 "I felt like she put up": Interview, informed source.
217 "When I was in New York": Interview, Mandy Merck.
218 "Let's assume some": Dick Morris, KABC Los Angeles, 1/27/98.
218 "I do not believe Hillary is gay": Dick Morris, New York Post, 1/28/98.
218 One particularly peculiar: Interview, informed source.
218 According to one source: David Brock, The Seduction of Hillary Rodham (New York: The Free Press, 1996), p. 63.
219 "I had a good friend": Interview, informed source.
219 "You take two people": Interview, informed source.
219 "A decent, honest guy": Interview, Ernie Dumas.
220 "The subject was clearly": Interview, Terry Guzman.

CHELSEA AND THE GARY HART PROBLEM
223 "a terribly inhospitable environment": David Maraniss, *First in His Class* (New York: Simon & Schuster, 1995), p. 440.
223 "I can't think of a thing": Interview, Max Brantley.
224 "The apple of their eye": Interview, Meredith Oakley.
224 "I was always touched": Interview, Carolyn Yeldell Staley.
224 "My recollection is": Brantley, op. cit.

CLINTON VS. BUSH

227   "We went to the john": Interview, Warren Maus.

227   "It was May 1991": Interview, Garrick Feldman.

227   "This was about four months": Interview, Max Brantley.

227   "We ran into them": Interview, Gene Lyons.

228   "The paper closed": Brantley, op. cit.

229   "My sense was": Interview, Kwan Kwan Wang.

230   "This man seemed": Interview, Eric Rozenman.

230   "Clinton ran for president": Interview, Ernie Dumas.

233   "He didn't ask me to go": Interview, David Matthews.

234   "Sometime after the Dover speech": Ibid.

234   "I felt such a powerful sadness": Interview, Mauria Jackson Aspell.

235   "He called me to check": Interview, Mandy Merck.

236   "We thought, an Arkansan": Interview, Melinda Gassaway.

236   "We were waiting for": Marla Crider, op. cit.

POLITICAL GAFFES, PERSONAL TRAUMA

240   "It was amazing": Interview, Dr. Stephen Van Devanter.

241   "You're going to have": Interview, Nick Petula.

241   "I was going over to see": Interview, Paul Fray.

242   "I'm the idiot": Gail Sheehy, *Hillary's Choice* (New York: Random House, 1999), p. 234.

242   "Hillary left Little Rock": Fray , op. cit.

243   "It was such a bizarre": Petula, op. cit.

243   "My father used to": Interview, Natalie Solfanelli.

243   "He talked about having": Interview, Oscar Dowdy.

244   "I think it's very weird": Interview, Cecille Champagne.

244   "The president drove the": Interview, Joseph X. Flannery.

245   "Cancer was my problem": Virginia Kelley with James Morgan, *Leading with My Heart* (New York: Simon & Schuster, 1994), p. 263.

245   "If they ask, you tell": Ibid, p. 266.

245   "People would ask her": Interview, Rachel Heffernan.

245   "My mother had a big sprawling life": Interview, James Morgan.

246   "I think the reason Bill's": Interview, Melinda Gassaway.

246   "I said, we want to make": Interview, Pat Roddenberry.

246   "We stayed real late": Interview, Mauria Jackson Aspell.

246   "We went down memory lane": Ibid.

247   "He said several times": Interview, Marty Elam Walker.

247   "Bill and Hillary and Chelsea": Interview, Melinda Barran.

248 "It was a really low point": Interview, Ernie Dumas.

248 "It's like that clown": Aspell, op. cit.

248 "I guess if you grow": Interview, David Matthews.

248 "Ultimately some of her": Interview, Max Brantley.

249 "She really manifests": Interview, John Brummet.

THE INTERN

Details about Monica Lewinsky's childhood years through her college years are, for the most part, based on *Monica's Story*, written with Lewinsky's cooperation, by British journalist Andrew Morton and published in 1999 by St. Martin's Press, New York.

The comparison between the Lewinskys' and the Rodhams' home life, appearing on page 252, is based on author research and interviews that are detailed in earlier chapters of *State of a Union*, such as "Portrait of a Marriage."

The quote beginning "Other than their mutual love," appearing on page 254 is from an author source.

Details of Lewinsky's White House employment and her relationship with President Clinton are, for the most part, from the Starr Report.

LIES, DENIALS, AND REBUKE

A portion of this chapter is based on material from the Starr Report; *Monica's Story*; Jeffrey Toobin's book *A Vast Conspiracy*, published in 1999 by Random House, New York; and reports in the *New York Times*, the *New York Post*, and the *New York Daily News*.

262 "Of course, Bill spent the entire": Interview, informed source.

262 "It was a tough": Interview, David Matthews.

262 "It was hell": Interview, informed source.

263 "Bill was an emotional wreck": Interview, informed source.

263 "Aunt Dorothy had": Interview, Oscar Dowdy.

268 "their time, their hearts": Interview, Melinda Gassaway.

268 "He embarrassed Hillary": Interview, Marge Mitchell.

268 "Arrogance, arrogance, arrogance": Gassaway, op. cit.

268 "Where's Monica?" Interview, Beckie Moore.

269 "Everyone else was gone": Interview Carolyn Yeldell Staley.

269 "There is a part of me": Interview, Marla Crider.

HILLARY ON HER OWN

News events described in this chapter are based on Hillary Clinton's senate campaign coverage in the *New York Times*; the *New York Daily News*; the *New York Post*; and the *New York Observer*. Comparisons with the senate race of Robert F. Kennedy Jr. and details from that campaign are from the author's book *The Other Mrs. Kennedy, Ethel Skakel Kennedy: An American Drama of Power, Privilege, and Politics*. Quotes from, and description of, President Clinton's 1998 and 1999 state of the union addresses were based, for the most part, on the reportage of the *Washington Post*.

INDEX

[The abbreviation HRC refers to Hillary Rodham Clinton and the abbreviation WJC refers to William Jefferson (Bill) Clinton.]